Introduction

Anthropological research in Nepal extends over barely two decades. Until 1951, the year which saw the fall of the century-old regime of the Rana family and the re-emergence of the monarchy as the focus of political power, Nepal persisted in a self-imposed isolation, more complete in some respects than that of its great northern neighbour Tibet. While foreign travellers and such scholars as Guiseppe Tucci had been able to traverse large parts of Tibet and collect information on conditions in the countryside as well as in Lhasa, the rulers of Nepal restricted the movements of foreigners to the narrow confines of the Kathmandu valley, and even the number of those permitted to visit the capital was severely limited. The only foreign envoy was the British resident, and he and the members of his staff were subject to restrictions similar to those imposed on other foreigners. As a direct result of this policy of isolation reliable anthropological information on the inhabitants of Nepal was virtually unobtainable. The only source of a limited knowledge of the people of the regions outside the Kathmandu valley were interviews with men serving in the Gurkha regiments of the British-Indian army, but compilations of such information for the use of British Gurkha officers were inevitably sketchy and unreliable.

In the year 1953, when the first professional anthropologists began work in Nepal, an expanse stretching from the northern border of India to the southern border of Tibet, and from Kumaon in the west to Sikkim in the east, was ethnographically virtually *terra incognita*. The first task anthropologists had to undertake was to establish the nature and distribution of the main ethnic groups, and this was to be followed by the study of selected populations representative of the main regions and groups. In pursuance of this aim my wife and I surveyed in the course of two journeys in 1953/54 and 1957/58 the middle-ranges and some regions of high altitude of Eastern Nepal; in 1962, 1966 and 1972 we extended this work to parts of Western Nepal. Intensive studies of the Sherpas of Eastern Nepal and the Thakalis and some Bhotia groups of Western Nepal, as well as a study of Nepalese Hindu caste society, were among the results of this work. In 1956/57 Colin Rosser, then of the School of Oriental and African Studies, undertook a study of the Newars of the Kathmandu valley and in 1964/65 Lionel Caplan, also of the School of Oriental and African Studies, studied the interrelations between the tribal Limbus and the high Hindu castes in a district of Eastern Nepal. In 1970 Lionel Caplan undertook a study of a small market town in the middle-ranges of Western Nepal while Patricia Caplan worked among the Hindu castes of a nearby village. At about the same time

Barbara Aziz studied immigrant Tibetans and Sherpas in Solu, and Nicholas Allen undertook research among a group of Thulung Rai. Among other students of the School of Oriental and African Studies engaged in research in Nepal were Stephen Greenwold, who investigated certain aspects of Newar society, and Alan Macfarlane who produced a comprehensive anthropological and demographic study of a Gurung village.

From 1958 onwards French anthropologists such as the late B. Pignede, Corneille Jest, Marc Gaborieau and Alain Fournier were engaged in fieldwork in several parts of the country, and A.W. Macdonald undertook extensive research in conjunction with the same project. In the years 1965-67 a large German research team under the leadership of Professor Friedrich Funke studied the Sherpas of Solu and Likhu Khola, and Adràs Höfer and W.D. Michl undertook research among Tamangs and Chantels.

In 1953 a Japanese group under the direction of Jiro Kawakita undertook anthropological investigations among various communities of high altitude dwellers in Central Nepal and in 1958 Kawakita, R. Takayama and Shigeru Iijima visited Dolpo and subsequently produced the first detailed ethnographic account of the pastoral economy of that region. Since then several Japanese anthropologists have done fieldwork in Nepal.

The American contribution to anthropological research in Nepal began with John Hitchcock's study of Magars, and the large number of American scholars who have since worked in Nepal include Charles MacDougal, James Fisher, Rex Jones, Sherry Ortner, Joe Reinhard, Don Messerschmidt and Barry Bishop.

Until recently anthropology had no place among the studies pursued in Nepalese institutions of higher education, and for this reason it is not surprising that the number of Nepalese anthropologists is still relatively small. The first Nepali to take an interest in social anthropology was Dor Bahadur Bista, the author of *Peoples of Nepal*, and his example was followed by his brother Khem Bahadur Bista. Other Nepalese scholars professionally engaged in anthropological research are Bihari K. Shrestha, Bed Prakash Upreti and Naveen Kumar Rai. Several specialists in other disciplines, such as Dr. Harka Gurung and Dr. P.R. Sharma have also contributed to anthropological studies.

In view of the manifold data on the anthropology of Nepal accumulated within the last two decades it was felt that a meeting of those most immediately concerned with the pursuit and planning of research would be useful, and it is gratifying that a large number of scholars accepted the invitation of the School of Oriental and African Studies to a symposium on the Anthropology of Nepal. This symposium was held from the 28th June to the 3rd July, 1973, and the following scholars participated in the Meeting:

Nepal: Harka B. Gurung, Prayag Raj Sharma, Bihari K. Shrestha, Naveen Kumar Rai, Hikmat Bahadur Bista.

U.K.: Nicholas Allen, Barbara Aziz, Lionel Caplan, Patricia Caplan, Christoph von Fürer-Haimendorf, Stephen Greenwold, Alan Macfarlane.

U.S.A.: Barry Bishop, James Fisher, John T. Hitchcock, Rex Jones, Don Messerschmidt, Sherry Ortner.

France: Alain Fournier, Marc Gaborieau, Corneille Jest, A.W. Macdonald.

Germany: Walter Frank, Wilhelm Hellmich, Andràs Höfer, R. Kaschewsky, Wolf Dieter Michl, M. Oppitz.

Sweden: Bengt Borgström, Hakan Wahlquist.

The papers contained in this volume are not a complete collection of those presented and discussed at the symposium. Some of the participants had already committed themselves to publish their manuscripts elsewhere while a few wanted to revise and amplify their contributions but were unable to do so before the volume had to go to press. The collection nevertheless constitutes a balanced cross-section of the data and problems discussed at the symposium, and thus reflects the research interests of a representative group of anthropologists specialized on Nepal. It is a matter of regret that owing to practical problems none of the Japanese scholars invited to the symposium could participate, and that this volume hence lacks contributions from a group of anthropologists noted for their long-standing interest in Himalayan studies. Their absence was felt all the more as a symposium on Himalayan anthropology held in 1968 in Kyoto in conjunction with the 8th International Congress of Anthropological and Ethnological Sciences had stimulated the idea of periodic meetings of specialists on Nepal and the adjoining regions.

It is not the function of the editor of a varied collection of papers to comment on the contents of individual contributions, and readers will be able to draw their own conclusions about the main trends in present-day anthropological studies in the Himalayan region. Yet, it would seem useful to point out some of the problems which arose in discussions and are perhaps not fully covered by the papers prepared for publication. Several of these problems are not only of academic interest but also of practical importance, and scholars concerned with the historical and traditional cultures of Nepal as well as with the contemporary developments can hardly afford to ignore them.

The increase of population and the resulting economic effects present one of the greatest national problems. Between 1930 and 1961 the population of the kingdom grew from 5,532,574 to 9,753,378, and the forecast for 1975 is a population between 11,750,000 and 13,100,000. If the present trend continues the 25 million mark may be reached before the end of the 20th century. This rate of increase presents a serious challenge in a country where the overwhelming majority of the population has always depended on agriculture. While in some regions, such as the relatively sparsely populated high altitude regions of Jumla, there is still scope for an extension of cultivable land, in others there is no or little vacant land to accommodate growing communities. In the virtual absence of other than agricultural occupations surplus populations must hence seem employment outside their home villages, a process which is liable to extend gradually to a large part of Nepal. Even today many thousands of villagers from regions such as Jumla migrate every winter to India in search of work, and while most of them return to their home-villages within a few months, it is not unusual for men to stay for a year or more in India. A similar situation was encountered by the Caplans in Dailekh district even though in that part of the middle ranges the expansion of trade in the local bazaar-towns and employment in enlarged government offices has provided some opportunities for villagers unable to make a living on inadequate land.

In many areas the dramatic increase in population has resulted also in the disappearance of most of the forest, because parts of the village land previously used as wood reserves had to be cleared of tree growth and brought under cultivation in order to accommodate the expanding population. This process has been studied by Alan Macfarlane among Gurung communities and by Nicholas Allen among the Rais of Eastern Nepal. In the past the forest used to provide the Rais with many of their necessities, and its depletion will inevitably result in a change in the pattern of living. Deforestation is one of the greatest dangers throughout the middle ranges, and many parts of central and eastern Nepal inhabited by Hindu castes are already nearly bare of any substantial tree growth.

Among the Bhotia populations in the areas of high altitude along the Tibetan frontier the growth of population appears to have been slower than in the middle ranges. The Sherpas of Khumbu, for instance, have not greatly increased in the past 15 - 20 years, but a substantial increase took place there in the 19th century, and it would seem that given the limitations of the environment the population of Khumbu has already reached the maximum which the land can support.

The changes in the economy and general pattern of living of the Bhotia populations brought about by the disruption of trade with Tibet and the shrinking of the market for Tibetan salt is discussed in detail in my contribution to this volume. But even though the improvement of communications and the spread of education has resulted in much social change, there is reason to believe that nowhere in Nepal has there been a wholesale relinquishment of traditional ideas and attitudes. There is, however, a general readiness to incorporate modern goals within the traditional value system. Responses to change have, on the whole, been in the nature of gradual adaptation rather than of revolution, and this applies to inter-caste and inter-tribal relations as much as to the reorientation of trade where outside forces destroyed the viability of the old system. The full effect of the newly instituted system of education are not yet apparent but as the young people now leaving school will reach maturity their impact on their respective communities will undoubtedly increase, and in tribal groups this may involve a process or Nepalisation as well as of secularisation. The continued observation of the process of social change now entering a new phase will be an important task of anthropologists in the years to come.

The symposium was financed by a generous grant from the School of Oriental and African Studies, which made it possible to provide hospitality to the participants and to meet the travel expenses of the Nepalese scholars. For further support thanks are due to the Dr. Fritz Thyssen Stiftung, which has a long history of financing research in Nepal and met the expenses of the German participants in the symposium.

At the end of the symposium the hope was expressed that in three years' time a further meeting may be held in Kathmandu and the Nepalese participants agreed to work towards the organisation of such a conference.

Christoph von Fürer-Haimendorf
School of Oriental and African Studies,
University of London.
February 1974.

The Ritual Journey, a Pattern underlying certain Nepalese Rituals

Descriptive accounts of Himalayan ritual often make use of the term "shaman", but there are many problems in giving it an exact definition. According to Eliade the defining feature of the shaman is his command of the techniques of ecstasy; by ecstasy he means that "His (the shaman's) soul can safely abandon his body and roam at vast distances, can penetrate the underworld and rise to the sky" (1964:182). Others have considered that while ecstasy is indeed fundamental to shamanism, soul projection should not be overemphasised at the expense of the ability to become possessed (Schröder 1955). Evidently this focus on the actual or putative mental state of ritual officiants raises interesting questions, and in the comparative study of Himalayan ritual one possible approach is to classify the ethnographic facts into shamanistic and non-shamanistic on this basis. But psychological criteria are not the only possible basis for a classification, nor is there any guarantee that they will be the most revealing. The Eliadean shaman is not only someone who is subject to ecstasy; he is also someone who in the course of rituals goes on journeys. The present paper concentrates on this second aspect, and by examining a range of different types of ritual journey, attempts to place the shaman's undertaking in a broader perspective. The comparisons which arise in the course of this approach turn out to have an interest of their own independent of any bearing on the notion of shamanism, and the implication is that the ritual journey is a useful ethnographic category in its own right.

Some of the journeys examined have been extracted from the literature, but the majority were recorded in the course of field research among the Thulung Rai of east Nepal.[1] I have described certain aspects of Thulung ritual life in two previous papers (in press a, in press b) which it would be wearisome to refer to below at every point where they have some bearing; other aspects I hope to go into in more detail elsewhere. Thus for the present purpose some of the journeys will only be described summarily.

Over recent centuries, and more intensively over recent decades, Hindu influences have been affecting the Thulung to such an extent that their traditionally non-literate culture now has something of the character of a survival, one might even say, of folklore. Though close neighbours of the Sherpas, they have never been Buddhists, but in a number of ways their traditional culture is related to that of pre- or extra-Buddhist Tibet. The maintenance of this tradition is recognised by the Thulung to be particularly the responsibility of the class of officiant I shall

Contributions To

THE ANTHROPOLOGY OF NEPAL

Edited by

CHRISTOPH VON FÜRER-HAIMENDORF

Proceedings of a Symposium
held at
THE SCHOOL OF ORIENTAL AND AFRICAN STUDIES
University of London
June/July 1973

ARIS & PHILLIPS LTD., Warminster, England

ISBN 0 85668 021 4

Printed in Great Britain by
Biddles Limited, Guildford, Surrey

CONTENTS

Introduction 1

NICHOLAS ALLEN *University of Durham*
The Ritual Journey, a Pattern underlying certain Nepalese Rituals. 6

BARBARA AZIZ *University of Edinburgh*
Some Notions about Descent and Residence in Tibetan Society. 23

LIONEL CAPLAN *School of Oriental and African Studies, London*
Inter-Caste Marriages in a Nepalese Town. 40

ALAIN FOURNIER *Centre National de la Recherche Scientifique, Paris*
Notes préliminaires sur des Populations Sunuwar dans L'Est du Nepal. 62

WALTER FRANK *University of Cologne*
Attempt at an Ethno-Demography of Middle Nepal. 85

CHRISTOPH VON FÜRER-HAIMENDORF
School of Oriental and African Studies, London
The Changing Fortunes of Nepal's High Altitude Dwellers. 98

MARK GABORIEAU *Centre National de la Recherche Scientifique, Paris*
Les Récits Chantés de L'Himalaya et le Contexte Ethnographique. 114

STEPHEN GREENWOLD *University of Birmingham*
Monkhood versus Priesthood in Newar Buddhism. 129

JOHN HITCHCOCK *University of Wisconsin*
A Shaman's Song and some Implications for Himalayan Research. 150

ANDRÁS HÖFER *University of Heidelberg*
A Note on Possession in South Asia. 159

Is the *bombo* an Ecstatic? Some Ritual Techniques of Tamang Shamanism. 168

CORNEILLE JEST *Centre National de la Recherche Scientifique, Paris*
La Fête des Clans chez les Thākālis. Spre-lo (1968). 183

DON MESSERSCHMIDT *University of Oregon*
and
NARESHWAR JANG GURUNG
Institute of Nepal and South Asian Studies, Kathmandu
Parallel Trade and Innovation in Central Nepal : The Cases of the Gurung and Thākāli Subbas Compared. 197

WOLF MICHL *University of Heidelberg*
Shamanism among the Chantel of the Dhaulagiri Zone. 222

MICHAEL OPPITZ *University of Cologne*
Myths and Facts : Reconsidering some Data concerning the Clan History of the Sherpa. 232

PRAYAG RAJ SHARMA
Institute of Nepal and South Asian Studies, Kathmandu
The Divinities of the Karnālī Basin in Western Nepal. 244

refer to as the tribal priest. Bodic speakers seem generally to have focused their maximum ritual emphasis on death,[2] and although Eliade gives equal emphasis to the shaman's two roles of psychopomp and healer, our own culture is surely unusual in allowing the doctor equality with, or even precedence over the priest. So we shall start with the journey of the dead soul.

A Thulung death chant

When someone dies in the ordinary course of events it has traditionally been the duty of the priest to perform a rite a variable interval after the burial to conduct the dead spirit to its final resting place. For all Thulung, this destination, *bebdu pabdu* "the place of the grandfathers and fathers", is quite precisely located in geographical space. Its Nepali name is Kotunje, which is a village lying about two days journey to the south-west, "the other side of the Maulung Khola", as it is often put; there are grounds for thinking that the Thulung ancestors, or some of them, may in fact have lived in that region.[3] The journey is accomplished by means of a chant which on the occasion observed was intoned by the priest three times with different melodies in the course of the day's ritual. The priest in Mukli village had no objection to his chants being tape-recorded but was unwilling to assist in interpreting them. However in spite of the many problems of word-by-word analysis, it is clear enough that the chant starts from the village where the rite is taking place and progresses via various named hamlets and across certain rivers by a more or less straight route to Kotunje; the soul is told that it has reached its destination and the journey is then reversed. The priest is immobile throughout his chant.

The undertaking is undoubtedly psychopompic in its general character. The verb ordinarily used to describe the activity of the priest is *puryāunu* Nep. meaning "to complete, escort, deliver", or more fully (translating definition 2 in Sarma's dictionary), "to accompany someone or something for safety to ensure that there are no obstacles èn route"; neither in Nepali nor in Thulung is it customary in this context to use the ordinary verb for "to send". In the chant itself many of the verbs are in the first person past causative, e.g. on the journey out *hunubetto* "I have caused to fly", and the priest was in fact wearing a feather headdress, an evident symbol of magical flight. The text relates Kotunje to the heavens, and some say that one climbs the hill there to reach heaven. The most obvious interpretation of the return journey is that it is that of the priest coming home.

In spite of all this, the journey can hardly be called

shamanic in Eliade's central Asiatic or strict sense of the word. The fundamental difficulty is that there is no question of the priest being in any sort of trance. No elaborate initiation is necessary to perform the ritual and if for some reason no priest is available, a layman with sufficient knowledge of the chants may act as substitute. It was suggested to me that the object of the return journey was actually to teach the spirit the route which he would have to follow at ceremonies when the ancestors are recalled to their natal hearth to exercise their potentially beneficient influence. Thus if it were put to them I think most Thulung would accept that in describing the priest's activity as "escorting" or "seeing off" the dead man, they were speaking metaphorically, and that all the priest's faculties remained with his body throughout.

One thing that is certain is that the dead man is not supposed to be making his journey alone, and the chant refers in successive lines to the fowl, pig and buffalo that accompany him. In principle these animals are killed earlier in the course of the day's activities, and are eaten by the participants. Of the three it is the buffalo that was most often mentioned by Thulung in discussions about death ritual, and although on the occasion I witnessed no buffalo was available in reality, it retained its place in the chant.

Mukli HuTpa rite

Once a year the same officiant performs a comparable rite on behalf of the collectivity. HuTpa literally means "the flyer" and refers to the evil force which is to be disposed of. Informants are vague as to its exact nature, but the chant addresses in successive lines Gelbu, Lokpa and Ciunba, in each case as a royal couple (i.e. first as *rājā*, then as *rānī*). The ritual paraphernalia are laid out on and around a mat in the courtyard of a house and the officiant stands still on one side of it. He intones two chants. The first includes a journey eastwards to the Tamur river and to Chatra (near Dharan), while the second includes a much more detailed itinerary leading northwards. The first half dozen place names refer to hamlets within the village; thereafter they are more spaced out. Two of the river crossings are noted. Namche is the 25th name, though according to one informant several had been omitted. The journey up to this point was quite familiar to older informants since up until about a generation ago most households sent a member northwards on an annual trading expedition to bring back Tibetan salt in exchange for grain. After Namche the chant mentions the putting on of garlands (this being a method of honoring a departing guest), and the itinerary terminates at Tingri Maidān in Tibet. As this final journey begins, the officiant, now facing north, is flanked by two assistants who swing winnowing fans to waft the evil away in that direction. In this case no return journey was chanted, and the only animals involved were minute fragments of meat or fish (*jium*) laid on small piles of grain on the mat.

Lokhim HuTpa

Four hours' walk to the east, in Lokhim village, the context of the rite is rather different. The officiant is not a priest but a medium; the distinction is a complex one but the basic point is perhaps that the medium is effective by virtue of a personal relationship with a certain spirit, while the priest's power is of a different nature and closer to being simply a matter of knowledge. In Lokhim the HuTpa is a household rite, held indoors in the early evening, and the medium may lead on from it into an ordinary nocturnal seance. However there are clear and basic similarities to the Mukli ceremony: the paraphernalia laid in front of the officiant, the absence of possession, drum or feathered headdress, the vocabulary and progress of the chant. The journey to the east may stop at Mayungma[4] but a knowledgeable officiant may go much further - on one of my tapes he reaches the Tista river and Gangtok. Northwards the chant reaches Pangboche, then mentions, without further details, a cave dwelling, a monastery, (i.e. gompa), and a "place of origin and fertility". After arrival at Namche a very small fragment of wild boar is roasted on a miniature spit. This time the journey back is detailed.

Several informants agreed that HuTpa was a Bhotia divinity, and there is no doubt that this rite, like certain other elements of Thulung myth and ritual, derives from the Sherpas (perhaps via the Khaling Rai), and hence ultimately from Tibet. It would be irrelevant to elaborate on the point here, but it is of interest in suggesting a possible explanation for the fact that there are eastward journeys as well as northward ones in the HuTpa. The New Year celebrations in Lhasa have often been described (earlier sources are synthesised by Frazer 1925: 218ff). The account by Nebesky-Wojkowitz (1956:508ff) mentions that in the course of the ritual two human scapegoats are despatched: one of them, after setting off to the south-east, turns east to end at Tsethang, while the other (who for some centuries was omitted) sets off to 'Phenyul, which lies north of Lhasa. The Thulung nowadays of course follow the national (i.e. Hindu) calendar, but the date of the Mukli HuTpa, March 30 in 1970, could be counted in favour of the suggestion that it derives from the Tibetan New Year rite. It is normal in India and Tibet to enumerate the cardinal points clockwise starting from the east, so the order of the Thulung journeys, first east, then north, makes one wonder whether at some stage in the rite's history, perhaps in Lhasa itself, the two intermediate cardinal points may have been omitted.

Danced Journey at nocturnal seance

Whereas the good dead are conducted to Kotunje as described above, those who die unnatural deaths are disposed of by the medium; their destination is somewhat obscure. Such seances are regarded as particularly difficult, but particularly important, and are supposed to be repeated a year after the death. Outwardly similar journeys are undertaken also at seances held for therapeutic or prophylactic purposes, and in all cases their general character is much more typically shamanic than in the three rites considered so far. While the Thulung priest is often compared locally to the Brahman, the Thulung medium is assimilated to the Nepali-speaking *jhā̃kri*, and like the latter is generally regarded as subject to altered states of consciousness. A shamanic drum (which drowns the chant, making analysis difficult) is obligatory, as is the feathered headdress. Symbols of ascent may be involved, for instance a ladder. There are some unsolved ethnographic questions as to the exact local exegesis of the medium's psychological state, and of his relationship to the bird or animal which may be hung at the top of the ladder, and to the birds whose movements he mimes during his episodes of dancing. However in one of his steps he imitates the movements of a man paddling a boat across a river, and it is clear enough that we have to do with a journey that is primarily acted rather than verbal. In the one such mortuary journey that was observed, much of the action took place under a cover in the courtyard since the interior of the house was too cramped, but the dances themselves were circular and there was no net movement or progression in any physical sense.

A Thulung mortuary procession

An interesting comparison is offered by a journey which occurred in the course of the normal final death ceremony with which we started. The previous day relatives and neighbours had built a stone resting place (*cautārā* Nep.) beside a steep path a few minutes walk from the house. In the morning the pig already mentioned as notionally accompanying the dead spirit to Kotunje had been killed and cut up, and its tail, together with some strips of cloth, was attached to the top of a tall bamboo pole *(tharseng)*. The pole was carried to the *cautārā* and planted in front of it. Some of the pig's blood was scattered at its base, and the priest intoned the Kotunje chant for the first time. Accompanied by five mourners and a medium,[5] he then danced anticlockwise around the pole, continuing to chant, but to a new melody which was drowned by cymbals. The dance was repeated around the *cautārā*, then around a spear which was planted in the ground at three "pauses" (*ngelung*) on the short journey back to the house, then once in the courtyard, and finally inside the house. This made seven in all, a number which was said to be the correct one, and must, I think, be related to the widespread belief in seven stages planes or steps on the route to heaven or hell (though I did not meet this interpretation locally). One informant summarised the Kunje chant as saying to the deceased "Now you are dead you must depart", and we may reasonably interpret the pole, at least on one of its levels of meaning, as representing the dead soul's route to heaven, with the pig's tail representing his companion on the journey as it were vanishing into the clouds above. In any case, in making their journey from the pole to the house the dancers were evidently doing more than simply shift from one ritual location to another. As the informant put it, in case the spirit did not stay in heaven, they were showing it the way back to a shelf in the house where offerings would be made to it. But his explanation is not to be taken as referring only to the four minutes' worth of physical path; the latter is symbolic of the metaphysical route from the other world to domestic reality, and those who travel it are not only forming a procession but also doing something akin to what the medium achieves by his dancing at a seance.

Two apparent inconsistencies deserve notice. The outward procession to the *cautārā* was unceremonious, where symmetry would appear to demand a passage through the same seven stages as are to be passed through on the return journey. One is reminded of the absence of any return journey from Tibet in the Mukli HuTpa. Since the return journey is present in the Lokhim HuTpa, it might be thought that we were dealing with abbreviations or variants of little analytical interest. This would be overhasty, as we shall suggest later. Secondly, it might seem to a logician that it was redundant to send the dead soul both vertically up a pole and horizontally overland to Kotunje. However this sort of doubling up is commonplace in Himalayan ritual, and indeed no doubt in ritual generally.

A western Bhotia mortuary procession

We have now considered briefly five sorts of ritual journey among the Thulung, ranging from the purely verbal to the physical but symbolic. We turn now to those Bhotias who live in the extreme north-west corner of Nepal and the adjacent part of India. Like the Rais, they are somewhat Hinduized, non-Buddhist Bodic

carries away a load of sin (Leviticus xvi). But "sickness, death and sin are identical from the religious viewpoint" (Hubert and Mauss 1964:53), and a communal rite can easily become a household one, as has surely happened to the HuTpa among the Thulung. Moreover the exact date of the Bhotia ceremony is fixed in conjunction with the village elders, so the rite has at least a certain communal aspect.

Journeys with Model Animals

As Buddhists, the Sherpas avoid killing animals, but this by no means implies that they avoid sending them on ritual journeys. On the contrary, animals in the form of dough models carried by humans and thrown away, play a major part in their ritual. In a rite performed in Khumbu twice a year on behalf of the collectivity, a three-headed figure (pig, ox, tiger) was taken to the southern end of the village where it was abandoned and two small boys were told to strike at it with their weapons. A similar rite is often held on behalf of a household eight days after a death, and it also forms the climax of the Dumje, the major collective calendrical ceremony of the Sherpas (Fürer-Haimendorf, 1964:252-4.237,201ff). Among the Junbesi Sherpas the picture is again similar, though distinct names are reported for the tiger-pig-yak three-headed figure prepared after a child's death and the pig-yak-snake figure discarded at the Dumje festival (Funke 1969:141,132).

We cannot examine all the details of the family likeness between these Sherpa rites and the journeys considered earlier. For instance there is no doubt a connexion to be explored between the tricephalic models and the three animals who accompany the Thulung deceased to Kotunje. A triad of animals (sheep, horse, yak) was already playing a central part in Tibetan death rituals a millennium ago (Stein 1970), but it might be a mistake to restrict attention to the Bodic-speaking area, or indeed to animals as distinct from diving trinities generally. Another interesting connexion is the name of the Sherpa model, which in all the cases reported from Khumbu appears to be called the Lokpar *gtorma*. We have already met this name in the Thulung HuTpa rite, where Lokpa *rājā* Lokpa *rānī* is invoked as the second of three pairs. The fact not only further supports the view that the Thulung rite derives from the north, but also sheds light on the changes it has undergone. The name Lokpar apparently comes from Tib. *bzlogpa* "cause to reverse direction" (ibid: 130,308). This implies a two-way journey, the second leg evidently being that in which the model is carried to its destruction. The first would thus be the spontaneous attacking movement of the evil force, combined perhaps with its involuntary entry into the figure (the "consecration" of the figure), which results from the officiant's coercive ritual. We can now suggest why the Mukli HuTpa journey has only one leg expressed in the priest's chant: it is because the first leg is implicit, and the chant replaces the second. On this view the return journey in the Lokhim chant is perhaps a secondary addition. The Thulung are of course not aware of the etymology of the name, and it is curious to note how what began as the name of a process, came to be applied to a model scapegoat, and has ended up as the name of a god.

I have never seen Thulung use dough models, but most seances include an episode in which four bamboo slivers are stuck into each of a number of potatoes to represent nominally nine "horses and elephants", which are discarded a couple of minutes' walk from the house. Sometimes this is done at a crossroads, but by no means always. Occasionally a drawing may be treated similarly. One example showed an anthropomorphic figure with a small horse below and a bird above. In the Sherpa journeys the role of bearer of the models is an unpopular one as the bearer is so closely associated with what he bears (one recalls the relationship of the *ya* to the Bhotia deceased). I have no explicit evidence of this attitude at Thulung seances, though in practice it was younger people who tended to undertake the role.

Whether it is a human or animal scapegoat that is driven out, or a two- or three-dimensional model that is discarded, the underlying idea is evidently the same, and the Tibetans apply to the material object or being the same term, *glud*, in either case (Nebesky-Wojkowitz 1956, especially p.507). The translation in Das' dictionary, "a thing given as a ransom", is not entirely happy. The word "ransom" - ultimately from the Latin literally "buying back", implies a situation involving four elements: (i) the party A who pays it, who has been deprived of something, (ii) the party B who controls what A lacks, (iii) the ransom or prestation that is paid by A to B, (iv) that which is redeemed, the counterprestation, which passes from B to A. The situation underlying the scapegoat consists of only three elements: (i) the party A who is afflicted with something he desires to be rid of, (ii) the space B into which he may discard it, (iii) that which is discarded, the scapegoat and whatever is associated with it. Viewed in abstraction, the second situation is quite different from the first, and simpler. However the ethnographic picture is much less clear cut, and it may be helpful to imagine how the simpler situation could merge into the more complex, typologically or chronologically.

The simplest possibility seems to be the following sequence.

Suppose first that the space B is personified, for instance by talking of the Guardians of the Four Quarters, of the Lord of Chaos. This means that what is discarded can be interpreted as a prestation from A to B. The second step would be to reify the absence or negation of what is discarded, for instance by conceiving of the absence of sin as grace, or the absence of illness as health. The reified concept is automatically a counterprestation from B to A, and the situation is now one of reciprocity. The personification logically precedes the reification since inert space cannot give counterprestations.[9]

An alternative route of transformation is as follows. The scapegoat has a dual aspect in that although it is so closely associated with evil, it is also the means through which good is achieved. The success of the rite depends upon it. It is a small step from regarding the animal as an instrument to regarding it as an agent, or representative of an agent. If it is taken, the successful outcome is the counterprestation, and elements of the ritual, e.g. the consecration, can be interpreted as prestations. This transformation is less neat than the first, since the ultimate fate of the former scapegoat becomes paradoxical once the animal has become the giver of success and the receiver of worship. But collective representations need not transform themselves in the neatest manner, and there are hints of this sort of paradox in the present status of HuTpa. Even without the comparative evidence from the Sherpas, the progress of the rite is sufficient to demonstrate its essentially scapegoat character. But HuTpa is referred to as a *deutā*, and his rite is called a *pujā* (the Thulung language offering no equivalent indigenous expressions). These Nepali terms are just the same as apply to the mass of Hindu gods and godlings who receive offerings or sacrifices in exchange for favours, and it is difficult to imagine that many Thulung are aware of the sharp theoretical distinction we have drawn between the two different ways of relating to the supernatural. It is possible that there are many other gods, in the Nepali sense of the word, who began their careers in equally close association with scapegoats.

In any case a purely prestational interpretation of the *glud* is not easy to reconcile with the facts. It is true that the Thulung potato models are sometimes described as offerings to Jemarāj, Lord of the Dead, but the personification is distinctly shadowy. The medium or his deputy does not set off in any particular direction, nor is the point where he chooses to discard the models regarded as a matter of importance. He does not necessarily make any invocation when the objects are discarded, an omission that would be inconceivable at any ordinary sacrifice. The natural interpretation is simply that the evil localised in the objects is taken on a journey away from the house and its immediate environs. Similarly the word *gtorma*, as in Lokpar *gtorma*, is often rendered "sacrificial cake" or "sacrificial offering", but this too is potentially misleading, and for the same reason. Doubtless there are occasions when it can be described as an offering to some clearly conceptualised deity, but there would be no point in the two small Sherpa boys striking at the Lokpar model if it were a gift. A prestation cannot meaningfully be the object of one's hostility. The verbal root in *gtorma* actually means "scatter, strew, throw, dissipate", i.e. the word has a connotation very different from, for instance *sbyinpa* "gift, alms" or *mchodpa* "offering, libation". The models have to be related, not so much to notions of this sort, but rather to the dismemberment of animals, or of the shaman during his initiatory crisis.

This selection of ritual journeys could be enlarged more or less indefinitely, and whatever stopping point was chosen would be somewhat arbitrary. In particular, we have not considered the ritual hunt (Pignede 1966:308, Macdonald 1955), which bears to the shamanic search for the lost soul much the same relationship as the physical journey of the *ya* does to the spiritual journey of the psychopomp in the central Asiatic sense of the term. Another omission is the *jātrā* Nep, in the sense both of individual pilgrimage and of communal procession, particularly perhaps the Newar processions with their large wheeled ritual structures comparable to the Juggernaut (Macdonald 1952). A third direction to explore would be journeys made by sliding down ropes, as reported from Lhasa and the western Himalaya. Any full investigation of the subject would certainly also have to include the journey on which the yogin conducts the snake or goddess Kundalini, up from the base of his trunk through the six *cakra* to the seventh and transcendent *cakra* at the top of his head. While noting some similarities, Eliade (1958: 330) contrasts the yogic and shamanic journeys as enstatic to ecstatic. But how much weight to give to such differences in mental state depends on one's purpose, and the whole thrust of the present paper has been rather towards emphasising the similarities of pattern. The Thulung youth discarding potato models a minute's walk from the house might seem a far cry from the central Asiatic shaman "roaming at vast distances", but I hope to have brought out the underlying similarity of the two undertakings.

All the rituals we have considered involve the traverse of the space between two termini, the one where the benefit is to accrue (village, household, etc.), and the one that symbolises "the beyond" (Kotunje, the pole at the *cautārā*, the spot where the models are discarded, etc.). Thus ritual journeys might be regarded as one variety of rite of passage. However this seems artificial since many of the ritual journeys involve two distinct transitions, that of the beneficiary (from a state of risk to one of security) being more important than that of whatever makes the journey. In any case such considerations would bear on the relationship of the ritual journey to yet broader and more abstract categories, whereas the main objects of this paper have been to recognise the pattern itself and to envisage its relationship to narrower categories.

As to the pattern, a striking feature has been the importance of birds and animals (sometimes grouped in triads). Whatever else may travel, they do. The least clear instance was the Mukli HuTpa, but one informant certainly interpreted the *jium* in this manner. Although the exact role of animals at the Thulung seance remains unclear, they surely belong in the same general class as the shaman's familiar or helping spirits, the majority of whom have animal forms (Eliade 1964:88-95). If we were right in suggesting that other gods have followed the same career as HuTpa, then the class would also include the prototypes of the animal or bird vehicles of the gods, the *vahana* which are so prominent a feature of Indian iconography.

The classification of ritual journeys adopted above has been into chanted, danced and walked, soul projection being most closely associated with the danced category. It would be exaggerated to claim that in such a perspective "shamanism" is simply dissolved and ceases to be a recognisable ethnographic category, as Spencer (1968) would wish. It is still legitimate to single out a class of shamanic ritual journeys, defined by particular criteria: for instance, those performed by someone who is believed (i) to be sending his own soul on the journey, and (ii) to have this power by virtue of an individual initiatory experience which a westerner might term psychopathological (an experience which is often itself a journey). Some such constellation of features may indeed have been historically important. But it appears less strange and more intelligible when seen as a segment of the broader category that includes the other types of ritual journey.

It might be prudent to stop at this point. But given that a number of ritual undertakings can be regarded as logical transformations of each other, some of the particular changes are likely to be more plausible historically than others. After all it is generally agreed that the use of dough models derives historically from the use of live animals, and there can be little doubt that the purely verbal journey of the Thulung HuTpa derives ultimately from earlier processional journeys such as are still made with the Lokpar model. It is one thing to point to a particular local sequence, and quite another to speculate about general trends from one type to another. But it is hard to avoid feeling that a psychopompic chant is more likely to be a verbalisation of a mortuary procession than a procession is to be the acting out of a chant. In similar vein, the soul projection journey is more plausibly seen as the transposition into mental life of a physical journey than of a purley verbal one. This would leave it open whether the soul projection and verbal journeys were alternative etherealizations of the physical journey, or whether the latter was first internalised and then reduced to words alone.

In either case the yogic journey is typologically one in which the travelling has been internalised to a greater degree even than by the shaman. The history of yoga is a matter on which specialists disagree (Filliozat 1955), but for Eliade many of its roots lie in extra-Aryan spirituality, and its incorporation into the body of Sanskritic culture is one aspect of the "radical Asianisation" of the Indo-Europeans (1958:360). We know also that the Indo-Europeans were relatively uninterested in shamanic ritual journeys (idem 1964:378-9). Processions transporting images of the gods are less marked a feature of folk religion in the north of India than in the less Aryan south (Crooke 1914: 145b), and become prominent again (together with other types of ritual journey) as one moves north into the Bodic speaking zone. The relative neglect of the ritual journey by the Aryans makes sense in the light of their intense emphasis on the sacrifice, a prestational rite involving at most only the upward journey of the burnt offering. No doubt also a traditionally pastoral and nomadic people finds it less natural to project transcendental journeys onto the horizontal plane than do traditionally sedentary and agricultural ones. Thus reliance on ritual journeys is perhaps one of the major underlying historical differences between the ancient East and the Indo-European West, comparable in importance to the recognition of a specific relationship ("alliance") holding between the children of siblings of opposite sex.

Nicholas J. Allen

NOTES

1. In connection with the field research (1969-71) I gratefully acknowledge the financial support of the SSRC and the encouragement of Professor C. von Fürer-Haimendorf. Some helpful criticisms of earlier drafts of the present paper were made by Dr. A. Höfer of Heidelberg and Dr. R. Jain of Oxford.

2. Why Hindu culture and our own prefer to give greater emphasis to marriage is an interesting question.

3. The south-west is of course the direction associated in Hindu tradition with Yama, god of the dead, but this is probably irrelevant. For one thing the Thulung, though much concerned with north and south (identified with up and down), generally attach little significance to the other cardinal or intercardinal points. For another, it was said that the Rai of the Okhaldhunga area, who are probably more Hinduised than the Thulung, send their dead not towards the south-west, but towards Halesi, which lies to their south-east.

4. Probably the Mayām Dānda of the map published by the Ministry of Defence (2nd edition 1967, sheet U 462 east).

5. The intervention of the medium Simbure in his ritual attire is interesting since it was generally claimed that mediums are only concerned with the disposal of the bad dead (and he was not a particularly close relative of the deceased). The association of disparate types of officiant is a characteristic feature of Himalayan tribal death rituals (e.g. Lepcha, Gurung).

6. It is not clear whether the four journeys of the *ya* are along the same route, or whether, as one might suspect, they are directed successively one to each of the four cardinal points.

7. Cf. Kumaoni *lukuṛā* "clothes" (Turner 1931 s.v. *lugā*).

8. Emigré Thulung near Darjeeling used to place a pig's tail in the hand of the dying man, ostensibly to serve as a fan against the scorching heat of the spirit's upward journey (Hosten 1909:670). The explanation is fanciful and does not accord with eschatological ideas usually expressed in the Thulung homeland. It appears to show the influence of a literate religion, possibly of Christian missionaries such as Hosten himself.

9. We have spoken as if the one- way movement of the scapegoat

is necessarily represented in spatial terms whereas the two-way exchange of prestations occurs "in one place", i.e. without any journey. This seems the natural use of the words. In fact in both cases one can imagine the contrary (e.g. a scapegoat being consigned to flames at the point where it was consecrated), and it is difficult to be certain whether there is anything to justify the feeling that one of the two notions is inherently more suited to spatial projection than the other. If there is a justification, then any abbreviation of the journey of the scapegoat would bring it closer to the possibility of prestational interpretation.

REFERENCES

ALLEN, N.J. in press a. Approaches to illness in the Nepalese hills. To appear in forthcoming ASA volume on Social Anthropology and Medicine.

ALLEN, N.J. in press b. Shamanism among the Thulung Rai. To appear in projected volume on Shamanism in Nepal under editorship of J. Hitchcock.

ALLEN, N.J. in press c. Byansi kinship terminology: a study in symmetry. To appear in *Man*.

CROOKE, W. 1914. Images and idols (Indian). *Hastings encyclopedia of religion and ethics 7:* 142 - 6.

ELIADE, Mircea. 1958. *Yoga: immortality and freedom* (trans). London.

ELIADE, Mircea. 1964. *Shamanism: archaic techniques of ecstasy* (trans). London.

FILLIOZAT, J. 1955. Review of French edition of Eliade (1958). *JA 243*: 368 - 70

FRAZER, Sir James. 1925. *The scapegoat* (Part 6 of *The golden bough*). London.

FUNKE, F.W. 1969. *Religiöses Leben der Sherpa.* Innsbruck.

FÜRER-HAIMENDORF, C. von. 1964. *The Sherpas of Nepal.* London.

HITCHCOCK, John T. 1966. *The Magars of Banyan Hill.* New York.

HOSTEN, H. 1909. Paharia burial customs (British Sikkim). *Anthropos 4*: 669 - 683.

HUBERT, H. and MAUSS, M. 1964. *Sacrifice: its nature and function* (trans). London.

MACDONALD, A.W. 1953. Juggernaut reconstruit. *JA 241*:487 - 528.

MACDONALD, A.W. 1955. Quelques remarques sur les chasses rituelles de l'Inde du nord-est et du centre. *JA 243:* 101 - 115

NEBESKY-WOJKOWITZ, René de. 1956. *Oracles and Demons of Tibet.* London.

PIGNEDE, Bernard. 1966. *Les Gurungs*. Paris.

SCHRÖDER, Dominik. 1955. Zur Struktur des Schamanismus. *Anthropos 50:* 849 - 81.

SHERRING, C.A. 1905. Notes on the Bhotias of Almora and British Garhwal. *Mem. Asiatic Soc. Bengal 1:* 93 - 119.

SPENCER, Robert F. 1968. Review of C.M. Edsman (ed). Studies in Shamanism. *Am. Anth. 70*: 396 - 7.

STEIN, R.A. 1970. Un document ancien relatif aux rites funéraires des Bon-po tibetains. *JA 258*: 155 - 185.

TURNER, R.L. 1931. *A comparative and etymological dictionary of the Nepali language*. London.

Some Notions about Descent and Residence in Tibetan Society

A fundamental feature of any society is its system of descent, and related to that the pattern of residence. Through identifying what is the particular type of descent system operating in a society anthropologists are able to decipher other aspects of a social structure; jural relations, marriage patterns, stratification, political units and the rules according to which people are recruited to any number of groups in their society. But what happens when, as is the case in Tibet, there is a limited notion of descent which seems to throw no light on other social structures in the society?

Historians and travellers have written a considerable amount about the social life of Tibetan peoples, but a few anthropologists have contributed some details on the subject. Most of these writers have noted that as a general rule Tibetan people are organized into lineages and clans, and patriliny is accepted as the principle of descent operating throughout Tibet. Some writers, realizing the weakness of the data in regards to this rule, qualify their statements by saying the notion of patriliny was not a strong one, or simply that Tibetan society was 'generally patrilineal'. Recently Goldstein[2] with some awareness of the inadequacy of those explanations, and basing his remarks on more recently acquired data describes the Tibetan descent system as 'parallel'. However, he retains the notion of lineal descent.

Significantly no details have ever been provided to illustrate just how the patrilineal (or parallel if you wish) descent system actually operates among Tibetans. Instead we have been presented with a sizable body of general data about other than lineage/descent aspects of Tibetan social life: social stratification, marriage patterns (particularly the varieties of plural marriage), kinship terminologies, peasant-type economy and of course the religious. The absence of reference to descent in all that literature should have alerted us long ago to question our assumptions about the reality and theory of lineal descent in Tibet[3]. Contrary to the usual anthropological approach to social structure, in none of the discussions of Tibetan family and community life is the ideal or practice of descent investigated with the result that there has been no explanation of Tibetan social structure *per se*. The lack of any basic understanding of this kind has no doubt perpetuated the mystical, fragmented quality that Tibetan culture continues to possess. The assumptions about the existence of a 'generally patrilineal system' has also inhibited any research that might have investigated other forms of social organisation.

Alternative models had never been considered, and meanwhile, anthropologists studying Tibetan-type societies south of Tibet have found that they are distinctly patrilineal.[4] A range of Buddhist societies: in Ladakh, west Nepal, Solu-Khumbu and Sikkim, all exhibiting a culture very similar to that of Tibet supported earlier contentions about Tibetan social structure. Of these Himalayan societies, whose people all claim to have originated in Tibet proper and retained a strong resemblance and relationship with Tibetan society, it was natural to assume they had also acquired their patrilineal features from the Tibetan.

The well established practice of patrilocality in Tibet is no doubt another factor for our unquestioned assumptions about a patrilineal descent system. And Tibetan informants, probably most of whom were male, must have been describing their society with an ideal either of lineal descent or male dominance that was interpreted by investigators as the former.

The unfortunate result of these series of erroneous assumptions is our continued limited understanding of Tibetan social structure. In this paper I want briefly to re-examine the notion of descent as it operates, or does not operate, in regard to Tibet. After exploring just what are the limits of the ideal and role of descent in the social structure, I propose to consider an alternative, namely the factor of residence, in defining and explaining social relations of Tibetans.

Unilineality

First, acknowledgement of the existence of a limited descent principle is due. Historians are not entirely incorrect in expounding the existence of patrilineality in Tibet. Lineages and ideas about descent through males exist among Tibetans, and are explicit in geneological records from ancient and recent Tibet. They are mainly confined, however (as might be expected), to the Tibetan aristocracy and the class of hereditary priests *(sṅags-pa)*.[5] However, these two groups comprise a minor and elite sector of Tibetan society, and we cannot apply the rules of descent practised among them to the *mi-ser* (commoners) Tibetans who constitute the vast majority of the society.[6]

In Tibet, four basic endogamous groups can be identified: *sger-pa* (aristocracy), *sṅags-pa* (hereditary priests), *mi-ser* (incl. agriculturists, nomads, labourers, traders) and the *yawa* (outcastes).[7] These categories are for the most part endogamous although there is some marriage between members of the first two ranks, the aristocrats and priests, and less frequently, between low *mi-ser* and the *yawa*. A Tibetan belongs to one of these groups his or her membership being defined by paternity. The group is one's *brgyud-pa*[8]. *Brgyud-pa* as far as I understand passes through the bone (*rus* in Tibetan) which is equated with the male. The strength of the notion of paternity and of the lineages resulting from it varies from one group to another. It seems to be strongest among the *sṅags-pa* where priests (usually called lama) are organized into ancestor focused lineages. Each male possesses a special spiritual power, referred to as *gdun-brgyud*[9], and assumes the role as religious functionary, heading an estate as well. Whether or not an encumbant employs his spiritual power and exercises his role is a matter of choice, but both the power and right pass through successive generations. The royal priestly family of Khon in Sa-skya is one of the best known *sṅags-pa* lineages.[10] I am told that in Nanchen (eastern Tibet) patrilineal clans are extant, with people there tracing descent to six early ancestors and forming large corporate units, but this type of social organization seems to be particular to the east. In central southern Tibet, even the aristocratic families do not form corporate unilineal groups.

As among the higher ranked groups, there is a limited notion of patrilineal descent recognized among the lowly outcaste *yawa*. An individual who acquires his outcaste status through his father[11] (the mother may be non-*yawa*) is considered of full *yawa* status and therefore more polluted or defiled than one whose mother is a *yawa* (but whose father is not). While it is sometimes possible for the latter to marry by stages into the *mi-ser* group I am told it is almost impossible for a patrilineally descended individual to do so. Indeed in most cases of marriages of mixed ancestry I collected, the *yawa*-member was matrilaterally related to the outcaste group.

Membership in one of these four endogamous groups, and possession of the powers and status of that group, whatever the case may be, are where the limits of patrilineal descent in Tibet rest. Ancestor cult, clan land, moiety marriage, hereditary leadership, lineage gatherings for ritual purposes and other well recognised manifestations of unilineal descent are lacking in Tibetan culture.[12] This, I would argue supports my contention that lineal descent is in the case of Tibetan material, largely the notion of its writers, limited in actuality to the minimal position described above.

A Tibetan's social relations are for the most part contained within his endogamous group, and after initial membership is established in it there is no further reference to lineal descent. This is what I have found in my analysis of Dingri society.[13] Dingri is a district in south Tibet bordering Nepal. Up to 1959 it was inhabited by about 12,000 people most of whom were agriculturalists, traders and labourers belonging to the mi-ser class.[14] Dingri and its people exhibit a culture, dialect, economy and history that is their own and serves to define the society as a distinctive socio-economic unit. However, one can see in Dingri many of the features that have been described for other parts of Tibet. Furthermore the Dingri people consider themselves Tibetans in every respect, often drawing analogies between themselves and other Tibetan peoples. Tibetans from the central or eastern regions of the country think of Dingri people as Tibetan, at the same time as they recognise the distinctive features of Dingri society. Its size and the intensity of social interaction within Dingri makes it possible to observe intra-family relations, those between families, and further - between villages. It is also possible to record interaction between the various economic groups, to locate certain core families from which others emerged, and trace the development over 4 or 5 generations[15] in families of varying status.

What becomes clear at an early stage in the analysis of Dingri society and culture is the almost total absence of the notion of patrilineal or any other type of descent system in defining the relations of the Dingri people with each other and with the outsiders (in other parts of Tibet and in Nepal). At the same time one becomes aware that there is another social principle operating to give Dingri society the order it exhibits. This is the rule of residence and the solidarity of the household. The remainder of this paper then is devoted to setting out and examining what is the role of the household in Dingri society.

House Names

The name by which one is known in one's own locality and in the wider community in Dingri is that of one's natal or affinal house. Every house of a particular status is assigned a name in Dingri, and it is the name of the house together with that of the locality.[16] The household group is both a residential and kinship unit, however its name and that of its inhabitants bear no relation to a lineage or clan or any other descent concept. Although the housename is commonly employed to identify individuals in the community, all those people who are members of a kindred cannot be identified as kinsmen by reference to their housenames.

Housenames rather than personal names are employed throughout

Dingri in all social contexts. It is not an ancestor's title, but the name of one's residence (*groṅ-miṅ* or housename[17]) that places a man socially and economically; it defines his status in the family, the village, and in the wider community. Each house is assigned a name when the dwelling is first constructed. Usually that name is arrived at by adopting features from physical-geographic location. We find in Dingri names such as *khaṅ-kyi* (central house), *tashi khaṅ-sar* (auspicious new house), *tarap* (auspicious best), *O-ba* (lower one), *baro* (superior).[18] This name, prefixed to a title (house rank, kin term, occupation) or personal name serves to identify any particular individual. Within the household unit of course it is not applied, but outside the housename is invariably used. One finds people referred to as *Tarup* Tensin, *Takra* Conzom, *Chalek* Jola, *Gurukpa* Nama, *O-ba* Agu. (The housename is placed first, followed by a personal or kin term.)

In the wider geographic context, a housename is often prefixed by the name of its village; thus: *Tashi-zom Tarap-wa, Partso Takra, Yuldong Gurukpa, Gangar Chalek*. Although a village name if often combined with the housename the latter remains of greater importance. It is rarely omitted, for it is the most relevant indicator of one's socio-economic status. The wealthiest families of Dingri are well known in their own right, enjoying such elite status that no village name is necessary; *Ta-ser-a, Dashan, Se-nemo, Tarap-wa,* and *Kong-tsa* are a few houses of this rank.

One's housename is acquired by birth, marriage or adoption. Even in the case of marriage or adoption, where one's residence has changed, the natal housename will be retained and frequently used, usually to indicate previous high status. A girl born in *Gurukpa* for example, after marriage into *Ashan* house will be known both as *Gurukpa po-mo* (daughter of *Guruk* house) and *Ashan Nama*[19] (bride or wife of *Ashan* house). The house from which she has been received continues to have social relevance for her; it indicates status, and enables people to trace her ties to members of her kindred linked by birth or marriage to that house.[20] As we shall see later, kinship terms alone are insufficient for identification of the kindred. And in the absence of lineage names of symbols the housename is the significant link.

It is by the fact of one's birth in a house that one acquires the right to employ its housename. One takes the name of one's natal residence, not of one's father.[21] Of course, with the rule of patrilocality, it is usually the case that the housename of one's father and one's natal residence are one and the same. It is only when there is no patrilocal residence, and by implication no legitimate marriage, that we are able to recognise that the rule is one of residence and not descent. In cases of illegitimacy although certain problems arise for an unmarried mother, no great shame accrues to the girl. A pregnant girl usually remains with her own family, and her child is born in her natal residence. This is known as the house of the *a-źaṅ* - the mother's brother (MB) - who will likely have taken the household over from the mother's father. If the illegitimate child is a boy, it is often the case that he is absorbed into the household of the MB. Upon reaching adulthood he may acquire equal rights with the MB's sons sharing his MB's property. This will include the sharing of the *nama* who is brought in as the wife of that generation of males remaining in the house.[22] Sometimes the sister's son is so completely absorbed into the household that after one or two generations his original paternity has been forgotten, and other kinsmen will not know he was not originally a full son of the household head. If a sister's son is not accepted into the household, a place will still be found for him among her kinsmen; often such a child is sent to live in a monastery with one of his mother's kinsmen, becoming a monk in due course.

The housename carries with it the status of the family, and within Dingri (there are about 1,200 households in the district) most people will know what is the status of any household. First, the mere possession of a housename signifies a certain socio-economic status. The commoners *(miser)* that comprised most of the Dingri population are divided into three economic classes: the *khralpa* or *groṅ-pa* (agriculturalist), the *tshoṅ-pa* (trader) and the *dud-chuṅ* (labourer).[23] The *groṅ-pa*, settled in the Dingri villages are the most conservative and longest settled of the Dingri people. Despite heavy tax obligations and lack of outright ownership of land, some hereditary land rights obtain to them; they exhibit a strong family structure, and enjoy status and wealth. A mark of their status is the possession of a housename, referred to as *groṅ-miṅ*.

The *dud-chuṅ* are a shifting class of labourers and artisans. They are characterized by their loose family structure (small nuclear family units without property rights) and the absence of a *groṅ-miṅ*. Several members of this class, when asked their housename replied "We have no housename, we are *dud-chuṅ*". They equate housename with *groṅ-pa* status, and its absence with their own position. The two are exclusive of one another, but there is some mobility from one status group to another through marriage and economic power.

The traders, most of whom were resident in the commercial-administrative centre of Dingri Gangar, unless they have migrated from an agricultural *groṅ-pa* community, possess no housename either. In lieu of a housename many use the title of their administrative rank, or the name of the locality (outside Dingri) from which they have emigrated. Others of this class marry into local Dingri families and adopt the names of the latter; *dud-chuṅ* in similar situations do likewise.

Usually the housename or rank name of a family is sufficient to identify it socially. But when an additional claim is made in regard to an individual's status, more often it is his house that is described, not his ancestry or paternity. An individual would be said to be of *mi-tshaṅ phyug-po* or *mi-tshan che* (a wealthy or a big family). *Mi-tshaṅ*, literally translated is 'people-nest'. The household is a 'nest of people'. It suggests that the residential factor is central, not that of kinship. Members of a *mi-tshaṅ* reside in the same household unit. Even the closest of one's kindred are not included if they do not share the same residence. The Tibetans' use of the word *mi-tshaṅ*, suggests this term in addition to denoting household, also means 'family'. In Tibetan societies there is no kinship unit larger than the household that could be described as a family. (Indeed I could not identify any term other than *mi-tshaṅ* that refers to a family unit.) If the suggestion of family=household is accepted, it surely implies some significant change is due in our analysis of Tibetan societies. A discussion of the implications this equation holds for our understanding of the Tibetans' system of inheritance, of plural marriage patterns, etc. may emerge later in the discussion.[24]

Kinship terminology in the kindred and the household.

Tibetan kinship terminology has never been adequately described, neither as it bears on the social structure, nor the patrilineal descent system which was claimed to exist. Now, recognizing the limits of the descent system in Tibetan societies, this earlier confusion about Tibetan kinship is understandable. However, it still remains to elucidate the meaning and form of the kinship terminologies employed by Tibetans. With the central role of the household in mind, new meanings and order emerge.

There are two naming systems common in Dingri, one is a bilateral system; the other is a system of ranks within the household. They are combined in such a way, it is only when we recognize the household as the fundamental social unit, that the terminologies employed reflect and elucidate the way Tibetan people see each other. First I shall describe the bilateral system. We shall see that in itself, it does not offer a complete explanation of what is going on in the family.

Tibetans first of all distinguish kinsmen from those who are not. All kinsmen, those related consanguineally are referred to as one's *spuns*.[25] This includes all of one's mother's kin as well as one's father's. There is no generic term for each of these groups. Those related through the mother are referred to as *a-ma'i spuns*; those through the father are known as *pha-pa'i spuns*. Full siblings are distinguished as *spuns pha-źig ma-źig* (kin of the same mother and father). The degree of consanguinity is not reflected in the terminology. But there is a distinction made between close kinsmen *(spuns ne-po)* and those who are not close *(spuns ma-ñe)*.

Although people recognize the *spuns* according to whether they are matrilaterally or patrilaterally related, there seems to be no preference shown for one side over the other (except for locality of residence) in the assignment of rights and obligations. Kinship terms distinguish the sides, but there is no set of rules regarding inheritance of property, or choice of in marriage partner that indicates a preference for one side over the other, or through one line more than another. I was unable to find any case where preference is made to a line of descent, male or female.

For selecting one's marriage partner, the kindred on both sides are equally important in defining the exogamous group. In Dingri there is a strongly enforced rule of exogamy; sexual relations (and therefore marriage) with any other member of one's kindred (including both matrilateral and patrilateral kin) is prohibited. This kindred is an extensive group, encompassing all those people to whom one is related on both sides extending back through about six generations. (Some informants cited 5 generations as the minimum, but others claimed it extends to 7 and 9). All those people recognized as kinsmen, both agnates and cognates, constitute the exogamous unit in Tibetan society. Those people to whom one cannot trace descent (to those limits) are simply non-kin, and, as such, they are potential affines.[26]

For defining the exogamous unit then, descent is a basic factor, but the side of descent is not. It is interesting that while they distinguish between the maternal and paternal sides, and as we shall see, express the difference in their kinship terminology, one side does not seem to play a special role. The bilateral kinship terminology employed throughout Tibet has been described by other writers.[27] However, it seems to me that they never reduce it to its basic and simple nature. I therefore take this opportunity, using the Dingri material to clarify it. As a development of the fundamental distinction of sides, the factors of age and sex further define which kinship terms Tibetans employ. All classificatory father's brothers in the ascending generation are *agu*, all father's sisters are *ani*. The head of the household in each generation has the rank of *pha-la* (F), *po-la* (FF), and *yaṅ-po* (FFF). Complementary to this: *ama-la* (M), *mo-la* (FM), and *yaṅ-mo* (FFM) are reserved only for the senior woman in each generation.

The mother's side follows the same pattern. Here all classificatory mother's brothers in the ascending generations are called *a-źaṅ*, and all one's mother's sisters are *a-sru* (or *sru-mo*).

These kinship terms are employed when the speaker is younger. To those younger than himself, a person simply uses a personal name or the diminutive *pu* (for boys) and *pu-mo* (for girls). Whether one uses *agu/ani* on one side or *a-źaṅ/a-sru* is determined not by line but by side. A person, X, for example, if a woman, will be addressed *'ani'* by her brother's son or daughter, *'a-sru'* only by her brother's daughter's children.

Dingri informants often follow these rules and explained the simple system carefully and with an awareness of its logical pattern. However, in my observations of the common everyday forms of address, I noted many deviations from these rules; sometimes there are complete contradictions. For example, persons are often called *agu* and *ani* although they bear no kin relation to the speakers; sometimes people related matrilaterally address each other by those so-called patrilateral terms, and in a few cases a child calls its pater, *'agu'* (FB). Furthermore kinship terms are often assigned to people who are one's affines, and affinal terms are occasionally applied to one's kinsmen.

The initial impression of chaos and inconsistency disappears, however, when the position of monks, nuns, and married priests is understood, and finally when we recognize how household ranking is applied. The terms *agu* and *ani* (father's brother and father's sister) are commonly employed in addressing monks and nuns; they are used regardless of relative ages of speaker and addressee and between kinsmen as well as non-kinsmen. If a man becomes a monk he is addressed by the term, *agu*. It often happens that a man leaves the monastic life after some years. Still people continue to call him *'agu'*.[28] Even after a junior brother in a household succeeds to the elder brother's position, he will be called *agu* by kinsmen as well as others.

Certain titles are due to men of rank; for example *pha-la* is a term reserved for senior men, and will be employed by all villagers - some kinsmen, others not - of all ages. Conversely, some men by virtue of their religious rank and the ideal of celibacy cannot be called *pha-la* even though they may marry and have children. There are two well known Dingri priests *(lama)* who have married; in both cases, while the villagers and their kinsmen address them "Lama", their own children call them *agu*, not *pha-la*!

Finally considering the household ranks applied within the residential unit, interesting patterns emerge, and explain some of the inconsistencies in the bilateral system. Within each household individuals are ranked according to age, sex and political status. The terms applied are listed below; without the additional housenames before them as would appear in ordinary use.

Dingri kinship-household terminologies

Father's father	*po la*
Father's father's elder brother	*agu che*
Father's father's younger brother	*agu rgen*
Father's mother	*mo la*, or *ama rgen*
Father	*pha la*
Father's brother	*agu la*
Father's younger brother	*agu + name*
Father's sister	*ani* (she will be patrilocally resident if she is a nun)
Mother	*ama*
Mother's sister	*ama chuṅ* or *ama* + name (if she is a coresident junior wife)
Elder brother	*jo la* or *cho jo* (lit. *gcen po)*

Elder brother's wife	*nama* (the wife of elder brother but shared by all his junior brothers in the same residence)
Junior wife	*tshud ma*
Younger brother	*agu*, or personal name
Elder sister	*a che*, or *che je* (lit. *gcen mo)*
Younger sister	*ani* (if a nun) or personal name
Son	*pu* (+ name)
Daughter	*pu mo* (+ name)

These terms above are those usually employed among members of a household; other members of their village including their agnates, cognates, and their affines use them as well. It can be seen that some of these are kinship terms. Others however are not; rather they are household ranks used in the same way as kin terms. There are certain ranks of which there can only be one per household. For example, in any house there is only one person addressed *pha-la*, one *ama*, one *jo-la*, and one *nama*. The position of the *nama* is particularly interesting. This term is reserved for the bride who enters the household in each generation to become the shared wife of all males in that generation residing patrilocally. If she is barren or dies young a second wife, (often her own sister) will be brought in to the house. The latter, however, will never acquire the rank of *nama*;[29] it is only the *nama* who is received with a dowry and enjoys certain rights in the house she enters. A woman received as a *nama* retains that title as long as her son is unmarried. As soon as the latter receives a bride, the new wife is addressed as *nama* and the former *nama* becomes *ama*. The same rules apply for the *jo-la* rank. When the senior brother receives the *nama* on behalf of his household, he is entitled to be addressed as *jo-la*. He retains that title until his own eldest son receives a *nama*. (Of course his own parents will always call him by name, or *pu*, and his children will address him *pha-la*.)

In Dingri the term *jo-la* is reserved for the sons of the households recognized as superior rank. Within such a high-status house, *jo-la* is employed as a kinship term for the eldest brother; it is inextricably bound up with the unity and social status of that household. I once heard a teenage girl reprimanded by friends for addressing her own brother as *jo-la*. That term, it was pointed out, should have only been used for higher status *groṅ-pa*; her own house was not of high enough rank to sanction its use. Villagers say, when they recognize a family has reached a certain political and economic status in the community, they begin to employ these special household ranks. *Nama* are also ranked. Differential status of brides arises out of the practice of hypogamy through various ranks of Dingri households and a variety of terms for bride designate the rank of her original house. While these might also be thought of as kin and affine terms, they are inextricably related to the ranks of the donor a and receiving households. From the particular form of address applied to a Dingri *nama*, it is possible to determine the rank of her natal household vis-a-vis that of her husband's house.

While recognition of the kindred is important in defining the exogamous unit, frequently the details seem to be overlooked. Often people do not know what is their precise kin affiliation. Usually only the household name of their common ancestor is cited being all that is deemed necessary to verify the kin relationship. However, that does not seem to be important. One woman, defined her relation to a man in the village simply saying she was his *a-źaṅ* (classifactory mother's sister). She could not supply the precise details of their kinship, but noted the common household from which her mother and his mother's mother had originally come. That house held high social status in Dingri. That is what seems more important and Dingri people are able to remember kinsmen among families of higher status households better than those in lower ones. This is another clear illustration of the precedence the household takes over the notion of descent and kinship.

Political, economic, and ritual dimensions of the household

It is hardly necessary at this point that I urge a re-examination of the economic and political systems of the Tibetans. Indeed writings on those subjects seem to have proceeded without reference either to unilineal models or to family and social life. However a more thorough and useful analysis of the Tibetan economic and political systems might be forthcoming if the corporate nature of the household unit were approached as one important variable in the systems. Rules of inheritance, succession to political office, bridewealth and dowery, economic co-operation and taxation among other institutions when seen in terms of the household group should become more than the nebulous or fragmented composite of Tibetan social structure that we have so far had to deal with.

The Tibetan household as a ritual unit is another new area for consideration. The abundant literature on Tibetan religion is surprisingly devoid of reference to household religion,[30] and before any extensive analysis can be undertaken, new material will have to become available. Even with the limited material I obtained from Dingri on household ritual practices, there is a strong suggestions that the household plays an important position in defining ritual beliefs and practices. One of the most obvious examples is the general rule that for all life crisis ceremonies, the household of the individual concerned must be the sponsoring unit. As well as an individual shrine in each household, there are said to be a company of spiritual beings residing in the house, who are ranked according to certain parallel household positions. Further research will probably show that those rituals performed in the household reflect beliefs about intra-household relations as well as the relationships between the housemembers and their supernatural cohabitants. I observed that when there is either a birth or death[31] the household in which it occurs enters a state of tabu, during which time all household members are isolated from the rest of the community. Together, after a period of confined ritual relations, these people undergo a cleansing ritual in the house. Only after these are completed are outsiders, kinsmen as well as others, allowed to enter the house.[32] It is not possible to elaborate further on these rituals here; I mention them briefly with the intention of inviting further research and dialogue on this aspect of Tibetan religion as well as to point out supportive material on the centrality of the Tibetan household in diverse facets of its culture.

One problem that emerges out of these findings is the relation Tibetan social structure bears on the Buddhist Bhotia societies bordering Nepal. Those societies are patrilineal in nature, and good empirical evidence of the realities of this descent principle are indisputable. Now, the implications are that in their process of migration from Tibet into various parts of Nepal, the Bhotias have experienced fundamental changes in their social structure, perhaps involving the developing of a new type of descent system. This is not a totally inacceptable hypothesis; there are other studies (Freedman 1966)[33] shows that with migration to a new area, the lineages strengthen. If there is a shift from an essentially Tibetan bilateral household oriented culture, to a patrilineal Bhotia one, then we must direct our attention more on that process of migration. The points at which new migrants from Tibet are being absorbed into the highland peoples of Nepal might be re-examined.

Barbara Aziz

NOTES

1. Material presented in this paper was collected in Nepal during 1970 and 1971. I am grateful to the SSRC of GB for their financial support of my research in Nepal. My thanks are also due to C. von Fürer-Haimendorf for his assistance and advice.

2. Goldstein, M. 1971. 'Stratification, Polyandry, and Family Structure in Central Tibet', in *Southwestern J. of Anthropology*, Vol. 27, p.65.

3. Prince Peter of Greece, 1963, *The Study of Polyandry*, Mouton; Stein, R.A. 1962, *La civilisation tibétaine*, Dunod; Bell, C. 1931, *The People of Tibet*; Ekvall, R. 1968, *Fields on the Hoof*, Holt, Rinehart and Winston. These are the major studies to which I am referring.

4. Cf. C. von Fürer-Haimendorf, The Sherpas of Nepal, 1964, G. Gorer, Himalayan Village, 1938; Kihara (ed.) Nepal Himalaya, 1957.

5. This and all other Tibetan words used in the text are transliterated according to the Library of Congress system. Where a more simplified phonetic spelling is used, it is so stated in the text.

   In regards to *ṅags-pa*, 'hereditary priests' is only a rough translation to facilitate some initial comprehension of what is involved and is not to be taken as a final translation of this word. Other writers have translated *ṅags-pa* as tantricist but this is meaningless in sociological as well as religious terms.

6. I would suggest these percentages as a rough estimate of the proportional representation of each class in Tibetan Society: *mi-ser* 90%; *yawa* 8%; *ṅags-pa* .5% and *sger-pa* .5%. These are based on data from Dingri.

7. Other names applied to members of the outcaste society of Tibetans are: *spaṅ-go*, *gdol-pa*, *śan-pa* (butcher), and *ragyaba* (after Das and Lhandon). In the beliefs concerning them and their rank in society, they seem to be much like the Sherpa *khamendu* (C. Fürer-Haimendorf, op. cit.). They are treated at much greater length in my doctoral dissertation, 1974, University of London entitled: The People of Dingri.

8. I translate this as line of succession, or heredity. There is some confusion in the literature about this word as there

is about the existence and form of lineage structure. *Brgyud-pa* is most often found translated as lineage, but Bell renders it as 'genealogy', and Buck offers 'tribe' and 'family' under this listing. The lexical confusion over all words having to do with group structure of the Tibetans is a manifestation of the misunderstanding of the social system itself.

9. Bell (1920, English-Tibetan Dictionary) lists this as lama's genealogy; there seems to be a certain agreement that this is a quality pertaining to married priests.

10. The history of this family is presented in Cassinelli and Ekvall, 1969, *A Tibetan Principality*.

11. The quality attributed to all *yawa* is *grib*, translated as defilement.

12. For a fuller discussion, cf. my doctoral thesis, op.cit.

13. Dingri, with the rest of Tibet proper has been subject to severe changes as a result of the new Chinese administration recently established there. All of my material dates from before 1959 when my informants, presently settled in Nepal, still lived in Dingri.

14. The *mi-ser* class, as noted constitutes 90% of the total population; therefore for the most part Dingri social relations are confined to members of this group. What I am describing throughout this paper unless otherwise stated are *mi-ser* social relations.

15. Most families can trace descent in Dingri back only four generations and some less than this. All inhabitants claim to be migrants, having moved to Dingri from another part of Tibet. Their knowledge of their ancestors is usually limited to those who have lived in Dingri only.

16. One's locality, called *yul*, is usually confined to the cluster of houses which constitute a village. They are discreet economic-political units to which most individuals' social relations are confined, and people have strong emotional as well as structural ties to their *yul*.

17. Also called *khaṅ-miṅ*, or simply *mi-tshaṅ-kyi-miṅ*.

18. Proper names listed here are spelled phonetically and not according to the transliteration system.

19. *Nama* is also spelled: *mna'ma* and *phag-ma*.

20. There is also the implication in this practice that certain ties between the girl and her house are maintained after her marriage out. Indeed a girl's brother continues to exert power over her (and her children) and sometimes her husband as well.

21. That is to say, neither the pater nor the genitor.

22. This practice of fraternal polyandry is common among the Dingri agriculturalists and has been recorded as extant in all parts of Tibet and the Himalayas.

23. These three classes are common throughout Tibet, and have been noted throughout the literature. These are not exclusive however as they do not include either the aristocrats or the nomadic peoples who as it happens are not represented in Dingri.

24. The complete discussion on these issues are contained in my thesis, op.cit.

25. Note the similarity of this with the Hindi term for kindred: *sapinda*. Cf. Berreman, 1963, *Hindus of the Himalayas*, pp. 179-180.

26. This implies of course that the exogamous unit is very large. As one might expect to happen after a few generations of residence in an area, it becomes increasingly difficult to find affines. This may be a factor in the degree of variation in marriage patterns we find between affines in Tibetan society, viz. once an affine is found, all of his kinsmen become potential sexual partners.

27. *Bendict*, P. 1941, Tibetan and Chinese Kinship Terms, in HJAS Vol. 6, pp. 313-331, and Prince Peter of Greece, op.cit.

28. Dingri people often pronounce this *a-wo*

29. The title of the junior wife is *tṡhud-ma*, whether or not she is the younger sister of the *nama*, but she is not generally addressed this way.

30. With the exception of Nebesky-Wojkowitz R. de, 1956, *Oracles and Demons of Tibet*, Mouton. Even in this study material on household rituals is fragmentary and of little use.

31. The pollution of the house brought on by a birth is called *son-grib* or *skye-grib*, and that by death is *ži-grib*. I have heard another term, *sno-sib* (sp.?) also used in connection with the birth pollution. Cf. Das' Dictionary for *grib* p244.

There is an ancestral god, *ma brgyud skyes lha* which is invoked at a birth rite.

32. The washing ceremony for both should be undertaken by a celibate monk, but a married priest may perform it. The general term of the rite is simply, *'khrus-gsol*. The period of tabu after birth is at least one week, but may be as long as a month; after the washing ceremony, a secular festival called *baṅs-gsaṅ*. The period observed after a death is usually about three days, but in a few Dingri villages, the purification rite is performed immediately after the death occurs and people may enter and leave the house from then on.

33. Freedman, M. 1966. *Chinese Lineage and Society*, Athlone.

** The Tibetan-English dictionaries consulted are:
Das, C. 1970 ed. Motilal Banarsidass, Delhi.
Buck, S.H. 1969. Catholic University of America Press.
Bell, C. 1920. English-Tibetan Colloquial Dictionary.

Inter-Caste Marriages in a Nepalese Town

Among anthropologists concerned with South Asia the view is widespread that endogamy is a fundamental feature of any definition of caste. Many would agree with Karve that while there might be a 'few exceptions', castes are essentially intra-marrying groups (1965:5). Thus, although their definitions differ in other respects, both Berreman (1960:120) and Sinha (1967:94) characterise a caste system as a hierarchy of endogamous divisions. Atal, moreover, identifies intra-marriage as the pivotal attribute (1968), while Mandelbaum seems to suggest that intra-*jati* marriage is virtually a categorical imperative. He writes: '... all of a person's kin by descent and marriage, both actual and potential, are within his *jati;* none are outside it' (1970:33). In this he appears to echo Leach who, in his introduction to *Aspects of Caste in South India, Ceylon and North-west Pakistan* observes that 'the kinship peculiarity of caste systems does not lie in the internal structuring of kinship, but in the total absence of kinship as a factor in extra-caste systemic organisation ... kinship relations are exclusively internal' (1962:7). In a different paper, Leach again notes how 'each individual is born into a particular named group which is the same as that of <u>both</u> his parents ...' (1967:9) (my emphasis).

Dumont and Yalman, however, find such statements which suggest that endogamy is the basic or even unique principle of caste overly simplistic. Both prefer to regard its occurrence rather as the net outcome of individual decisions generated by the more fundamental principle of hierarchy (cf Yalman 1962:95; 1969:127; Dumont 1964:91). According to Dumont, 'castes are self-reproducing because this is a condition for the application of the hierarchical principle by which they are arranged in order' (1964:113). This principle, moreover, 'does not stop at the outward boundary of each particular caste-group, it permeates it ...' (ibid).

In this view, therefore, hypergamy may be seen as a feature of the caste system no less paramount than isogamy, and marriages across caste boundaries need not be regarded as deviations from an ideal form.

But while Dumont regards the entire system as permeated by the notion of hierarchy, he is concerned to distinguish the significance of isogamous from hypergamous marriages. His argument is that a difference of status and legitimacy is recognised between unions and between the offspring they produce according as whether the couple are of equal or unequal rank (1964:87). Because of the need to maintain the status of the group, men's principal and women's primary unions must be isogamous, and only then, in their subsidiary or secondary marriages can hypergamy be tolerated (Dumont 1966:115-16).

This paper considers some implications of a relatively high incidence of inter-caste unions in a small administrative town in western Nepal.[1] The discussion is offered as a complement to what Barth has called the 'purely scholastic explanations' of this phenomenon (1962:132). My interest here is in the demographic and politico-economic background to inter-caste unions, in the nature of the links between kinsmen and affines belonging to different castes in the town, and finally, in the consequences of such unions for townsmen's perceptions of hierarchy. The view I take, which draws both from Barth (1962) and Pocock (1972) is that inter-caste marriages (provided they do not link groups across the 'pollution barrier') do no violation to the status hierarchy in the community - and so need not occur only after preliminary, isogamous unions have been concluded - because there is an unambiguous principle of status conferment.

To begin, I describe the physical and historical setting of Belaspur Bazaar, the pseudonym of the town.

The Setting

Belaspur Bazaar is situated in the south-central portion of Belaspur district of which it is the administrative and market centre. The district is part of the far western hills of Nepal, one of the more economically backward areas of the country. The region's poor soil and inadequate rainfall conspire to produce the highest per capita deficit of grain in the kingdom. The far western hills are physically isolated from the main centres of commerce and administration, as well. It is a week's journey on foot from the bazaar to the nearest major town in the terai, the source of most manufactured goods found in the shops and homes of Belaspur district, and the immediate destination of most of its (mainly dairy) exports.

Prior to 1962, Belaspur was one of 35 districts into which the country had been partitioned in the early part of the 19th century. At the time of the 1961 census it contained an area of approximately 1,800 sq. miles, and a population of roughly 300,000. In 1962, a major administrative reorganization which divided the kingdom into 75 new districts reduced the area and population of what had been Belaspur by more than half; by 1969, at the time of my fieldwork, numbers in the newly bounded unit were an estimated 137,000.

The district's population, like that in most parts of Nepal, may be divided into a number of caste *(jat)* groups, each of which is associated with one of three main, ranked ritual categories. At the top of the hierarchy are the *tagadhari* castes, who wear the 'sacred thread' of Hinduism. These are internally ranked with the Brahmins, who monopolise priestly services, accorded the highest status. The Jaisis, who are descended from the marriages of Brahmin men and Brahmin widows claim a place immediately below the priestly group. Members of both castes are referred to, and refer to themselves as *bahun*, but the Brahmins prefix the term 'Upadyaya' which indicates their superior status. The Jaisis do not serve as household priests, although they provide most of the astrologers in the region.

A place next to the Brahmins is also claimed by the Thakuris, who assert Rajput ancestry and, of greater importance, have been associated for centuries with royalty both nationally and regionally. The area of what is now Belaspur district was part of the Malla empire which emerged around the tenth century and ruled over much of present-day western Nepal and western Tibet (Tucci 1962). With its collapse some three centuries later, that part of the empire which extended over western Nepal was gradually replaced by a number of petty states established by Hindu immigrants fleeing the Muslim invasions of North India, and ruled by Thakuri rajas. Much of Belaspur district was a part of one such state until the middle of the sixteenth century, when the latter was divided into several units and the area in the immediate vicinity of what is now Belaspur Bazaar became an independent principality with its own Thakuri ruler.

Belaspur, along with all the states of western Nepal, fell to the Gorkha armies[2] during the final two decades of the eighteenth century, and the rulers lost their sovereign rights in their former territories. Most, however, like the Belaspur *raja*, were given small grants of land which allowed them either to enjoy the cultivation rights and a degree of tax relief on these lands, or assigned them the taxes paid by the cultivators. Along with the latter kind of grant went the privilege to exact corvée from each cultivator household. These privileges, in modified form, were passed on to their patrilineal descendants (called *chautariya)* and were only finally abolished with the establishment of the *panchayat* system in 1960-61. By virtue of their association with these rulers Thakuris have been regarded as a kind of 'aristocracy' in the area, and have provided some of the most prominent families in Belaspur. Under the pre-1961 system of tax-collection operating in the district, 10 of the 16 senior headmanships *(jimmawal)* were held by Thakuris, although they probably constituted no more than 15 percent of the district population then as now.

By general agreement, the Chetris rank below both Jaisis and Thakuris, even if the wealthiest among them would acknowledge ritual inferiority only to the Brahmins. As the largest group in the district (see Table 1) the Chetris may be regarded as a 'dominant caste' and nowadays the wealthiest and most influential peasants are as likely to be Chetris as Thakuris.

The Joggis - mainly the offspring of ascetics who gave up their celibate lives and became 'householders' (cf. P. Caplan 1973) - are commonly recognised as the lowest of the 'twice-born' castes, although strictly speaking, they do not wear the sacred thread and the Nepalese Law Code *(Muluki Ain)* introduced by the Ranas (and replaced only in 1963) ranked Joggis as a separate category below the *tagadhari* castes.

The groups collectively referred to as *matwali* or 'drinking' castes comprise the next category in the ritual hierarchy. This is the level at which Nepal's indigenous 'tribal' groups such as the Magars and Gurungs, have been absorbed into the caste system. In addition, the Newars who, in their native Kathmandu Valley, have an elaborate system of stratified groups (cf. Fürer-Haimendorf 1956; Rosser 1966) are, with a sole exception noted below, classified in the Belaspur context as a single *matwali* caste, and ranked above the others. None of these groups wears the sacred thread but all are regarded as ritually 'clean', so that they are served by Brahmin household priests *(purohit)*, and members of twice-born groups will accept water from their hands. *Tagadhari* castes, however, will not normally eat ritually relevant foods e.g. rice cooked by members of *matwali* groups.

The lowest place in the ritual hierarchy is assinged the 'untouchables' *(pani na calne jat)* who are considered ritually impure, so that those associated with the two higher categories will accept no food or water from them nor allow them entry to their homes. In this area, the untouchables include, in addition to Sarkis (Leatherworkers), Damais (Tailors and Musicians) and Kamis (smiths) found throughout the country, both Muslims and Newar Kasais (Butchers). According to the pre-1963 Legal Code, however, the latter two groups were ranked marginally higher than the former (Gaborieau 1972).

Table 1 gives the relative ranking of each caste and ritual category in the district. The percentages they represent of the total district population of 137,000 are shown in brackets.

Table 1

Ranking and Population of ritual categories and castes in Belaspur district.

'Clean' Castes (73.0%)

'Twice-born' *(tagadhari)* castes (59.9%)

Brahmin (1.7%)
Jaisi (10.5%) - Thakuri (13.0%)
Chetri (32.8%)
Joggi (1.9%)

'Drinking' *(matwali)* castes (13.1%)

Newar (.4%)
Gurung (.8%) - Magar (11.8%) - Other (.1%)

'Untouchable' castes (27.0%)

Kasai/Butcher & Muslim (.4%)
Kami/Smith (18.8%) - Damai/Tailor (5.0%) - Sarki/Leatherworker (2.8%)

All the evidence points to the establishment and growth of Belaspur Bazaar following the incorporation of the area into the Nepalese state. In the southern portion of the town is its most prominent structure, a hexagonally-shaped stone fort which dominates the bazaar and surrounding region. It was almost certainly built by the conquering Gorkha forces as one of a series of military posts to protect the far western sector of the newly forged kingdom.

Very little is known of the administrative organisation of the country during the 50 year period following its unification under the Thakuri dynasty of Gorkha, save that it was based on military forts such as the one in Belaspur. During this period, however, the kingdom was divided into a number of districts which, with a few subsequent adjustments, were to serve as the principal units of administration for the next 150 years (Kumar 1967). The bazaar thus arose as the official capital of Belaspur district, and gradually became a small market and service centre as well.

Today the population of Belaspur Bazaar totals just under 1,000 persons. Table 2 gives the numbers in each caste.

Table 2

Population of Belaspur Bazaar

	Numbers		Percentages	
'Clean' castes				
'Twice-born' castes				
Chetri	143		15.2	
Thakuri	50		5.3	
Joggi	10		1.1	
Jaisi	4		.4	
		207		22.0
'Drinking' castes				
Newar	267		28.4	
Magar	14		1.5	
Gurung	11		1.2	
Other	4		.4	
		296		31.5
		503		53.5
'Untouchable' castes				
Leatherworker	173		18.4	
Tailor	147		15.6	
Smith	66		7.0	
Butcher	51		5.4	
		438		46.5
		941		100.0

The caste composition of the bazaar is clearly quite distinct from that in the district as a whole. Whereas twice-born groups make up almost 60 percent of the district's population, they constitute only slightly more than one-fifth of the town's inhabitants. Drinking castes, by comparison are 13 percent in the district, but 31.5 percent in the town, and the overwhelming majority of the latter are Newars, who are virtually unrepresented outside the bazaar. Finally, against an untouchable population of 27 percent in Belaspur district, almost half of all townspeople (46.5 percent) are so ranked.

Briefly, then, in contradistinction to the demographic pattern in the district as a whole, the town is characterised by a predominance of castes at the lower end of the ritual hierarchy, which are, moreover, otherwise sparsely represented in the area at large. Townsmen and villagers have traditionally occupied different economic roles as well (although during the past two decades these differences have been diminishing). The latter have been largely self-sufficient agriculturalists. The former, by contrast, have been associated with commerce and administration, in the case of clean castes, and with craft services, in the case of untouchables. Since this paper will consider inter-caste unions between members of clean castes only, I shall omit further discussion of the untouchable groups.

Settlement

It is impossible to be certain about the history of settlement in the bazaar, but it is probable that the earliest permanent inhabitants of clean caste were Newars. The majority trace their origins several generations back to Kathmandu Valley. Most came originally as part of the personal entourage of a senior member of the administration, usually the Rana governor. Depending on personal abilities and the strength of ties to the patron, these men were, on arrival in the district, assigned jobs in his living quarters or posts in the offices of the administration, including the local militia. Those who stayed on in the town after completion of their tour of duty, or resigned the protection of a patron-official on the latter's return to Kathmandu or transfer to another district, did so for several reasons.

For one thing, many Newars settled in the town because of the poverty of their home environment, since most who left Kathmandu in the first place, as clients of officials, did so out of economic necessity. Early administration records support the statements of informants that those who remained to settle were by and large from a number of low and economically depressed castes, such as Nau (Potter), Kau (Blacksmith) and Bada (Coppersmith).

Secondly, settlement in the bazaar was stimulated by a commutation of taxes on house sites in the town, a policy designed to encourage permanent residence in small urban centres throughout the country. A third reason was the growing attractiveness of petty commerce, an occupation which bazaar residents often adopted after completion of their government service. Finally, in more recent times, a number of unattached men were encouraged to settle locally by the possibility of marrying local brides and benefiting from attractive 'dowries'. Thus, a number of Newar settlers who became merchants owed the establishment of their shops to the assistance of well-to-do fathers-in-law.

The other clean castes - Chetri, Thakuri, Joggi, Jaisi, Magar and Gurung - are more recent arrivals in the town. In no case is the first immigrant more than one generation back. A few simply abandoned homes in distant areas and settled, like the Newars, after completing a tour in government service in the district. Most, however, have migrated from villages within Belaspur district, and about half the adult members of these groups now in the bazaar have come in their own lifetimes. Insufficient land to meet a rising population can help to explain the growing interest in the bazaar on the part of these former peasants. (In the 40 year period up to 1961 the population of Belaspur had tripled.)

But the motives bringing Belaspur villagers to reside permanently in the town must also be sought in the circumstances of the migrants themselves. Personal biographies reveal a number of motives for the decision to move residence from the village to the town. One frequently cited is family quarrels over inheritance claims leading to bitter and irreconcilable divisions between brothers. Another relates to marriages which are not readily tolerated within village society. These usually take place between members of different castes and may lead to the establishment of a residence for the woman in the bazaar, to her children being born there and regarded, as well as regarding themselves, as 'bazaariyas'.

Marriages of townspeople

The growth of an administrative and commercial centre in the midst of a traditional peasant society presented new settlers in the bazaar - most of whom were men - with difficulties relating to the establishment of affinal ties with members of their own castes in the district. For Newars there was simply a dearth of members of the same caste in the villages of Belaspur district. Early immigrants of non-Newar groups, for different reasons outlined below, could not find suitable partners of equivalent status in the rural areas. A large proportion of townsmen, therefore, made and have continued to make alliances within the bazaar itself. Approximately 40 percent of all clean caste marriages - and almost half of Newar unions - about which I have information, have linked together households in the town.

But the possibilities for intra-bazaar unions are necessarily limited by the rule prohibiting marriage in the male line; even Newars, who have no named descent groups *(thar)* do not marry for at least three generations, and generally five. About a third of townspeople's marriages, therefore (again, particularly those of Newars) have been made out of the district, usually in other administrative centres of western Nepal, where enclaves of the same caste, often facing similar problems, can be found. This has led to the creation of marital links as far away as seven days' walk from Belaspur Bazaar. Moreover, about one-fifth of these out-of-district unions involve local bazaar women (most of them Newars) who have married officials from other parts of the country posted temporarily to the district administration. In addition, a few locally resident government employees have imported wives married while they were serving in other districts.

The same factors which have led townspeople to look for partners mainly inside the bazaar or outside the district have also encouraged unions across caste lines. Over 15 per cent of their marriages have involved partners of different clean caste. Table 3 presents the configuration of these unions.

Table 3

Made by:		With Thakuri	Chetri	Newar	Magar	Gurung	Other	Total
NEWAR	Men		4		9	2		15
	Women	5	6				3[a]	14
THAKURI	Men		1	2				3
	Women					1		1
CHETRI	Men			6				6
	Women	1		3				4
MAGAR	Men					2	1[b]	3
	Women							
GURUNG	Men							
	Women		1					1

[a] A Brahmin, a Rai and a Joggi

[b] A Thakali from west-central Nepal

The numbers of inter-caste unions involving Newars would be even higher if account were taken of those marriages within the

Newar community itself, between persons of different status. I have already alluded to the variety of clean Newar castes who settled in the town. Whereas in Kathmandu Valley they would not normally have married with one another, local demographic considerations resulted in a not too great concern for such norms among the immigrants in Belaspur Bazaar. This led, however, to the obliteration of distinctions between these groups and their common self-identification as 'Shrestha'. In this connection, the Shresthas resemble the Patidars of Gujerat who, Pocock notes, are subject to infiltration at the lowest levels and tolerate a considerable degree of heterogeneity ('graduality') within their ranks (1972:54). All Newars save the untouchable Butchers who were not already so became 'Shresthas' on or shortly after arrival and no record remains of the precise affiliations of the earliest settlers.

Table 3 shows that 28 (16.6%) of men's marriages are across caste boundaries, as are 20 (14.0%) of women's marriages. Of the men's inter-caste marriages, 21 are hypergamous, two isogamous (between Magars and Gurungs) and five are hypogamous. Of the women's marriages, 15 are hypergamous and five are hypogamous.

Most inter-caste unions in which Newar men are involved have been with tribal women, principally Magars. The offspring of such unions are sometimes referred to as 'Nagarkoti', but for all intents and purposes they are treated as Newars and marriages between them are regarded as isogamous.

Newar women who have married outside their caste have, with a single exception, married hypergamously. Moreover, they have established these unions either, as in eight cases, with members of the administration posted temporarily to the district or, as in six cases, with members of the administration from outside the district who settled in the town. But whereas - because of virilocal residence norms - the majority of unions in the first category found their way out of the area when the men were posted elsewhere, the second have had a significant effect on the pattern of relations among members of clean castes within the bazaar. Furthermore, they have contributed to shaping the links between townsmen and villagers as well, because the origins of these unions can be sought in the attitudes of villagers to marriages with those claiming equal ritual status who settled originally in the town from other parts of the country.

The Brahmins, Thakuris and Chetris of the countryside surrounding the town were reluctant to create marriage alliances with settlers in the bazaar claiming twice-born status both because of their uncertainty about the latters' caste credentials, and the relative poverty of the immigrants. The refusal of these villagers to offer their women to the earliest of their caste fellows from outside the district compelled the newcomers (who were, on the whole, males) to take women of lower castes as wives. Fürer-Haimendorf rightly attributes to demographic factors the tendency of new arrivals from distant regions to conclude unions with women of different castes (1964:102). The founding settlers (a Brahmin, a Thakuri and five Chetris) of the seven clan groups of *tagadhari* status in the bazaar which originate outside the district, wed as follows: five married Newar women (one of these also took as his second wife a Gurung); one married the daughter of a former slave, ranked as a Gharti Chetri;[3] and one married a village woman of 'pure' Chetri standing.[4] In the last instance the Chetri migrant had come with substantial financial resources and established a business in the bazaar. His wealth and success quelled the initial fears about his uncertain ritual status.

Generally, the accumulation of wealth and, *mutatis mutandis*, acceptance of caste claims takes a generation or two. Thus, a Thakuri, whose ancestral home was far to the east of Belaspur, came to the bazaar as a minor government official in the entourage of a Rana governor. His marriage to the younger sister of one of the bazaar's most prosperous Newars, enabled him to establish a small shop on leaving government service, and he soon became a relatively wealthy man. His three sons, ranked as Thakuris, married Thakuri women from surrounding villages, and one also took a Chetri as his second wife. Their children, males and females, have all married into 'pure' Thakuri families in Belaspur and adjacent districts.

In a not dissimilar instance, an impoverished Brahmin came to the bazaar as cook for a district governor and remained after the latter had left. His marriage to the daughter of a well-to-do Newar in the town provided the impetus for his sons, ranked as Khatri Chetris, to join the bazaar's wealthiest circle of residents. Their sisters and children, as they themselves, have as affines only 'impeccable' Chetris, some of these among the districts most prosperous and respectable families, as well as other bazaar residents who, like themselves, have vastly improved their financial positions over time.

Both these examples illustrate how the refusal of high-caste villagers to acknowledge the claims of new bazaar immigrants to equal status exposed the latter to pressures from Newar families - confronted by their own problems resulting from demographic imbalances - to accept their women as wives. On the whole, however, these Newars offered moderate wealth and the influence which went with near monopoly of administrative posts open to local residents. Immigrants of twice-born status had to offer in return only their higher ritual status. This is clearly at variance with the situation in a Ceylonese village studied by Yalman. There he notes that while 'a very rich low-caste woman can always obtain a high-caste consort' there is little temptation on either side to enter into cross-caste unions since 'neither she nor her children will thereby become high caste' (1962:94). In Nepal, the children of such marriages do stand to gain a great deal.

The cases cited above also suggest that wealth and other forms of power affect the assessment of ritual standing and enable better marriages to be made in the succeeding generation than in the previous one. Where the descentdants of migrants have been less than successful economically or politically, marriage choices have been correspondingly more restricted. In one case, the migrant Chetri was a former clerk in the district administration who married a Newar woman from a well-to-do household and settled in the town. Both spouses died soon after, leaving a small son (ranked as a Chetri) who spent most of his early years as a servant or herd boy in the homes of bazaar residents and administrative officials. On reaching manhood, in poverty, he was able to arrange a marriage with a village girl of Gharti Chetri, i.e. ex-slave standing. The Ghartis are more than ready to offer their women to Chetris of higher standing than themselves, including the children of inter-caste unions. The female offspring of such marriages may then go on to marry 'pure' Chetris. Thus, the grand-daughters of the original Chetri-Newar marriage cited above, i.e. the daughters of the Gharti woman, have married into 'pure' Chetri families, although relatively poor ones. The grandsons, on the other hand, still burdened by poverty, and their association with the lower standing of ex-slaves have continued to marry with the Ghartis.

The Status of Inter-Caste Marriages

Inter-caste unions, save in the case of those which unite two partners of twice-born status, marrying for the first time, involve no wedding rite, nor any custom of bridewealth or dowry, although it is by no means unusual for some transfer of property to take place at the time of or following the establishment of the union - usually from the bride's family to the bridegroom's, or to the bride herself. The marriage is signified by the couple taking up residence together, and the woman is thereafter referred to as the man's wife *(swasni)* and he as her husband *(logne)*. Strictly speaking, then, such marriages are not sanctified by Hindu religious 'authority', but should not, because of this, be considered as instances of concubinage and therefore as productive of illegitimate children. The marriages are recognised by the community and, indeed, should another man seduce the woman, he is liable to pay compensation *(jarikal)* to the cuckold.

Such inter-caste unions, it should be noted, are not invariably secondary marriages, made possible only after primary, isogamous ones have been forged. Dumont propounds such a view partly on the grounds that 'there must be in a house a woman whose cooking the family can eat before a subsidiary wife can be admitted' (1964:93). The facts of the situation in Belaspur Bazaar belie this reasoning. In the first place all but a handful of the inter-caste marriages noted above are primary or principal unions (indeed, in most cases, only unions). Moreover, where men do take more than one wife, stringencies of the kind cited earlier sometimes compel the initial union to be made with a woman of lower caste, and only later, when the personal circumstances of the husband improve can he enter a subsidiary marriage which is isogamous.

Secondly, the question of cooking and inter-dining in households containing hypergamous unions is less problematical than Dumont would suggest. In a community where such unions are not exceptionable pressures to conform strictly to commensal regulations within the household are light, and there are few husbands who would consistently refuse to eat even ritually important foods prepared by their lower caste wives in the privacy of their kitchens. Still, as Fürer-Haimendorf notes, some men who are of higher status than their spouses do cook for themselves, and certainly all would claim <u>publicly</u> to do so (1964:99). This is surely not so unusual: Yalman reports that in the Ceylonese village he studied persons of high caste occasionally take food prepared by persons of low caste but he remarks that 'this would be vehemently denied in public' (1962:96).

Dumont also raises the important question of gradations of legitimacy and status as between the offspring of isogamous and hypergamous marriages. Here, it would seem, there are important if not fundamental distinctions to be made on the basis of the affiliations of those involved in marriages across caste lines. Firstly, there are conjugal unions across the line of pollution, uniting partners of clean and untouchable castes. Such unions, on the whole, result in the virtual excommunication of the partner of clean caste, the relegation of the latter to untouchable status, and the allocation of any offspring to a similar place in the ritual hierarchy.

Secondly, we have to note those unions between Brahmin men and women of inferior status. While the children of such marriages suffer no legal disabilities (e.g. inheritance), they are nevertheless relegated to a status lower than their fathers: Jaisi (in the case of marriage with a Brahmin widow or a Jasai woman); Hamal (in the case of marriage with a Thakuri woman); or Khatri-Chetri (in the case of marriage with a woman of *matwali* or Chetri rank). Thus, not only the purity but the very continuity of the Brahmin caste is threatened by hypergamous unions, and can only be maintained by marriages of an isogamous nature. Fürer-Haimendorf (1971) points out how Brahmin men of Jumla make principal marriages with Brahmin maidens, and then are 'free' to marry beneath themselves; a similar procedure obtains in the villages of Belaspur (P. Caplan 1972).

For other clean castes, however, a different principle of status conferment obtains. Here a marriage outside the group does not carry with it degradation of status. The offspring of all such marriages are affiliated to the caste of their fathers. While it is recognised that, let us say, the Chetri son of a Chetri man and his Newar wife may not enjoy precisely the same standing within the caste as the son of two Chetri parents, this does not constitute a difference of status (cf. Pocock 1972:52). Given the passage of time and an improvement in financial circumstances, such disabilities are either forgotten or overcome, as I have shown.

The assignment of the father's rank to the children of non-Brahmin men is explicable not by reference to any textual authority, but to the articulation of a caste model which serves local conditions. In this connection it is significant that in Belaspur Bazaar no distinction is recognised between *jharra* ('pure') and non-*jharra* Chetri status as reported for other parts of Nepal (cf. Fürer-Haimendorf 1971). Townspeople disclaim any knowledge of such a formal dichotomy among Chetris, as they do of the term '*jharra*' itself. They would not agree, moreover, that 'Thakula' refers here, as it does elsewhere, to the slightly degraded offspring of a Thakuri man by his *matwali* wife (Fürer-Haimendorf 1971). Furthermore, 'Nagakoti', as I have already noted, while referring to the children of Newar men and their tribal spouses, carries notstigma nor any suggestion of a status less than that enjoyed by 'pure' Newars.

Clearly, a proliferation of terms for identifying minute

distinctions among offsprings based on parental associations exists which could, and in parts of Nepal does, serve as a blueprint for the creation of an elaborate caste hierarchy. Townsmen compelled by demographic and economic circumstances to make a substantial number of cross-caste unions, ignore the possibilities for fragmentation provided by such distinctions and employ instead a simpler, less differentiated model.

Local circumstances can also help to explain the considerable tolerance for hypogamous unions in the town (again, excepting those which involve clean caste women and untouchable men). The numbers of such unions are small, but they occur without the dire consequences suggested by some writers. Relations between the woman and her natal group do not cease, nor does the union go unrecognised (Dumont 1964:96). Moreover, the children of such marriages are not outcasts (untouchables?) as Stevenson seems to imply (1954:57). In Belaspur Bazaar, they take the caste of their father and suffer no legal or social disabilities. Most instances of hypogamy have brought together Newar residents of the town established in commerce or local administrative employment with the sisters or daughters of poor Chetri newcomers to the town who, for reasons already noted, could make no ritually 'suitable' alliances in the district.

Thus the same kinds of pressures encourage hypogamous as well as hypergamous inter-caste unions. The former occur less frequently undoubtedly because of the strong opprobium attached to *pratiloma* unions.[5] But while townspeople are aware of the scriptural abhorrence of such practices, and admit that because of this the reputation of the women's family, in particular, suffers, the evidence suggests that the stigma is ephemeral and quickly forgotten.

Inter-caste relations

Having examined the attitudes to and assessment of marriages between persons of different status, we might now discuss the effects on inter-caste relations and on the cultural divisions between these groups of such unions.

Almost one in five households of clean caste in the bazaar at present (14 out of 75) contains members of more than one caste who are related to one another. Two of the most 'mixed' domestic units in the town are illustrated in Figure 1.

Figure 1

Two Multi-caste households

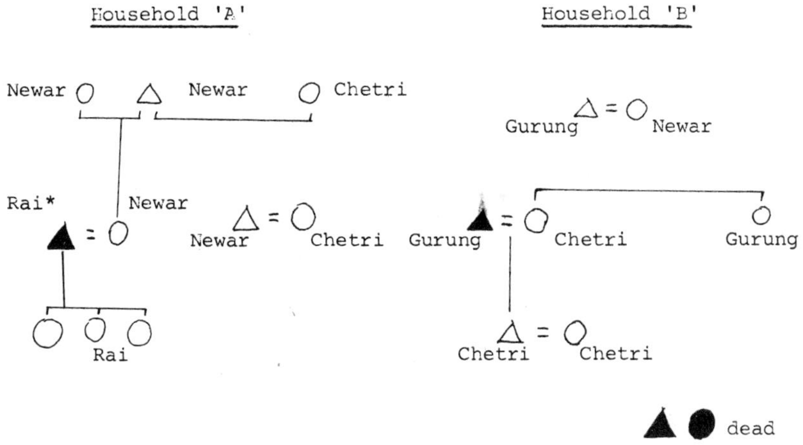

* The Rai was a government servant from East Nepal. His Newar wife returned to Belaspur Bazaar with her small children after his death.

A bald statement of even such a relatively high proportion of multi-caste households fails to convey the full extent of links among townsmen of different groups. There are also various ties between uni-caste households created by multiple marriages. The children of one Chetri government official from outside the district are related through their locally resident mothers (a Gurung, a Newar and a Chetri) to other bazaariyas belonging to these groups, while one Newar woman married first to a Gurung and then to a Thakuri has generated close kinship ties between the households to which her children of different castes are affiliated. The combination of affinal, matri- and patri-lateral ties among members of the same and different castes are therefore exceedingly varied and complex; households are so interwoven that the vast majority of clean-caste townsmen could, without projecting very far into the past, be located on a single genealogical chart.

There is, moreover, a sense of close attachment between affinally-linked households, which are expected to cooperate with one another, provide assistance of various kinds (including loans), and, in political contexts, give support when required. Inter-caste marriages, then, involve more than simply two individuals, although they may not be 'alliances' between sets of kinsmen, if by this we mean that the connection is intended to be perpetuated in the next generation (Yalman 1962:95).

The notion of a uni-caste household must be understood in the context of how caste membership is determined. We would have to regard as uni-caste, for example, a domestic group containing a married pair each of whom is in fact 'half-caste', viz., the Newar husband might be the child of a Gurung mother, and his Newar wife of a Chetri mother, but both are Newars because each had a Newar father (who may himself have been the son of a Magar woman). In other words, despite constant hybridisation, caste affiliation is clear and consistent, and based on the principle that the child of a marriage between members of different clean castes - save those involving Brahmin men - assumes the status group of its father.

The significance for inter-caste marriage of status allocation by patrifiliation has recently been noted by Pocock who suggests that 'where the paternal side is the valued side in descent ... violations of endogamy are more common than is often supposed' (1972:55). Earlier, Bailey had pointed out that rank ascription at birth does not necessarily entail endogamy: 'the same effect is achieved by an unambiguous descent rule' (1963:111). Furthermore Barth has objected to the notion that endogamy is primarily related to concepts of pollution and so must be regarded as an integral feature of caste systems. He suggests that 'Only those intercaste relations which would create ambiguity in the principles of status ascription are incompatible with the structural features of a caste system. It follows logically from this that a pattern of caste endogamy is vital in any system of kinship only where rights and status are transmitted to children from <u>both</u> their parents.' (1962:132). In the Pathan case the stress on patrilineality 'serves to make matrilineal and matrilateral kinship irrelevant to status and authority ascription, and thus obviates the need for caste endogamy' (ibid.) With the exceptions already noted (hypergamous unions of Brahmin men, and any unions between clean and untouchable individuals), Barth's statement fits the Nepalese situation here described.

This view raises questions about Berreman's stress on the cultural plurality of castes. For him, an important function of endogamy lies in its implications for the distinctiveness of these groups. By restricting inter-marriage and interaction generally, he argues, a caste system ensures that the constituent groups will remain culturally distinct (1967a; 1967b).

In Belaspur Bazaar interaction between clean caste groups is clearly anything but restricted and one result is a broadly uniform set of customary practices. All speak Nepali as a first language (including Newars), wear the same dress, celebrate the same festivals and household rites, utilise the same category of ritual specialists, live in the same neighbourhoods, or even households, and so on.

Still, despite this uniformity, perhaps because of it, there is a sense in which we may speak of cultural distinctiveness. It is not the fruit of separation, as Berreman suggests, but rather arises from a common belief in and perception of difference imposed by a system founded on hierarchy. Indeed, Berreman makes much the same point when he notes - in a statement seemingly at variance with his argument noted above - that even 'when interaction between castes is maximal and cultural differences are minimal, the *ideal* of mutual isolation and distinctiveness is maintained and advertised among those who value the system' (1967a:52) (my emphasis).

It is assignment at birth to membership of specific castes which confers this difference. And whatever their matrifiliation or their private behaviour within a household, men behave and purport to behave publicly in a manner commensurate with their ritual status. At public gatherings they eat only foods appropriate to their caste, prepared by persons of proper rank and served in an acceptable manner. They follow established mourning procedures normally associated with their status, so that a Thakuri son of a Magar woman mourns his Thakuri brother for 13 days, but his mother for only three. Again, whatever their matrifiliation, men ranked as Thakuris and Chetris wear the sacred thread of Hinduism conferred publicly by Brahmins. Bazaar residents (such as Newars) who rank below the *tagadhari* groups make no attempt to belittle them, but if anything acknowledge their ritual superiority (even though they may be the closest of relatives) and accord them the respect which is thought to be their due. There is, then, a dissociation of marriage practice and ritual status. The latter is conferred by patri-filiation and validated by reference to shared values and symbols.

Despite the close unity wrought by kinship and affinity, townsmen regard themselves as composed of distinct caste groups, hierarchically ranked and, by virtue of their ritual differences, culturally distinct.

Conclusion

Leach invites us to consider 'just how far a social system can differ from the orthodox Hindu prototype yet still deserve the cultural label "caste"' (1962:2). If a crucial feature of the 'orthodox Hindu prototype' is caste endogamy must we conclude that, when marriages across caste boundaries occur with some frequency, we cannot speak of a caste system?

This paper has examined some implications of a not insignificant rate of such unions in a single peri-urban community. The incidence of marriages between members of different caste groups was related to demographic and economic considerations. The effects on relations among residents of clean castes in the town was also noted, but notwithstanding the close links of kinship and affinity which bind together persons belonging to different ritual groups, their collective perception of caste hierarchy and difference is fundamentally unaffected. This was attributed to the manner in which caste status is conferred, by affiliating the offspring of inter-caste unions involving members of other than Brahmin and untouchable groups to the caste of the father - thus making it irrelevant whether or not these marriages are primary or secondary.

This interpretation seems to reinforce one view of the caste system which finds rigidity of belief and action at its extremities - the Brahmin and untouchable poles - but flexibility at the 'intermediate' levels of the hierarchy. This flexibility is clearly seen in the attitudes of villagers to the inter-caste marriages of townspeople. The former choose an 'orthodox' cultural model against which to measure castes in the bazaar, and denigrate (especially) those claiming ritual equality with themselves. They compare the purity of their own castes which result from endogamous marriages with the 'counterfeit' *(nakali)* groups produced by hybrid unions in the town.

Lionel Caplan

NOTES

1. Fieldwork in western Nepal in 1969 was sponsored by the School of Oriental and African Studies, University of London.

2. Gorkha was, until the middle of the eighteenth century, one of the numerous Thakuri-ruled principalities west of Kathmandu.

3. Slavery was abolished in Nepal in 1924, and the former slaves granted the sacred thread and the status of Chetri by government decree.

4. Pocock (1972) distinguishes 'standing' within the caste from 'status' as between castes.

5. Tambiah suggests that aside from ritual constraints, hypogamous unions are likely to occur infrequently because it makes no sense for women of superior status who are endowed with property (viz. dowry) to marry men of lower status and inferior economic position (1973:67).

BIBLIOGRAPHY

Atal, Y. 1968. *The changing frontiers of caste*, Delhi.

Bailey, F.G. 1963. 'Closed social stratification in India', *European Journal of Sociology*, 4.

Barth, F. 1962. The system of social stratification in Swat, North Pakistan. In E.R. Leach (ed), *Aspects of caste in South India, Ceylon and north-west Pakistan*, Cambridge.

Berreman, G. 1960. 'Caste in India and the United States', *American Journal of Sociology*, 66.

Berreman, G. 1967a. Stratification, pluralism and interaction: a comparative analysis of caste. In A. de Reuck and J. Knight (eds.) *Caste and race: comparative approaches*, London.

Berreman, G. 1967b. 'Caste as social process', *Southwestern Journal of Anthropology*, 23.

Caplan, P. 1972. *Priests and Cobblers: a study of social change in a Hindu village in western Nepal*, San Francisco.

Caplan, P. 1973. 'Ascetics in western Nepal', *Eastern Anthropologist*, 26.

Dumont, L. 1964. 'Marriage in India: the present state of the question', *Contributions to Indian Sociology*, 7.

Dumont, L. 1966. *Homo Hierarchicus: the caste system and its implications*, (Eng. transl.), London.

Fürer-Haimendorf, C. von 1956. 'Elements of Newar social structure', *Journal of the Royal Anthropological Institute*, 82.

Fürer-Haimendorf, C. von 1960. 'Caste in the multi-ethnic society of Nepal', *Contributions to Indian Sociology*, 4.

Fürer-Haimendorf, C. von 1964. Comment on Dumont, L. 'Marriage in India', *Contributions to Indian Sociology*, 7.

Fürer-Haimendorf, C. von 1971. 'Status and interaction among the high Hindu castes of Nepal', *Eastern Anthropologist*, 24.

Gaborieau, M. 1972. 'Muslims in the Hindu kingdom of Nepal', *Contributions to Indian Sociology*, (N.S.), 6.

Karve, I. 1965. *Kinship Organization in India*, Bombay.

Kumar, S. 1967. *Rana Polity in Nepal: origin and growth*, Bombay.

Leach, E.R. 1962. Introduction: What should we mean by caste? In E.R. Leach (ed) *Aspects of caste in South India, Ceylon and north-west Pakistan*, Cambridge.

Leach, E.R. 1967. Caste, class and slavery: the taxonomic problem. In A. de Reuck and J. Knight (eds) *Caste and Race: comparative approaches*, London.

Mandelbaum, D. 1970. *Society in India*, Berkeley.

Pocock, D. 1972. *Kanbi and Patidar: a study of the Patidar community of Gujarat*, Oxford.

Rosser, C. 1966. Social mobility in the Newar caste system. In C. von Fürer-Haimendorf (ed) *Caste and kin in Nepal, India and Ceylon*, Bombay.

Sinha, S. 1967. Caste in India: its essential pattern of socio-cultural integration. In A. de Reuck and J. Knight (eds) *Caste and Race: comparatove approaches*, London.

Stevenson, H.N.C. 1954. 'Status evaluation in the Hindu caste system', *Journal of the Royal Anthropological Institute*, 84.

Tambiah, S.J. 1973. Dowry and bridewealth and the property rights of women in South Asia. In J. Goody and S.J. Tambiah, *Bridewealth and Dowry*, Cambridge.

Tucci, G. 1962. *Nepal: the discovery of the Malla*, London.

Yalman, N. 1962. The flexibility of caste principles in a Kandyan community. In E.R. Leach (ed) *Aspects of caste in south India, Ceylon and north-west Pakistan*, Cambridge.

Yalman, N. 1969. 'De Tocqueville in India: an essay on the caste system' (review article), *Man* (N.S.), 4.

Notes préliminaires sur des Populations Sunuwar dans L'Est du Nepal

Les régions monatagneuses et boisées du Népal oriental ont servi de refuge à différentes populations *Kirāt* lorsqu'elles furent expulsées des vallées ou des plaines du Terai. Les Sunuwar qui se disent *kirāt*, racontent qu'ils durent abandonner Simraungarh dans l'Est du Terai, après sa conquête par d'autres ethnies. Prédateurs et chasseurs, les différents groupes se seraient séparés à un endroit appelé Chautara. Cette division se serati opérée entre les Surel (*jeṭhā*); les Sunuwar (*māhilā*); les Rai (*sāhīlā*); les Limbu (*kāhīlā*); et les Hayu (*kānchā*). Chacun de ces groupes auraient alors gagné son présent habitat après une longue migration.[1]

Les Sunuwar sont composés de divers groupes: les Sunuwar proprement dit, les Surel, les Jirel et les Bahing; les Bahing préférent se faire appeler Rai. Linguistiquement, les Sunuwar appartiennent au "groupe bahing, de la branche occidentale de la section himâlayenne orientale (dite aussi section *kirāt*) à l'intérieur de la division bodique" (R. Shafer).[2] Rappelons que les diverses ethnies rai ou limbu font aussi partie de cette section. Les Surel qui n'avaient jamais été encore étudiés, parlent un dialecte archaîque sunuwar. Les Jirel, par contre, ont une langue relativement proche du Tibétain de Tichurong et du Sherpa de Kerung.[3]

Les Sunuwar qui sont une population d'environ 20,000 personnes vivent dans une trentaine de villages, situés principalement entre les rives de la Khimti Khola et de la Maulung Khola. Les Surel habitent Suri, un village sur la rive méridionale de la Suri Khola, dans le *pañcāyat* de Suri-Tinekhu Haleshwar. Ils ont environ 140 locuteurs.[4] Les Jirel, qui sont environ 3,000, sont établis entre la Tamba Kosi et la Khimti Khola, dans quatre *pañcāyat*. Chhetarpa, Jhyankhu-Paldung, Jiri et Jungu-Yebo. On les trouve principalement dans les vallées de la Jiri et de la Sikri.[5] En résumé, les Sunuwar et ses deux sous-groupes, les Surel et les Jirel, vivent principalement entre les rivières de la Tamba Kosi et de la Maulung Khola, dans les districts de Dolakha et de Ramechhap dans la région de Janakpur, et dans le district d'Okhaldhunga dans la région de Sagarmatha. Cette aire sunuwar est appelée *wallo kirant*.[6]

Avant d'exposes l'organisation économique, sociale ou politique, et la religion des Sunuwar, il est nécessaire, semble-t-il de mentionner en détail la situation particulière des Jirel.

Au dèbut du XIX siècle, il y a maintenant sept générations, des Sunuwar du village de Rasnalu qui chassaient dans la jungle, aux pieds du Mont Chordung, rencontrèrent des Sherpani du village de Dhunge. De cette liaison naquirent des enfants qui furent rejetés par les deux communautés. Un lama tibétain qui parcourait la région, prit alors soin des nouveaux-nés et les éleva dans la vallée de Jiri. Les Jirel seraient les descendants de ce metissage. Les Jirel, néanmoins, se proclament Sunuwar. Mais pour ces derniers, par contre, les Jirel sont des sang-mêlés *(temsing)* et ils se marient rarement avec eux et refusent le riz cuit par eux.

L'ORGANISATION ECONOMIQUE, SOCIALE ET POLITIQUE

1. *Le Cadre de la vie économique*

Après la conquête du Népal oriental par les troupes de Prithwi Narayan, le domaine occupé par les Sunuwar ou les Surel fut reconnu comme étant leur propriété et fut déclaré *kipaṭ*.[7] Les chefs de village reçurent le titre de *mukiyā*. Selon les traditions, avant Prithwi Naryan, il apparait que les Sunuwar reconnaissaient la juridiction des Sen de Chaudandi, mais qu'ils étaient en butte aux visées expansionnistes du royaume Newar de Dolakhā. L'ouverture de nouvelles mines au XIXe siècle, en pays Sunuwar, entraina une forte immigration des différentes ethnies du Centre et de l'Ouest du Népal. Les Sunuwar qui pratiquaient l'agriculture itinérante sur brûlis, eurent alors à souffrir de cet afflux de population. Ignorant le népali et étant incapable de le lire, ils décidèrent de faire appel aux autorités népalaises. Sous le ministère de Jang Bahadur Rana, une délégation de douze villages alla demander à Kathmandou la permission d'y pratiquer l'hindouisme et sollicita la venue de familles brahmanes et chetris. Naturellement, ces dernières s'approprièrent les meilleures terres pour y cultiver le riz. Ce serait les Brahmanes et les Chetris qui auraient enseigné aux Sunuwar l'usage de l'araira. A présent, les Sunuwar cultivent, sur des champs en terrasse, les terres à flanc de côteaux, entre 1,300 et 2,000m. Les champs irrigués, au fond des vallées, sont souvent aux mains des "hautes castes". Les Tamang qui habitent sur les hauteurs, entre 2,000 et 3,000m., ont défriché la forêt et, en été, ils y cultivent du maïs, de l'éleusine, des pommes de terre et un peu de sarrazin.

Les Surel, qui furent dépossédés de leurs terres en 1918 par une famille chetri, sont à présent des métayeurs.[8] Les Jirel par contre, bénéficiant de l'aide d'ingénieurs-agronomes suisses, entre 1958 et 1970, ont transformé en rizières, les vallées de la Jiri Khola et de la Sikri Khola.[9]

L'élevage chez les Sunuwar, est une activité annexe, confiée aux adolescents. Ils accompagnent les bovins et les buffles sur les pacages au-dessus de 1,800m. Entre les mois d'Avril et de Novembre le bétail paît dans la forêt. C'est sur les champs moissonnés, près de l'habitation, que se passe l'hivernage. Les Sunuwar ne consomment pas le lait, mais ils le transforment en beurre clarifié, qui sera vendu ou échangé. Ils élèvent aussi des porcs, des chèvres ou des poules pour les sacrifices lors des festivités religieuses ou sociales.

Les Surel déclarent qu'autrefois ils possédaient d'importants troupeaux qui pâturaient sur les contreforts du Chordung; à présent, rares sont ceux qui ont une vache ou un buffle. Comme leurs voisins Jirel, les Surel n'ont pas de porcs.

Les Sunuwar, les Surel et les Jirel, sont très attachés à leurs terres et n'aiment guere voyager. Ils répugent à faire du portage et préfèrent se rendre à Darjeeling, au Sikkim ou au Bouthan, pour travailler pendant l'hiver comme manoeuvres sur les chantiers. A la suite de la transformation de leur *kipaṭ* en *birta* en 1918, plus de la moitié des familles de Suri émigrèrent à Gangtok ou en Assam pour s'y embaucher. Depuis 1909, les Sunuwar peuvent s'engager dans les troupes mercenaires "gourkhas". A Khaping, une vingtaine de personnes avaient servi dans l'armée britannique ou indienne. Le prestige dont jouit l'armée, est très mobilisateur, et de nombreux jeunes cherchent à devenir militaires ou à défaut, policiers à Kathmandou.

2. *Le village et les techniques de consommation*

Les villages Sunuwar sont formés de différents hameaux, habités généralement par un clan ou une lignée particulière. Certaines grosses agglommérations, telles que Bhuji (700 maisons), Khiji ou Rashalu, ont localement des noms distincts pour chacun des groupes d'habitations *(ṭol)*, séparés les uns des autres par des accidents de terrain. Cette unité territoriale basée sur un clan ou sur un lignage, donne une plus forte cohésion aux personnes qui l'occupent, l'unité minimale, tant sur le plan économique que sur le plan religieux.

C'est depuis environ une quarantaine d'années que les maisons sunuwar sont construites en pierre par un maçon. Cette habitation qui a généralement un étage, est souvent flanquée d'une grange-étable en pierre *(matān)*. Ces deux bâtiments encadrent la cour avec son séchoir à maīs. Le rez-de-chaussée sert de pièce d'habitation: c'est là où vit la famille nucléaire, le premier étage étant utilisé comme grenier. Dans le cas d'un fils benjamin, ses parents habitent au premier étage où ils cuisinent et dorment, tandis que le rez-de-chaussée est occupé par l'heritier de la maison, son épouse et leurs enfants.

Auparavant, les maisons étaient construites en torchis, et chez les personnes riches, elles étaient en planches. C'était une habitation basse, aux murs en torchis, épaulés par des poteaux et badigeonnés d'un mélange d'argils ocre et de bouse de vache. Le toit très incliné, était couvert d'herbes ou de bardeaux. Toute la communauté villageoise participait à sa construction et recevait du futur propriétaire de la nourriture et de l'alcool. Ce type d'habitation est encore en usage chez les Jirel et chez les Surel. On le rencontre de temps à autre, chez certains Sunuwar pauvres, mais les murs de torchis sont remplacés par des murs en pisé.

Les Sunuwar et les Surel sont des vanniers réputés qui vont vendre leurs productions sur les marchés *(hat)*, à Jiri ou à Sangutar, ou pendant les foires *(melā)*. Selon les besions, le tournage sur bois est pratiqué par quelques artisans sunuwar ou jirel, pour fabriquer les contenants à beurre clarifié ou à lait. Les femmes qui accompagnent leurs époux sur les marchés ou lors des foires, en profitent pour y vendre de l'alcool distillé ou fermenté; puis avec les bénéfices obtenus, elles achètent des étoffes de des bracelets.

Le tissage tend à être de plus en plus délaissé au profit des cotonnades indiennes, vendues sur les marchés ou au *bajār*. A Suri, il n'y avait que seulement deux femmes qui pratiquaient encore le filage et le tissage. Chez les Sunuwār, les Surel ou les Jirel, le métier à tisser est de type océanien. A Sabra, il y avait aussi des métiers à tisser de type indien à deus rangs de lisses. La ramie et le *bombax* qui étaient jadis colorés au moyen de teintures végatales, sont dorénavant remplacés par du fil de coton industriel de différents couleurs. L'ouverture du marché de Jiri depuis 1964, a transformée l'économie des Jirel, des Surel et des Sunuwar de la Khimti Khola. Les Sunuwar de la Likhu Khola sont restés plus isolés, et la monnaie n'a pas encore remplacé les échanges de service ou le troc.

3. *Le Clan*

Après être venus de Banepa et avoir traversé la Tamba Kosi près de Kiranticchap, les Sunuwar continuèrent leur migration vers l'Est, en laissant derrière eux les Surel qui s'installèrent sur les rives de la Suri khola. Les Sunuwar, qui devaient être probablement un petit groupe composé de plusieurs familles, se fixèrent à Haba sur la rive occidentale de la Khimti Khola. Comme la pays était inhabité, ils en colonisèrent les alentours. Chaque famille, en essaimant, prit le nom de l'endroit où elle s'était établie, et forma ainsi un clan distinct:

NOM DU CLAN	VILLAGE ET SITE		RIVE
Bamna-Yata	Sorke	(Bamna)	Khimti Khola orient.
Garshi-Yata	Haba	(Garshi)	Khimti Khola occid.
Jespotsa	Darkha	(Jespo)	Khimti Khola orient.
Lokutsa	Pharpu	(Loku)	Khimti Khola orient.
Katitsa	Kati		Khimti Khola orient.
Linu	Pahare	(Linu)	Likhu Khola orient.
Lukitsa	Pirti	(Luki)	Likhu Khola occid.
Tolotsa	Saiphu	(Tolo)	Likhu Khola occid.

et ainsi de suite ...

Il semble que des familles sunuwar se dispersèrent vers le Sud-Est et émigrèrent jusqu'en pays Rai où elles demeurèrent. Les Bahing qui se considèrent maintenant comme une population rai, parlent encore aujourd'hui un dialecte similaire à celui des Sunuwar. Selon leurs traditions, ils déclarent s'être séparés jadis des Sunuwar.[10]

Lorsque la population d'un village augmente et que les cultures se raréfient, un nouveau site est choisi et des membres du clan vont s'y installer, en créant un nouveau clan. En voici quelques exemples: "Il y a sept ou huit générations, des *Satwa-Jeti* quittèrent le village de Sapra, au Nord de Kati, et se fixèrent à Sabra. Ils étaient quatre frères qui donnèrent naissance à quatre nouveaux lignages". Lors de mon séjour à Sabra, il était question de transformer ces lignages en clans. "Les *Kuintitsa* habitent à Ragheni, une bourgade sur la rive orientale de la Likhu khola. Or, un jour, des villageois de ce clan décidèrent d'aller habiter sur l'autre rive, à Saiphu (Tolo). Ces émigrants prirent le nom de *Tolotsa*". De nos jours les *Kuintitsa* et les *Tolotsa* se marient fréquemment entre eux. Pourtant cette règle n'est pas uniforme: ainsi les membres des clans *Jespotsa* et *Lukitsa* ne contractent pas de mariage entre eux, car ils sont tous deux originaires du village de Pirti.[11] - C'est, me semble-t-il, le seul cas connu chez les Sunuwar.

La segmentation des clans, chez les Sunuwar, les Surel et dans une moindre mesure chez les Jirel, apparait comme l'un des traits dominants des *Kirāt*. Comme chez les Kulunge-Rai, étudiés par C; W; McDougal[12] la segmentation s'opère après sept ou huit générations, et chacun des nouveau segments se transforme automtiquement en clan. On peut, dès lors, s'étonner que certains auteurs aient parlé des *bāra thar* (douze clans) des Sunuwar. Peut-être faut-il y voir le souvenir des douze villages de la Khimti Khola qui allèrent négocier avec Jang Bahādur Rānā le venue des familles brahmanes. Actuellement, on peut affirmer qu'il y a un peu plus de 70 clans sunuwar. Les Jirel qui ont été appelés *das thar* (dix clans), en ont environ 20. A la suite du dépeuplement de Suri, entre 1925 et 1941, après l'émigration des deux tiers de ses habitants qui se trouvaient soudainement sans terre, il ne reste que seulement cinq clans sur les douze ou quinze clans qui l'occupaient auparavant. Ces clans sont les Darkatz; les Durbitz; les Ronku; les Gahorung (Gurung) et les Yata. (Ces deux derniers clans sont récents et n'ont guère plus d'une génération d'âge).

Le système des *thar*, tel qu'il est pratiqué par les "hautes castes" indo-népalaises, est inconnu des différentes populations sunuwar. Elles sont totalement ignorantes des noms de leur *gotra*[13] donnés par les Brahmanes. Néanmoins, quelque soit son clan, un Sunuwar se rend à la fête annuelle de son village. Presque tous les villages ont leur propre sanctuaire où l'on rend un culte aux génies protecteurs du lieu. A Sabra, par exemple, lors du *Baisak-purne*[14] les membres des clans *Satwa-Jeti*, *Bamna-Yata* ou *Wangdetsa* se rendent aux deux sanctuaires du *Caṇḍi* où sont sacrifiés des buffles. Les *Satwa-Jeti* revendiquent, par ailleurs, le *Caṇḍi* comme étant une déité propre à leur clan. En effet, certains clans semblent avoir des divinités tutélaires.

A l'intérieur de son propre clan, tout Sunuwar regarde d'abord son lignage, puis son hameau, c'est-à-dire le lieu de son lignage, et enfin la place qu'il y occupe.

4. *Le mariage*

Il y a un dicton sunuwar qui dit: "Nous sommes comme des oiseaux et nous nichons où nous voulons". L'étude de leur nuptialité fait mentir cet adage, car les Sunuwar contractent des mariages entre un segment de clan et un segment d'un ou plusieurs autres clans, chacun occupant une aire géographique particulière. Ces liens matrimoniaux entre les segments de différents clans créent alors un réseau d'alliance qui peut être utilisé dans les conflits entre villages.

Le mariage entre cousins croisés, tel qu'il est pratiqué dans les castes indo-népalaises (*Ṭhakuri*; *Gāine*; *Kāmi*; *Sārki*...) ou dans les ethnies de l'Ouest et du Centre du Népal (Thakali; Gurung; Magar; Tamang...) est interdit. Comme c'est le cas chez les Rai ou les Limbu, les Sunuwar et les Surel ont un profond dégoût pour ce type d'union.

La résidence est le plus souvent patrilocale ou virilocale, toutefois il n'est pas rare de rencontrer des personnes qui ont préféré s'établir dans le hameau de leur femme. Faut-il voir les vestiges d'une coutume ancienne? Il m'a été rapporté qu'autrefois, les fiancés pauvres contractaient souvent un "mariage par service".

La polygynie est rare chez les différentes populations sunuwar. Seuls les hommes riches ont la possibilité d'avoir plusieurs femmes, chacune devra habiter une maison particulière. Toutefois, s'il s'agit de soeurs, on peut les répartir à l'intérieur d'une même habitation: l'une occupant le rez-de-chaussée l'autre le premier étage. Contrairement aux Tibétain et aux Sherpa des Rolwaling, la polyandrie n'est pas pratiquée. Les enlévements et les divorces sont relativement fréquents. Certaines bourgades de la Likhu Khola sont célèbres pour leur mariage par capture: les habitants de ces villages ont de bonnes terres; ils sont riches et ils peuvent donc aisément payer les amendes compensatrices au mari outragé.

Les veuves peuvent se remarier, mais dans la plupart des cas, elles épousent le frère cadet du défunt. Si elles se remarient hors du segment de lignage, le marié devra verser un dédommagement à la famille du défunt et les enfants, nés du premier lit, resteront dans la famille de leur père.

5. *La Politique*

Depuis l'abolition du système foncier des *kipaṭ* et l'introduction des *pañcāyat*, les *Mukhiyā* sunuwar et surel, et les *Mijhār* jirel ont perdu une grande partie de leur prestige. Leur audience reste maintenant limitée à leur village et à leur ethnie. Néanmoins, comme à Sabra, lors de la fête du *Dasahara*, les forgerons *(kāmi)*, les tailleurs *(damāi)*, les savetiers *(sārki)*, les serfs affranchis *(bhujel)*, les Tamang et les Kagate qui vivent sur des terres de l'ancien *kipaṭ* du village, viennent prêter allégeance au *Mukhiyā* en lui apportant les prémices ou des présents symboliques; En retour ils reçoivent la *tikā*.

C'est le *Mukhiyā* ou le *Mijhār* qui tranchaient auparavant les différends à l'intérieur de l'ethnie ou les litiges entre les castes et les différents groupes ethniques, placés sous sa juridiction. Ils collectaient aussi les impôts et ils abaient le droit de bénéficier du travail gratuit des villageois pendant les semailles ou les récoltes sur ses propres emblavures.

Au moment des festivités, en l'honneur des divinités tutélaires du village, certains *Mukhiya* faisaient des dépenses somptuaires. Ils offraient des buffles, des porcs, des volailles et une large quantité d'alcool à la communauté. Maintenant que les *Mukhiyā* et les *Mijhār* ont perdu toutes leurs prérogatives, les Sunuwar, les Surel et les Jirel ont tendance à se remémorer avec nostalgie ces fêtes de prestige. Dans le systéme du *pañcāyat*, introduit en 1962, les nouveaux immigrants, principalement les Chetris ou les Brahmanes, ont utilisé la "démocracie directe" en jouant sur des rivalités ethniques, et en faisant élire des membres de leur caste. Sachant lire et écrire le népali, ces "hautes castes" bénéficient de l'appui de l'administration népalaise, elle-même aux mains de ces castes. Elles peuvent ainsi utiliser la loi aux dépens des minorités prot-népalaises analphabétes.

La suppression des titres fonciers en 1963, a permis l'achat des meilleures terres tribales par ces castes. La dépossession des droits coutumiers sur les tenures traditionnelles a sonné le glas de tout un pouvoir, qui bien qu'étant souvent autocratique, permettait pourtant à ces petites ethnies de conserver leur spécificité, et de résister à la transformation rapide de leur société.

LA RELIGION

Dans l'est du Népal, on est surpris par le pluralisme religieux qu'on y rencontre: les uns se disent bouddhistes, comme les Tamang, les Kagate ou les Sherpa; d'autres se déclarent hindous, comme les Newars, les Gurung ou les Magar. En pays Sunuwar les Jirel pratiquent à la fois un bouddhisme lamaïque et des rites magico-religieux propres à cette ethnie. Les Sunuwar et les Surel continuent de pratiquer des cultes qui leur sont particuliers, tout en se déclarant hindous.

1. *Le bouddhisme lamaïque*

Les Jirel qui sont des bouddhistes, font appel à des lamas jirel lors de certains rites domestiques, tels que l'octroi du nom, trois jours après la naissance, le mariage ou les funérailles. Formés par des lamas tibétains, il y a quatre ou cinq générations, la fonction des lamas jirel est héréditaire: c'est le père qui apprend à son fils des rudiments de tibétain pour pouvoir lire les livres religieux. Tous les rites publics se font à l'intérieur de la *dgon-pa* du village.

Vivant en bonne intelligence avec les lamas, on trouve aussi dans le village un autre officiant: le chamane *(Pem-bo* ou *Phombo)*. Ce chamane sert d'abord d'intercesseur entre les personnes et les esprits courroucés: il est capable de les exorciser. Par ailleurs, il connait le passé, le présent et l'avenir, et sait aussi bien discerner les maladies que retrouver les objets perdus ou égarés. Enfin, il est un détenteur des traditions et, lors des rituels jirel, il remplit la fonction de sacrificateur.

On peut se demander si les Sunuwar ou les Surel furent jadis des bouddhistes? On trouve de nombreux *mčhod-rten* en pays Sunuwar, mais il semble impossible à l'heure actuelle d'en connaitre les bâtisseurs. On est en droit de penser qu'ils ont dû être construits au siècle dernier par les Tamang qui vinrent s'installer près des mines de cuivre ou de fer, ou bien par des marchands tibétains descendant commercer dans la vallée de la Sun Kosi. Les Sunuwar et les Surel furent peut-être, à un certain moment des bouddhistes; mais à présent, ils ne paraissent pas avoir aucune attirance particulière pour cette doctrine.[15]

2. *Les croyances magico-religieuses propres aux Sunuwar ou aux Surel et l'hindouisme*

Chez les Sunuwar il y a deux types d'officiants spécialisés: le prêtre *(Naso)* et le chamane *(Puimbo)* ou la chamane *(Ngiami)*.

Le *naso*[16] est un conductuer de rituel. Il connait toutes les formules propitiatoires *(pidar)* pour invoquer les divinités du panthéon sunuwar. Lors des grands rituels publics ou semi-public, tels que le *Caṇḍi*, le *Ghil*, le *Khas* ou le *Tsaeta*, il effectue les sacrifices sanglants. Il est un homme de savoir, détenteur des traditions. En tant que ministre du rituel, il posséde le pouvoir et la force *(tung)* de la divinité invoquée, sans pour autant pouvoir l'incarner. Car un *naso* ne rentre jamais en transe, et c'est pourquoi, lors de différents rituels, il a besoin du concours d'un chamane.

La fontion de *naso* est toujours héréditaire, contrairement à celle du *puimbo* ou de la *ngiami*. Parmi ses descendants directs, un *naso* choisira le garçon qui lui semblera le plus intelligent ou le plus apte pour accomplir ce ministère. Son fils ou son petit-fils devra apprendre très jeune les *pidar* et les litanies, par des procédés mnemotechniques. A partir de l'âge de six ou sept ans, l'élève accompagnera son père ou son aïeul à divers rituels, en vue de se familiariser avec les séquences qu'il devra par la suite reproduire en rentrant chez lui. Il doit aussi apprendre tous les mythes et les traditions en les recueillant de la bouche même des anciens du village. Si son père ou son grand-père meurt avant qu'il ait complété son apprentissage, le jeune garçon doit alors demander aux villageois de l'aider à compléter sa formation en finançant son instruction chez un autre *naso*.

A la mort de son père, le jeune *naso* hérite de l'arc et des flèches sacrificielles, et c'est lui qui doit alors conduire les rites funéraires à la mémoire de son "*guru*".

Les attributs du *naso* sont très ordinaires si on les compare à ceux du *puimbo* ou de la *ngiami*. Lorsqu'il officie, il porte des vêtements de tous les jours. Autour de la tête, il a noué une longue bande d'étoffe blanche *(pheṭā)* donnée par le maître de la maison où la cérémonie s'effectue. Il porte sur le côté droit un petit sac à franges *(dun-tahilo)* décoré de quelques cauries. Pour les grands rituels publics, il est assis sur une peau de daim musqué *(Moschus mosciferícus)* ou sur une couverture, ou si celle-ci fait défaut, sur une natte *(gundri)*. Devant lui, on place une aiguière en cuivre rouge *(tamar)* où trempe une branche d'hopa *(Thysanalaena agrestis)* qui servira de goupillon pendant les *pidar*, et un encensoir en terre *(dhupauro)*, empli de résine de genevrier et de braises. A sa droite, il place ses deux couteaux: un petit *(lalukarda)* pour sacrifier les porcs, et un coupe-coupe *(lalutsub)* pour égorger les chèvres et les poulets.

Pendant le *Caṇḍi*, le grand rituel sunuwar qui a lieu chaque année, au moment de la pleine lune, entre les mois d'Avril et de

Mai *(Baisak-purne)*, le *naso* danse autour des victimes en frappant sur son tambour sacrificiel *(ḍhol)* avant de décocher avec son arc rituel, une flèche dans le coeur d'un buffle ou d'un porc.

Le *naso* doit savoir conduire une variété de rites qui peuvent se sub-diviser en quatre catégories:

1. les rites publics: *Caṇḍi; Ghil; Naesa; Khas...*

2. les rites saisonniers: les semailles *(jojor washi)*; les prémices *(nogi)...*

3. les rites privés ou domestiques: la naissance et l'octroi du nom; le mariage; les funérailles; le culte des ancêtres *(tsagu)...*

4. les rites préventifs ou curatifs pour les humains comme pour le bétail: *kalikā pujā; saguni; bhimsen; antim; aitabare;*

Après cette aperçu du rôle et des fonctions du *naso*, nous allons à présent nous tourner vers le *puimbo* et la *ngiami* et examiner ce qui les différencie.[17]

Comme nous l'avons déjà signalé, la fonction d'un *puimbo* ou d'une *ngiami* n'est pas héréditaire puisque chacun d'entre eux est l'élu d'un esprit. En fait la divinité choisit rarement en dehors de la lignée du possédé, mais elle peut négliger la ligne directe pour les collatéraux éloignés de plusieurs degrés. La vocation du chamane apparait évidente après une crise qui a généralement lieu entre l'âge de 10-13 ans. Un garçonnet ou une fillette gardant le bétail sur les hauteurs, tombe malade ou fait une chute dans la jungle. Il est possédé par un "esprit nain" qui vit dans la forêt *(banjhākri)*. Cet esprit le conduit à son domicile, le plus souvent une grotte, où il lui enseigne les rudiments de son ministère: formules propitiatoires, *mantrā*, et les techniques pour façonner son tambour chamanique *(ḍhyāṅro)*.

Par la suite, l'apprentissage se fera, soit sous la conduite d'un chamane confirmé, soit en retournant dans la jungle pour y retrouver son "esprit nain" tutélaire.

Lorsqu'il officie, le *puimbo* revêt un long vêtement particulier ou féminin *(jāmā)*, et il noue autour de la tête une large étoffe blanche. Dans ce turban improvisé, il glisse plusieurs piquants de porc-épic. Comme le *naso*, il a sur le côté droit, un sac à franges où il range des conques, un fémur humain, une corne de moufflon, dans lesquels il soufflera, et une ou deux petites fauçailles. Il porte en sautoir divers colliers faits de gros grains, de vertèbres de serpent ou de clochettes. Dans sa large ceinture en ramie, il porte son couteau rituel en bois *(phurbu)*. Pendant les cérémonies, il se sert de son tambour et parfois de cymbales. Lorsqu'il danse, il brandit sa lance rituelle *(tsiu-tek-bartsa)* ou son *phurbu*.

La *ngiami* posséde les mêmes attributs, à l'exception de la lance. Par ailleurs, elle porte une sorte de jupon *(ghāgri)* qu'elle passe par-dessus sa jupe.

Le *puimbo* ou la *ngiami* effectue divers rites:

1. les rites publics ou semi-publics: *Caṇḍi; Ghil; Khas; Pol*..

2. les rites saisonniers: *Rikhitarpani; Sri panchami;* les *Purne*

3. les rites domestiques: naissance et octroi du nom; mariage; funérailles; culte des ancêtres...

4. les rites propitiatoires privés: rite de chasse: de pêche; de sélection d'un site pour y bâtir une habitation; de fabrication de *dhyāṅro*......

5. les rites curatifs pour les humains et le bétail: *Amla tsinta; Iwa tsinta; Mewal tsinta; Tara tsinta; Tsedi*.....

Lors des rituels publics ou domestiques, le *naso* invoque les divinités, et c'est le *puimbo* ou la *ngiami* qui permet à l'esprit ou à la divinité de descendre sur le sanctuaire où le sacrifice se déroule. A la fin de la cérémonie religieuse, ce sera encore le chamane qui aura le pouvoir de le renvoyer vers les cieux. Le *puimbo* ou la *ngiami* n'ont pas le droit de faire des sacrifices sanglants.

Si l'on compare les tâches et les fonctions du prêtre et du chamane, on s'aperçoit aisément qu'elles sont complémentaires. En général, le *naso* officie et sacrifie le jour, tandis que le *puimbo* ou la *ngiami* préfèrent opérer la nuit. Si le *naso* invoque les esprits et les divinités bienfaisantes, le *puimbo* ou la *ngiami*, par contre, doit exorciser les âmes errantes des personnes mortes de mort violente, en les renvoyant dans l'au-delà, et bannir les fantômes ou les esprits courroucés qui importunent les vivants.

Lorsqu'ils font un rituel à l'intérieur d'une habitation, le *naso* occupe la partie privée de la pièce d'habitation, près du pilier central, tandis que le *puimbo* ou la *ngiami* occupe la partie publique, ouverte aux alliés, aux amis et aux visiteurs. Pendant le rituel, le *naso* est assis à droite et il utilisera l'un de ses couteaux; le *puimbo* ou la *ngiami* se trouvent à gauche avec son couteau magique en bois.

Si un *naso* ne peut exercer sa fonction qu'à l'intérieur de la communauté sunuwar, un *puimbo* et une *ngiami*, au contraire, peuvent servir d'intercesseurs entre le monde des esprits malveillants et des personnes appartenant à des castes ou à des ethnies différentes.

A sa mort, le *naso* est enterré debout et son *ḍhol* est placé sur sa tombe, tandis que le *puimbo* ou la *ngiami* sont inhumés en position assise avec leur *ḍhyāṅro* sur la sépulture. C'est depuis 1947-1948 que les Sunuwar sont incinérés selon le canon hindou.

Si l'on résume les rôles respectifs du *naso* et du *puimbo* dans un tableau *(tableau I)*, on peut voir l'opposition qui existe à l'intérieur d'un système dualiste, sous forme de termes opposés mais complémentaires.

Tableau I

NASO	PUIMBO - NGIAMI
homme	homme ou femme
héréditaire	non-héréditaire
droit	gauche
sacrifice	transe
sang	souffle
dans la journée	dans la nuit
vêtements ordinaires masculins	vêtements particuliers ou feminins
les vivants	les esprits
le cycle de la vie	le cycle de la mort
les bonnes morts	les mauvaises morts
les dieux, les esprits des ancêtres	les fantômes, les esprits malveillants
favorable	défavorable

NASO	PUIMBO - NGIAMI
la partie privée de la maison	la partie publique de la maison
rituels publiques ou semi-publiques	rituels privés
rituels préventifs	rituels curatifs
enseignement dans le village	enseignement dans la forêt
Sunuwar	multi-ethnique
sacré	profane
ḍhol, lalutsub	*ḍhyãṅro, phurbu*
inhumé debout	inhumé assis

Après avoir montré la dualité des fonctions religieuses, chez les Sunuwar, on peut ajouter que cette complémentarité des rôles sacerdotaux se retrouve chez les Surel, avec le prêtre *(nakso)* et le chamane *(poembo* et *giamini)*.

A présent, les Sunuwar de la Khimti Khola ont tendance à faire de plus en plus appel à des brahmanes pour accomplir les rituels et à se conduire en hindous. Les *naso* n'excercent plus aucun rôle dans la société, et les cérémonies proprement sunuwar sont abandonnées. Par contre, chez les Sunuwar de la Likhu Khola, où les traditions sont encore vivaces, le *naso* reste toujours un personnage très important. Face à l'hindouisme, on voit dans certains villages où les rituels avaient disparu, se manifester un renouveau liturgique. Le *puimbo* et la *ngiami*, au contraire, n'ont pas perdu une partie de leur audience, et ils continuent à pratiquer leur art, l'exerçant même pour des familles chetris ou brahmanes.

Si l'on se tourne vers les rites particuliers aux Sunuwar, on est surpris par leur diversité et leur extrême richesse liturgique. Le *ghil*, par exemple, est un rituels fait essentiellement en l'honneur des ancêtres lignagers. Il se déroule tous les 20 à 25 ans dans la maison lignagère. Cette cérémonie qui dure deux ou trois jours, est composée de différentes séquences gigognes, toutes empruntées à d'autres rituels (*Tsagu, Saguni, Khas...*) qui se combinent en s'emboitant les uns dans les autres. Chacun de ces rites forme alors un acte où les acteurs sont les prêtres *naso* et les chamanes (*puimbo - ngiami*). Les *puimbo - ngiami*, qui ont un rôle secondaire, sont néanmoins essentiels car ils permettent aux esprits, aux âmes des ancêtres, aux divinités invoqués de descendre sur la maison lignagère et sur toute l'assistance (le lignage stricto sensu). Par leurs transes et leurs appels, ils servent d'intermédiaire entre les vivants et l'au-delà. Le ou les *naso* conduisent les rituels, introduisent les séquences et sacrifient les porcs, les chèvres et les poulets aux déités. Le *ghil* prend fin par une large agape de tous les membres du lignage. Enfin les chamanes renvoient vers leurs demeure toutes les divinités. Le lignage s'est concilié les bonnes grâces des ancêtres et des génies tutélaires: il en attend la bienveillance pour une nouvelle génération.

Ces "notes préliminaires" sont le résultat d'une mission de recherche en pays *sunuwar* qui n'a pu dépasser six mois, compte tenu de la faiblesse des ressources financières qui lui avaient été allouées. Elles n'ont pour toute ambition que de décrire et d'expliquer l'originalité des divers groupes *sunuwar*, face à la poussée démographique des castes et des ethnies voisines, à l'influence de plus en plus profonde de l'idéologie hindouiste et à la disparition de leurs moyens de production.

En attendant les monographies qui un jour, développeront tous les aspects particuliers et spécifiques des Jirel, des Surel et des Sunuwar, nous espérons que cette modeste contribution apportera une meilleure compréhension à l'étude du Népal de l'Est.

Alain Fournier

NOTES

1. Mission effectuée en Août 1969 - Fevrier 1970, grâce à une allocation de recherche dans le cadre de la R.C.P. 65 du C.N.R.S. que dirigeait M. C. Jest. La translittération du népali est basée sur celle de R. L. TURNER, et celle du tibétain sur H. A. JÄSCHKE. Pour le sunuwar, le surel ou le jirel, elle m'est propre. Sur la langue des Sunuwar, et des Jirel, on se reportera aux diverses études récentes publiées par le linguistes de la Summer Institute of Linguistics: D. BIERI & M. SCHULZE et par E. STRAHM & A. MAIBAUM.

La bibliographie sur les populations Sunuwar est plutôt mince; on trouve cependant des reférences: B. H. HOGSON, 1847, pp. 1235 - 1244; H. H. RISLEY, 1891, II, 1, pp. 281 - 283; G. A. GRIERSON, 1909, III, 1, pp. 198 - 205, 254 - 270; W. B. NORTHEY & C. J. MORRIS, 1928, pp. 256 - 258; C. J. MORRIS, 1936, pp. 117 - 119; H. R. GIBBS, 1947, Chap. IX; R. SHAFER, 1953, pp. 356 - 374; M. HERMANNS, 1954, pp. 20 - 21; R. B. SUNUWAR, 2013, 70p.; R. SHAFER, 1957, p. 167; MINISTRY OF DEFENCE, 1965, pp. 114 - 116; B. PIGNEDE, 1966, p. 165; D. B. BISTA, 1967, pp. 64 - 69, 169; I. S. CHEMJONG 1967, pp. 86 - 87; R. SCHMID, 1969, 245p.; DOBREMEZ, J. F. 1972, pp. 9 - 24; A. FOURNIER, 1973a, pp. 147 - 165; 1973b, 22p.

Dans les premiers rapports de W. KIRKPATRICK, 1811, et de F. BUCHANAN HAMILTON, 1819, les différentes populations sunuwar ne sont même pas mentionnées. B. H. HOGSON, *op. cit*, signale que les Sunuwar "are mostly found west of the great valley and north of the Magars and Gurungs, near and among the Cisnivean Bhotias" (1237). Il faut attendre les observations de H. H. RISLEY, *op. cit.*, pour avoir des informations concordantes avec la localisation actuelle de cette ethnie. On peut se demander si B. H. HOGSON n'a pas été induit en erreur par la similitude des noms entre les Sunuwar et la "caste artisanale des orfèvres" (*Sunār*); les *Sunār* occupent l'Ouest de la vallée. De nos jours, nombreux sont les Népalais dans les collines qui confondent ces deux populations. C'est la raison pour laquelle les Sunuwar transforment souvent leur nom en *Kirāt*, lorsqu'ils viennent chercher du travail à Kathmandou ou en Inde.

2. R. SHAFER, *op. cit.*, p. 356.

3. E. STRAHM et A. MAIBAUM, 1971, p. 1.

4. En 1971, les Sunuwar avaient une population de 20.265 âmes. Cette information m'a été aimablement communiquée par le Dr. H. GURUNG que je tiens ici à remarcier. Les Surel ont été considérés à tort jusqu'à présent, comme un des clans des *das thar*, c'est-à-dire, comme une fraction des Jirel. Leur dialecte, leur superstructure et leurs traditions sont différents des Jirel et proches des Sunuwar. Je me propose de revenir plus tard sur cette population attachante.

5. Je compte publier prochainement mes notes de terrain sur cette ethnie. On consultera la *Note ethnologique sur la région de Jiri* de P. VALEIX, C. JEST, J. F. DOBREMEZ et J. STEBLER.

6. B. H. HOGSON, 1858, pp. 446-456. On remarquera que cet auteur nous décrit l'aire géographique (*wallo kirāt*) des Sunuwar, sans les mentionner.

7. Sur le *kipaṭ*, on s'en tiendra à la définition donnée par M. C. Regmi, 1965, p. 82: "Land is held on a tribal, village, kindred or family basis, and individuals have definite rights in this land by virtue of their membership in the relevant social unit. Hence, title to land has a communal character and it is usufructuary, rather than absolute".

8. Après avoir dépossédé les cinq *mukhiyā* de Suri de leur *kipaṭ*, en leur faisant signer une procuration où ils renoncaient à tous leurs droits, le Colonel Dal Bahadur Karka reçut en 1918, le *kipat* de Suri sous forme de *birta*, du gouvernement Rana, pour le récompenser de ses brilliants services. Selon la définition que nous donne M. C. Regmi, 1964, p. 2. : "*Birta* meant an assignment of income by the state in favor of individuals in order to provide them with a livelihood".

9. Sur l'agriculture des Jirel, on consultera B. MULLER, 1964. Je tiens à remercier M. J. Stebler pour les divers renseignements qu'il m'a communiqué lors de mes séjours à Jiri, qu'il en soit ici remercié.

10. B. H. HOGSON, 1857, pp. 486-522. Mlle. M. MAZAUDON, linguiste du C.N.R.S., qui travaille sur ce dialecte, a eu l'extrême obligeance de me fournir diverses informations sur ce groupe.

11. Cette particularité avait déjà été signalée par H.H. RISLEY, *op. cit.*, p. 281.

12. *Report on findings of field research on the Kulunge-Rais of the Hongu valley of Solukhumbu District*, 1965, 27 pages. (multigr.).

13. Sur l'usage de ce nom de clan, voir I. KARVE, 1965, pp. 51 sq., ou K. B. BISTA, 1971, pp. 65-68. Les noms de *gotra* de certains clans sunuwar sont donnés dans l'ouvrage de R. B. SUNUWAR, *op. cit.*, pp. 46-48. Ils sont sanskrits pour la plupart.

14. Pleine lune qui a lieu au mois de *Baisak* entre Avril - Mai. cf: D. B. BISTA, *op. cit.*, p.69.

15. F. BUCHANAN HAMILTON, *op. cit.*, p. 53, 56-57. Certaines vieilles personnes déclarent que dans leur jeunesse, le pays était beaucoup plus fréquenté par des lamas. A Sabra, un mausolée (*māne*) avait été érigé, il y a environ une dizaine d'années, pour le repos de l'âme d'une jeune femme sunuwar, liée par une relation d'amitiée rituelle (*mit*) à une Tamangni fortunée. C'est cette dernière qui l'avait fait construire. Chaque année, un lama vient y reciter des prières et il est reçu avec déférence dans la famille de la défunte.

16. Dans cette étude, nous ne parlerons que de *Duma Naso*, le *naso* le plus important. Les autres *naso* subalternes *(Sher-pa Naso, Dhupe Naso* ou *Shipe Naso)* sont les aides, les servants des *duma naso*. Ils ont néanmoins des tâches definies lors des grands rituels: le *sher-pa naso* assiste le *duma naso* lors du sacrifice, pendant que le *dhupe naso* récite les *pidar* et que le *shipe naso* frappe le *dhol*; voir ma communication: "The rôle of the priest in Sunuwar Society", 1973b, *I.C.A.E.S.; Himalayan Session*, 22 pages.

17. Sur la fonction du *puimbo* ou de la *ngiami*, voir A. FOURNIER 1973a, pp. 147-167.

18. Le Sunuwar, ainsi que nous l'avons vu, a été classé par R. Shafer, 1953, p. 356, dans la "Bodic Division, East Himalayish Section, Western Branch, Bahing Unit". Depuis quelques années, des linguistes de la Summer Institute of Linguistics ont commencé à faire paraitre le resultat de leurs recherches. Mais ni Mlles. D. BIERI et M. SCHULZE pour le sunuwar, ni Mlles. E. STRAHM et A. MAIBAUM pour le Jirel, n'ont encore publié la terminologie de parenté dans ces langues. Le dialecte surel, qui a été totalement ignoré jusqu'a présent, est pour la première fois offert aux chercheurs et aux linguistes.

Les vocabulaires qui suivent, ont été relevés rapidement; il n'était pas question, en si peu de temps, d'essayer d'etablir une phonologie sommaire de ces trois langues. La notation phonètique comporte sans doute quelques erreurs car aucune vérification ne m'été possible après avoir quitté le Népal. Mlles M. MAZAUDON et G. STEIN, linguistes aux C.N.R.S., et spécialistes des langues tibéto-birmanes de l'Himalaya, m'ont aidé dans la transcription phonètique et ont bien voulu revoir cette notation. Je tiens ici à leur exprimer toute ma gratitude, et à décliner leur responsabilité des fautes qui auraient pu s'y glisser. Je tiens aussi à remercier mes informateurs népalais, qui ont montré tant de bon humeur, de générosité et de patience avec moi, en particulier: à Suri, Rantsa Sunuwar, seconde fille de Tsone Sunuwar et épouse maintenant de mon ami Yam Bahādur Sunuwar, mon collaborateur à Sabra-Khaping; et enfin de Gaṇeś Bahādur Jirel à Sikri.

REFERENCES BIBLIOGRAPHIQUES

BIERI, D. & SCHULZE, M. 1971 — *A guide to Sunuwar Tone.* Kathmandu, S.I.L., Tribhuwan University, 38 pages, (Multigr.).

" 1971 — *A vocabulary of the Sunuwar language.* Kathmandu, S.I.L. Tribhuwan University, 40 pages, (Multigr.).

" 1971 — *Sunuwar phonemic summary, revised version.* Kathmandu, S.I.L. Tribhuwan University, 37 pages (Multigr.).

BISTA, D.B 1967 — *People of Nepal.* Calcutta, His Majesty's Govt. of Nepal, Ministry of Information & Broadcasting

BISTA, K.B. 1971 — *Le culte de Kuldevata au Népal en particulier chez certains Ksatri de la vallée de Kathmandou* Thèse de 3e cycle, University de Paris, 286 pages, (Multigr.).

BUCHANAN HAMILTON, F. 1819 — *An account of the Kingdom of Nepal, and of the Territories annexed to this Dominion by the House of Gorkha.* Edinburgh, Archibald Constable & Co.

CHEMJONG, I.S. 1967 — *History and Culture of the Kirat People.* Kathmandou, Pushpa Ratna Sagar. (3e. ed.).

DOBREMEZ, J.F. 1972 — Carte écologique du Népal II: Région Jiri-Thodung 1/50 000. *Cahiers Nepalais,* pp. 9-24.

FOURNIER, A. 1971 — Note préliminaire sur le Puimbo et la Ngiami, les chamanes Sunuwar de Sabra. *ASEMI* IV, 1, pp. 147-167.

" 1971 — The role of the priest in Sunuwar Society. *I.C.A.E.S. Himalayan*

Session, 22 pages.

GIBBS, H.R. 1947 *The Gurkha Soldier*. Calcutta Govt. of India, Central Publication Branch, Part III, vol. 1.

HERMANNS, M. 1954 *The Indo-Tibetans*. Bombay, K. L. Fernandes.

HOGSON, B.H. 1847 On the Aborigines of the Sub-Himalayas. *JASB*, XVI, pp. 1235-1244.

" 1857 Bahing vocabulary. *JASB*, XXVI pp. 486-522.

" 1858 On the Kiranti tribe of the Central Himalaya. *JASB*, XXVII, pp. 446-456.

JÄSCHKE, H.A. 1972 *A Tibetan-English Dictionary*. London, Routledge & Kegan Paul Ltd., (7e ed.).

KARVE, I. 1965 *Kinship Organisation in India*. Poona, Deccan College, (Deccan College Monograph Series, 11), (3e ed.).

KIRKPATRICK, W. 1811 *An Account of the Kingdom of Nepaul being the substance of observations made during a mission to that country in the year 1793*. London, W. Miller.

McDOUGAL, C.W. 1965 *Report on findings of field research on the Kulunge-Rais of the Hongu Valley of Solu-Khumbu District*. s. 1., 27 pages, (Multigr.).

MINISTRY OF DEFENCE 1965 *Nepal and the Gurkhas*. London, H.M.S.O.

MORRIS, C.J. 1936 *Handbooks for the Indian Army*. Gurkhas. Delhi: Manager for Publications, (2e ed.).

MULLER, B. 1964 *Untersuchungen über die wirtschaftlichen und sozialen Verhältnisse in den vier ostnepalischen Gebirgstälern Jiri, Sikri, Jellung, Khimti.* Jiri, SATA, 68 pages, (Multigr.).

NORTHEY, W.B. & MORRIS, C.J. 1928 *The Gurkhas, their Manners, Customs, and Country.* London, J. Lane.

PIGNEDE, B. 1966 *Les Gurungs une population himalayenne du Népal.* Paris La Haye, Mouton.

REGMI, M.C. 1964 *Land Tenure and Taxation in Nepal, vol II, The Land Grant System: Birta Tenure.* Berkeley, Institute of International Studies, U. of California.

" 1965 *Land Tenure and Taxation in Nepal, vol III, The Jagir, Rakam and Kipat Tenure Systems.* Berkeley, Institute of International Studies, U. of California.

RISLEY, H.H. 1891 *Tribes and Castes of Bengal.* Calcutta, Bengal Secretariat Press, 4 vol.

SCHMID, R. 1969 *Zur Wirtschaftsgeographie von Nepal. Transport und Kommunikation Probleme, Ostnepal im Zusammenhang mit der Schweizerischen Entwicklungshilfe in der Region Jiri.* Zürich, Juris Druck und Verlag.

SHAFER, R. 1953 East Himalayish. *BSOAS*, XV, pp. 356-374.

" 1957 *Bibliography of Sino-Tibetan Languages.* Wiesbaden, Otto Harrassowitz.

STRAHM, E. & MAIBAUM, A. 1971 *Jirel phonemic summary.* Kirtipur, S.I.L., Tribhuwan University, 81 pages, (Multigr.).

STRAHM, E. &
MAIBAUM, A. 1971 *A vocabulary of the Jirel language*. Kirtipur, S.I.L., Tribhuwan University, 17 pages, (Multigr.).

SUNUWAR, R.B. 2013 *Sunuwar jatiko vamsavali*. Benares, 68 pages.

TURNER, R.L. 1965 *A Comparative and Etymological Dictionary of the Nepali Language*. London, Routledge & Kegan Paul, (2e ed.).

VALEIX, P., JEST, C., DOBREMEZ, J.F., STEBLER, J. 1972 Note ethnologique sur la région de Jiri. *Cahiers Népalais*.

Attempt at an Ethno-Demography of Middle Nepal

In the 1960s, the Research Scheme Nepal Himalaya was investigating the Sherpas in Solu and Khumbu, East Nepal. After completing the project, it was planned to start research on the Tamang. But while the Sherpas were a comparatively small ethnic group with but a few tenthousands of people, the Tamang were estimated some hundred thousand persons. Thus, it seemed necessary to undertake a preliminary investigation about the number, distribution and settlement concentrations of the Tamang, before the main project could go into proper planning. To do this I went to Nepal in early spring 1969.

I had expected to find the results of the National Population Census of 1961 and to work on its data. But, on my arrival in Kathmandu, I found that neither were these results published by that time, nor were they available at the ministries and offices engaged on the matter. Indeed they were printed but half a year later, and even if I had had the time and patience to wait, their figures would have been of very little use for our purpose, since they were published on district level as the lowest level, while we wanted to know the population distribution on village level, to find our Tamang research areas.

Well - but as so often in science, what looked like an obstacle at first sight turned out to be very productive in the long run. Under the circumstances, we had to collect our information - population figures and settlement areas of the Tamangs - by field research in the country. And, thanks to the outstanding quality of my Nepali assistants, we found not only our Tamang data, but registered the entire population of our investigation area, considering the possibility that it may help saving the time and money of further research schemes on different ethnic groups within the same area.

Within the Panchayat administrative system of Nepal almost all the local activities are initiated and executed by district officials. Therefore we chose the district level for our investigations, and indeed we found all our materials at local district offices, including the data about the villages (Gaon Panchayats). As the Tamangs still were our main object, we were looking for districts containing relevant portions of Tamang populations. Amongst the 75 districts of the country we visited 18, commencing from Dolakha in the east to Kaski in the west, covering approximately 23% of the area of Nepal, and inhabited by about 3 million people, or 32% of her entire population.[1] To win the cooperation of the local officials we obtained letters of recommendation from the Ministries of Home and Panchayat, Land Reform and Health. These papers opened the files of the district offices for Panchayat, land reform and of local health authorities, where we found the required data.[2]

To give a clear impression of the conditions in our investigation area, it appears helpful to give a closer look at the administrative and geographical structure of the country:

Presided over by the King, as the highest authority, Nepal is organised into 4 levels. The lowest, the village level, is based on clusters of wards and villages, represented by 9 Panchas, 1 chairman and 1 vice-chairman, who form the Gaon Panchayat (village council). Panchas are chosen by means of local elections. The Gaon Panchas of a district, from within themselves elect the Panchas for the next higher level, the Jilh Panchayat (district council). From this level upwards, parallel to the elected Panchas, there is a system of civil service officials, responsible to the Ministry of Home and Panchayat in Kathmandu. On the next higher, the zonal level, the former Panchayat was abolished and its functions are taken care of by the Anchal Sabhá (zonal assembly), which is elected out of all the district Panchas of the zone. From within their ranks, the Anchal Sabha elects the Panchas for the Rashtriya Panchayat (national assembly, parliament). Only 90 of the 125 members of parliament are elected, while the rest are delegated by the King and the 'class organisations', including its president. The Prime Minister and his government are appointed by the King.

Geographically, Nepal can be divided into seven belts of landscapes, all of them stretching roughly from west to east. The low plains of Outer Terai are the northern rim of the Indian Gangetic plain. The next step is the Siwalik mountains (Churia Range). Between them and the following, considerably higher Mahabharat range, are the basins of Inner Terai. The Mahabharats are mainly separated by rivers from the broad belt of the middle ranges, which include the basins of the Kathmandu and Pokhara Valleys. The Great Himalaya then forms the border to Tibet, except in the west, where there follows a further system of highland valleys between the Great and the Lower Himalaya ranges.

Our investigation area covered all these landscape forms of Middle Nepal. In the South-East as in the South-West, our area touched the Indian border, but we left out the 5 Outer Terai districts between Chitwan and Danussha, since no Tamangs were expected in these parts of the country. From Kathmandu, which can be considered the very centre of the country in every respect, except a purely geometrical one, our area stretched east and westward proportionally to the dimensions of the whole country. The 18 districts of our area contained 951 village communities (Gaon Panchayats). We got the data about all of them, except 3 Gaon Panchayats in Danussha district. We also were able to ascertain the altitude of all the villages for later correlation with the ethnical distribution. For most of the districts we furthermore registered the number of households (families) to correlate them with the numbers of persons of the different ethnical groups.

Altogether we found some 60 different ethnic groups within our investigation area, several of them not even mentioned in the literature so far. Thus, a systematisation of the ethnical structure of the population of Middle Nepal appeared desirable.

Contrary to all comparable places in the world, there are hardly any areas in Nepal which can be considered to be the area of a certain ethnic group, and on the other hand, we find distinct differences from ethnic group to ethnic group if we look at the population as a whole. In single cases, sometimes it may be difficult to discover to which group a certain person belongs, and it may seem that differentiation by ethnic groups appears more or less fictional. But looking at the problem more closely and on a larger scale, it will be found that there are clear distinctions and that the people themselves are well aware of these distinctions, the most reliable being the clan names.

The situation is complicated by the fact that the population of Nepal is composed of ethnic groups belonging to at least three quite different 'racial' branches. But as the term 'race', applied to mankind, is somewhat ambiguous, I would prefer the term 'Formenkreis' (complex of anthropological features). Here in Nepal we find people of the Europoid type side by side with distinctly Mongoloid groups and some even with Melanide features. And the languages these people speak are correlated with their physical types. Thus a taxonomial systematisation seemed necessary. The only useful source found within the literature was Dor Bahadur Bista's 'Peoples of Nepal'. But even this book gives only a rough structure, since Bista's aim was rather to observe and to describe, than to work out a proper system of the collected materials.

The problem turned out to be of too great a complexity to be settled satisfactorily within the possibilities of our research project, so its proper solution must be left to a later attempt. Nevertheless a provisional but practicable solution had to be found for computation of our materials, and their presentation in a sufficiently logical order.

This task was comparatively simple concerning the names of ethnic groups. Tamang, Newar, Magar, Gurung; Brahman, Chhetri; Sherpa; Tharu etc. were distinct expressions in use by the people of Nepal themselves. It was more difficult to combine these groups in larger units, at least in some cases. Though it was clearly possible to find the differences between the Europoid peoples with the Indo-aryan Nepali language, the more or less Mongoloid peoples with Tibeto-Burman languages and the groups with Melanide features and languages of yet unknown nature (to be called autochthonous, unless more is known about them), there was no clear nomenclature of these larger families of groups, or clusters, to be found in Nepal. The people there have a number of names even for these larger ethnical units of typological, linguistical and cultural distinction, but these names are not used uniformly. Thus, in the way they are used in Nepal, they are rather a source of confusion than a means of systematisation. To avoid a further complication of the matter by producing further new terms, here the Nepali expressions are used nevertheless. But they had to be made handy for the purpose, by restricting their somewhat vague meaning, by joining these names to distinct main groups (clusters) of ethnic acquaintances. In this sense they are used in the following systematisation.

There is a rough analogy between the step-like geographical structure of the country and the ethnical structure of the population, since there are noticeable differences in the physical and cultural character of the inhabitants of the high Himalaya region, the middle ranges and the flat lowlands, or in altitudes: the people living above 7,000 feet, between 7,000 and 1,000 feet and below 1,000 feet. As the country is descending from north to south, this scheme also applies to these categories of the wind rose. At the northern border to Tibet, in the high alpine and alpine biotop of the Himalayas, their lofty valleys and the immediate fore-mountains, lies the domain of the Bhotia-people, a cluster of ethnic groups, who may be considered Tibetan in cultural, anthropological and linguistic respect. Bhot is the old name of Tibet. The Sherpa, Khamba, Bhotia, Manangba, etc. belong to this cluster.

The broad field of the middle hill area or Pahar houses a wide spectrum of ethnic groups. Although, by low land people, they are called collectively the 'Paharia', which means 'mountaineers', they are not in the least uniform in their ethnical nature. We can roughly divide them into at least two quite distinct clusters of ethnic groups. One of them is more or less Mongoloid in physical features and Tibeto-Burman in language, the other cluster is clearly Europoid in appearance and speaks the Indo-Aryan Nepali. These Indo-Aryan speaking Brahman, Chhetri, Thakuri and so forth call themselves and are called by others *Parbatiya*. This word 'Parbatiya' is sometimes translated as 'hill people', but in fact it is derived historically from the old kingdom of Parbat in the middle west of Nepal, along the middle course of the Kali Gandaki river, from where the Parbatiya penetrated eastwards into their present habitat. The Parbatiyas call their Tibeto-Burman neighbours *Paharia*. For this systematisation we shall follow this practice and use the term Paharia for the Tibeto-Burman cluster of ethnic groups only and *not* generally for all the middle hill people. The numerically leading ethnic group are the Tamang, followed by the Magar, Gurung, Thami, Sunwar, Chepang, Rai, Limbu, and some smaller groups. The Newar belong also to this group, although they seem to be a special case in almost every respect.

In the formerly malarious valley basins between the Mahabharat and Siwalik ranges we find a cluster of ethnic groups, called the *Awalia*, since they are supposed to be immune against the malaria, or *awal* fever. The Tharu are the main group of this cluster, but Danuwar, Majhi, Darai and others also belong to it. Their dialects are considered to be autochthonous with Austro-Asiatic elements, but nowadays comprise quite a number of terms from North Indian and Tibeto-Burman languages.

And finally, south of the Siwaliks in the plains of the Outer Terai, the population is similar to that of the neighbouring north Indian provinces, with languages such as Hindi, Maithili, Bhojpuri etc. and a complex Hindu caste society, therefore we shall call this cluster the Terai castes. But amongst them are living some smaller groups of Moslems, whose mother tongue is - or at least was - the west Indian Urdu. In our systematisation we call them the *Moslem* cluster.

In a paper like this one, only a very short summary of the results of our investigations can be included. Therefore I shall mention only a few facts about each one of the 18 districts.

Commencing from east to west, we start with *Dolakha*. In Dolakha within a total population of 133,258 people, the Chhetri form the majority, with 36.5% of the district population, followed by the Tamang with 16.5% and the Brahman with 12%. Altogether we registered 20 different ethnic groups in the 37 gaon panchayats of the district, but none of them except Chhetri, Tamang and Brahman reaches even near 10%. Dolakha is the home of the Thami; above 70% of all the Thamis within our investigation area are settled here. The Jirel-Surel, a small group of 3,125 people are living in Dolakha altogether and cannot be found anywhere else. They are particularly interesting since this nowadays quite autonomous ethnic group originates from inter-marriages between Sherpa and Sunwar. The issue of such liaisons were integrated neither into the Sherpa, nor into the Sunwar clan system. But without integration into any of the parent groups, they had no clear status. So they developed all the necessary tokens and formed a separate group. The difference between Jirel and Surel is merely local: the 2,950 Jirel are living in the Jiri valley, whilst the 175 Surel settle along the Suri Khola.

Ramechhap, situated between Sun Kosi and Likhu Khola, houses a Chhetri majority, making up 25.7% of the district population of 196,993 persons. Here too the Tamang are second with 20%, third are the Newar with nearly 12%. In 41 village communities we found 20 ethnic groups. 67% of all Hayu are living in Ramechhap. The ethnical nature of this group is not quite clear yet. They certainly were slaves until the 1920's. There are altogether only about 1,500 people known to be of this group. Further 78.8% of the Badi are living here, a very low caste of drum makers and drummers.

Sindhuli, between the Sun Kosi river and the Siwalik range, embodies the eastern Inner Terai or Madesh, here formed by the valleys of Marin Khola and Kamla Nadi. In 38 gaons we found 23 ethnic groups - altogether 110,780 people. Tamang are the majority (24.5%), followed by Chhetri (15.9%) and Magar (15.2%). This comparatively large Magar community in a middle eastern district is quite surprising, since the Magars mainland lies in the middle west, hundreds of miles away. On the northern slopes of the Siwaliks we find villages of the Danuwar and Majhi - the latter fishermen and boatsmen - both groups belonging to the Awalia cluster.

Nawakot lies just north of the Kathmandu basin. Although small in size the district has 49 gaons, with altogether 146,940 persons. 22 ethnic groups were registered, with the Tamang leading again (41.4%), followed by the caste of the Sanyasi, the descendants of Sanyasin and their progeny.

Whilst all the districts mentioned so far lie mainly in the middle ranges, *Rasua* is a triangle of valleys and slopes between Himalayan massifs, the Ganesh Himal in the West, Langtang Himal in the north, Jugal Himal and Doarley Himal in the east and Gosainkund Lekh in the south. It is the least populated of the 18 districts listed with only 14,897 individuals in 16 village communities. The Tamang form a vast majority of 88.9% amongst the 10 ethnic groups; all the rest are below 5%. We visited the very isolated Langtang valley, to clarify the nature of its "Tamang" population, and found they were all Sherpa and Bhotia. But as they are only 219 persons, their correct identification as Bhoti is of little relevance for the percentage within the whole population of our investigation area.

Kabhre Palanchok, just east of the Kathmandu valley, with 264,237 inhabitants is one of the most densely populated districts we found. 99 gaons are crowded on an area of moderate size, housing 462 people per square mile. Again the Tamang predominate among 29 ethnic groups; one-third of the district population are Tamang and they form 17% of the whole lot of Tamangs within our investigation area. Brahman (24.3%) and Chhetri (13.6%) are second and third, followed by the Newar (13.5%). Most of the Pahari (41.1%) are living here. They are a small ethnic group of the Paharia cluster, so the two names must not be confused. In Kabhre we also find 38% of the Bhujel, who are former slaves, thus are descending from forefathers of various ethnic groups. Their difference to the Gharti, the main group of former slaves, is that the Bhujel ran away before the abolishment of slavery in 1926, whilst the Gharti were freed by this act of law.

With 299,320 people *Kathmandu* is the most densely populated area in Nepal. Kathmandu city houses more than 40,000 persons per square mile and even the surrounding countryside more than 2,000. Here is the domain of the Newar; with a 46.7% majority they lead amongst the 23 ethnic groups, followed by Chhetris (18.8%), Brahmans (16.1%) and Tamangs (10.7%). The list of gaon panchayats names 83 communities.

Of the 113,692 people in *Bhaktapur* District (Bhadgaon) 55.2% are Newar, 20.9% Chhetri, and 10% Brahman. About 2,700 people live to the square mile in this district with 22 gaons and 13 ethnic groups.

Lalitpur (Patan) has 168,418 inhabitants of 18 ethnic groups in 40 gaons. Half of them are Newar (50.7%), 20.7% Chhetri,

11.6% Tamang and 10.1% Brahman. 30.1% of the small Pahari group live here. The deliniation of the district as you will find it on any printed map is incorrect. All these maps show Lalitpur district within the boundaries of the Kathmandu basin, but in fact about three-quarters of this district lies in the mountains south of the Kathmandu valley, as these parts were cut off from the area of the former district Chisupani Garhi, when it was transformed into the new district of Makwanpur. So Lalitpur is by no means a typical Kathmandu valley district any more, and its landscape is mainly Pahar.

Chitwan, neighbouring Makwanpur to the west, borders India at its southern brink. Two-thirds of the area are covered by the plains of the Central Inner Terai. The river Rapti cuts the district in two halves, whilst Trisuli Gandaki and Narayani form the northern and western boundary. Contrary to Makwanpur, the bulk of the population of 160,192 people is gathered in the low river plains, where most of the 42 gaon panchayats are found. With 28.7% the Brahmans are in the majority among the 31 ethnic groups, followed by the Chhetri (12%), the Tharu (11.4%) and the Gurung (10.6%). We registered more than 18,000 Tharu here - the main group of the Awalia cluster - 97.4% of all the Tharus we found. 47.8% of the registered Darai - another Awalia group - are also living in Chitwan.

Gorkha, just north of Chitwan, stretches up to the Tibetan border. All of the 63 gaon panchayats, except four, are found in the southern half of the district. 170,322 people belong to 27 different ethnic groups, the majority of them to the Brahman (22.7%), 20.7% to the Gurung, 11.4% to the Chhetri and 11% to the Magar group. There are two gaons with Bhotia populations in the alpine part of the upper valley of Buri Gandaki, where 99% of all registered Bhotia live. In Gorkha we also find 96.6% of all Barhamu, a group regarded as belonging to the Awalia cluster, but with many elements of the Paharia cluster. Here we also registered 30.6% of the Yogi, progeny of liaisons of Yogin and Yoginis and their descendants, who are not to be confused with the Jogi caste of the Newar society. In Gorkha we have the rare case of a relatively clear stratification within a district population, as the Bhotia live in the far north, the Gurung dominate the alpine and northern Pahar region just south of them, whilst most of the Brahman are found in the middle hill region around the town of Gorkha, and in the most southern part of the district, mainly on the northern slopes of Trisuli valley, there is a concentration of Magar settlements.

Lamjung is the neighbour district west of Gorkha. Its area is cut into a western and eastern half by the Marsyangdi river, the northern half is covered by Himalayas and their spurs, and thus no gaons are found there, whilst all of the 60 gaon panchayats are in the southern half. The 22 ethnic groups form a population of 132,226; most are Gurung (36.9%), Brahman are 20.2% and Chhetri 15.3%. The Durah people are found exclusively in Lamjung (100%). Their ethnical nature is not yet cleared satisfactorily, but there are some hints that they may have originated from Gurung-Magar intermarriages and their offspring. We registered 2,415 people of this group altogether.

Kaski, just west of Lamjung, is much like its neighbour, with the Annapurna massif and its spur in the north and the Seti Khola cutting the district from north to south, but the south-western part of the district is flat land; here stretches the plain of the Pokhara Valley, with several lakes. The 144,889 persons of the district population live in 60 gaon panchayats in the southern half. 22 ethnic groups are living here, dominated by the Brahman (36.4%). The Gurung make 20% and the Chhetri 15.4%. 75.7% of all Miyar were registered in Kaski. The Miyar are supposed to be a Moslem group, who are acquainted with the Muselman, but were separated from them, since they refused the veil for their women, but more research has to be done to clear their ethnical nature. Most of them live in the town of Pokhara.

Tanahun lies to the south-east of Kaski, north of Chitwan and north-west of Makwanpur. It is a typical Pahar district. 148,809 people of 23 ethnic groups live here in 42 gaon panchayats. The Magar are the dominating group with 22.5%, followed by the Gurung (15.4%), the Brahman (14.9%) and the Chhetri (12.6%). As in the neighbouring Chitwan, a big section of the Darai is registered in Tanahun (46.8%), and one-third of all Bhujel live here.

Danussha is the last of our 18 districts and is the only Outer Terai district of our investigation area. It stretches from the Siwaliks, which here form the southern boundary of Sindhuli, right down to the Indian border. All of its area is flat plain. Quite densely populated, we find here 219,628 individuals of 43 ethnic groups in 103 gaon panchayats. The vast majority belong to the cluster of Terai castes. Leading are the Goala (Gowala; cowherds, cattle dealers and dairy stewards) with 22%, second the Dhanuk (Kurmi, Kewat; former servants and menials) with 22% and third the Teli (oil-pressers) with 12.2% Fourth in the succession of group size are the 18,000 Musalmans (8.3%), the main group of the Moslem cluster. None of the rest of the ethnic groups make up more than about 5%; most of them stay below 1%.

Generally it can be said that the distribution of the larger ethnic groups within our investigation area is more uniform than may be expected. We may neglect the Bhotia people, since only a minority of this cluster is living within the surveyed region. We also may leave out the figures about the Outer Terai, because this is only one of the many Outer Terai districts comprehended in our material, hence it is by no means representative. Thus we have only to deal with the Pahar, including the Mahabharat range, and the Inner Terai for a survey of ethnic distribution.

Beginning with the Paharia cluster, we find Tamang majorities with about 25% or more in the districts of Sindhuli, Nawakot, Shading, Makwanpur, Sindhu Palchowk, Rasua and Kabhre Palanchok, and a further 20% and 16.4% Tamang within the district populations of Dolakha and Ramechhap. Altogether we counted 511,420 Tamang in our investigation area; they are in fact the largest ethnic group we found. The Newar count 492,320 in our files. Most of them live in the Kathmandu valley, but there are considerably colonies of Newar in Makwanpur and Ramechhap. In the townships of Pakhara (Kaski), Bandipur (Tanahun), Hetaura (Makwanpur) and Dolakha (Dolakha) they form the bulk of the population. The 191,404 Gurung live mainly in Lamjung, Gorkha, Kaski and Tanahun. Most of the 165,355 Magar we found in Tanahun, and a colony of 17,000 people as far east as Sindhuli, where they settle mainly on the slopes of the Sun Kosi valley. Of the 19,365 Sunwar - they should not be mixed up with the Sunar, as Toni Hagen did - two-thirds live in Ramechhap. The main settlement area of the Kirati (Rai, Limbu, etc.) is in the far east of Nepal, outside of our field; thus their figures in our material are not significant. Of the Thami we counted 13,606, about 10,000 of them living in Dolakha, where all of the 3,000 Jirel/Surel dwell. Almost 2,000 of the 4,697 Pahari are settled in Kabhre Palanchok, another 1,400 in Lalitpur. The Durah people are found exclusively in Lamjung - 2,415 persons. The main region of the 24,947 Chepang lies in the south-western corner of Dhading and the neighbouring areas of Makwanpur, Chitwan and Gorkha.

The Tharu - main group of the Awalia cluster - number 18,745 people, who, except for a very few, are all living in Chitwan. Of the 15,836 Majhi we found concentrations in Ramechhap, Sindhuli, Sindhu Palchowk, and Danussha, and of the 15,727 Danuwar in Makwanpur, Sindhuli, and Kabhre Palanchok. The 3,934 Darai are found in almost equal parts in Chitwan and Tanahun, with a small minority in Gorkha. Concentrations of the Kumhal were registered in Tanahun, Gorkha, Danussha, Chitwan, Dhading and Nawakot. Together with small minorities in neighbouring districts they make up 17,422 people. They must not be confused with the Kumale, the potter caste of the Newar. Almost all of the 4,334 Barhamu are found in Gorkha.

The situation looks quite different in regard to the Parbatiya cluster. Brahman and Chhetri, numbering respectively 494,754 and 464,754, are almost equally distributed all over our investigation area. The third of the high castes, the Thakuri, numbering only 21,029, are also found in every district except Rasua. In the medium strata of the Parbatiya caste hierarchy, the Gharti, those slaves who have been liberated by act of law in 1926, and their descendants, number 27,577 people within our field. We find them in every district, with a maximum of about 5,000 in Ramechhap. The Giri number 21,816, more than 6,000 of them living in Sindhu Palchowk. The Yogi, 2,434 persons, are mainly settled in Gorkha, Kabhre Palanchok, Tanahun, Kaski and Lamjung. Of the Hayu and Bhujel, both former slaves like the Gharti, numbering respectively 1,551 and 1,369; most of the former can be found in Ramechhap and the latter mainly in Kabhre Palanchok and Tanahun. Amongst the low castes or so called 'untouchables' the Sunar range highest. They are actually only the favoured stratum of the Kami, the caste of the blacksmiths, since their materials are gold, silver and other non-iron metals. We counted 7,036 Sunar, about one-third of them living in Chitwan, but as in some districts they are filed amongst the Kami, these figures may not be reliable. The Kami number 76,736 in our investigation area, distributed over the whole of the region, and this applies also to the 50,321 Damai (tailors and musicians) and the 71,513 Sarki (tanners and cobblers). Badi and Gaine - lowest caste of musicians - are only respectively 269 and 639 individuals, too few to be dealt with in detail.

Besides the figures of persons, the numbers of households (families) were also collected, enabling us to compute the data for average family sizes. But they were computed not only for the districts, but also for the whole of our investigation area. It is surprising how small the average family in middle Nepal actually is. But, of course, these figures like all figures of this investigation are minimum numbers. Several factors are to be considered to interpret these results correctly: first of all, very young children, mostly up to 3 years of age, are rarely counted since the death rate in these first years of life is very high. Secondly, the envy of the gods is feared, thus parents tend to underestimate their family size in official polls. This effect was found by other authors too (OPPITZ, BROOK, MORRIS). Nevertheless, there seemsto be further factors. There is the outstanding fact that the average family size is remarkably similar throughout the clusters and groups and castes and geographical areas. It is not possible, however, to discuss all aspects of the problem in this context.

As a further parameter of our material, we collected the data of the altitudes for all of our 951 Gaon Panchayats. We wanted to find out whether the impression is correct that there are layers of ethnical settlement stratifications within Nepal's population, related to settlement altitudes. Here too the results were quite astonishing. But again, only a glimpse of the results is possible here.

The generally preferred altitude of 1,300m, where 13.7% of the total population of our investigation area are living, is mainly formed by the population of the Kathmandu valley, the most densely populated area in the whole country - and one of the most densely populated areas in the world, with more than 40,000 people to the square mile in some parts of Kathmandu City! Computed for the mountainous regions, which form the bulk of the landscape of Nepal, we find most people in the altitude around 1,500m (10.3%). Considering a wider stratum of 1,300 - 1,500m, we find 32.5% of the population settling there. That the Bhotia cluster is found in the higher altitudes (the Thakali are not relevant here, for several reasons) was to be expected, since they mainly live in the Himalayas. The stratum for the Sherpa would be even higher, if their main areas in Solu and Khumbu were included in our data.

Comparing results proceeding from the main parameter of districts, several conclusions are possible. First of all it should be noticed that the districts are varying considerably in shape, area, number of Gaon Panchayats, number of ethnic groups living there, size of population, and population density. But with the exception of the districts of the Outer Terai and a very few districts situated north of the main Himalayan range, their landscape is medium mountainous, or what is called Pahar in Nepal, i.e. altitudes between about 1,000 - 1,300m in the valleys and up to 2,000m on the ridges. Even in the districts of the Inner Terai, we find this form of scenery, at least in their northern parts.

The average family size is noticeably uniform throughout the whole investigation area: from district to district the average family size varies only 0.5 below and 0.3 above the general average of 5.262 heads per family. This is quite surprising, since the distribution of ethnic groups is rather irregular over the area, as is the number of groups within the districts. Although most of the larger groups can be found in most of the districts, their percentages within the district populations differ. Also differing are the rates of population growth, which are highest in Kathmandu valley districts, namely in Kathmandu itself. There, not only are hygienic and health conditions improving more rapidly than in the rest of the country, but also there is a considerably migration from the hill area downwards. Unfortunately, only a few of the districts can be compared in their figures, since most of them have changed their shape and area since 1961, the year of the census, from which the comparative figures must be taken.

The computer printouts of our data piled up more than one foot and weighed 63 lbs. Naturally, not all of these results can be discussed in this article. Nevertheless, all of them can be made available to any scholar on request, including the data about any of the 951 Gaon Panchayats investigated.

On the other hand, the research I outlined in these pages is of the kind that never attains proper completion. Not only are population figures changing constantly, since people are born and die, marry and migrate, but also it is almost impossible to get really exact figures by field investigation under conditions as we find them in a country like Nepal. More than in any other research the words of the great British scientist and philosopher, Bertrand Russell, apply here, that "... the evolution of science is a steady progress from the larger to the smaller errors ...". Therefore I shall be very grateful for any additional information, supplementation and correction of my material by other scholars of the subject, professionals or laymen.

Concluding, I want to emphasise the urgency of continuing the ethno-demography of Nepal. I hope to be able to add the data of further areas of Nepal to the above mentioned 18 districts within the coming years. I also hope that a publication of coloured maps may be possible regarding the distribution of ethnic groups, district by district. Furthermore, I hope to be able to supply a systematical survey on the ethnic structure of the population of Nepal, which is under way presently. With all this I hope to be able to contribute my share to the attempt of reducing errors within our field of science.

Walter A. Frank

The Changing Fortunes of Nepal's High Altitude Dwellers

Until the middle of the 20th century the outside world had little knowledge of the Bhotia populations of Nepal's northern border-regions, and the rulers of the kingdom were then not greatly concerned with communities that lived in high valleys difficult of access and seemed perfectly capable of managing their own affairs. Speaking Tibetan dialects and professing lamaistic Buddhism, these Bhotias stood on the fringes of the country's Hindu dominated caste society. They freely moved across the border and deep into Tibet, and had established profitable trade relations not only with Tibetans of nearby districts but also with merchants in towns as distant as Shigatse and Lhasa. The pursuit of trade also took them to the grain-growing valleys of Nepal's middle-ranges and even further afield to the low-lying Terai. Kathmandu and the other towns of the Nepal valley, however, lay outside the grid of this trade route. Bhotias from eastern as well as western border-territories sometimes visited these cities in the course of pilgrimages, but such visits did not lead to lasting social or economic links with people in the heart-land of Nepal.

For centuries the economy of such Bhotia groups as the Sherpas of Khumbu, the people of Mustang and Dolpo, and the inhabitants of Mugu and Humla had been in equilibrium, resting on the three pillars of cultivation, livestock breeding and trade. The Tibetans of the arid plateaux to the north were in need of the grain and many other products of the middle ranges of Nepal, while they in turn were able to provide virtually unlimited quantities of salt as well as wool and certain types of livestock. Apart from being the natural channels for the exchange of the basic products of the zones extending to the north and to the south of the Himalayan main range, the passes on Nepal's border with Tibet served also the flow of trade in goods from the more distant lands of India and China.

In the past 15 years, however, the trade between Nepal and Tibet has been disrupted first by political events in Tibet, and later also by economic developments inside Nepal. The replacement of the conservative regime of the Dalai Lama by that of Communist China led to rigid control of all traffic across the Himalayan passes and to a ban on many imports into Tibet. At times the borders were entirely closed, and even when a modest flow of trade could be resumed Sherpas and other traders from Nepal were no longer allowed to go beyond the few official trading depots set up by the Chinese authorities close to the frontier. While these events had immediate depressing effect on the trading activities of all the Nepalese Bhotia communities, the improvement of communications in the lower regions of Nepal and particularly the construction of motor roads linking the middle ranges of Nepal with India gradually restricted the market for Tibetan goods. The influx of cheap Indian salt, above all, threatens the viability of the important grain/salt barter-trade on which the Bhotias have always depended for a large part of their income.

Ever since I began the study of the Sherpas of Khumbu in 1953, I was conscious of the vital importance of trade for the high altitude dwellers of Nepal, and subsequent research in Thak Khola, Dolpo and Jumla in 1962 and 1966 confirmed this view. In 1972 I undertook an exploratory tour through Humla, the region in the extreme north-west corner of Nepal which adjoins the Tibetan district of Purang.

In the 12th and 13th century Humla formed part of the Malla kingdom, which extended from Dullu and Kashikot as far as Guge and Purang in Tibet, and an important trade-route linking the rich rice-growing areas of the Karnali basin with the Tibetan trade-mart of Taklakot has ever since been leading through the Bhotia villages of Humla. The prosperity of their inhabitants depends to a high degree on the barter trade with Tibet, and the recent developments in this trade were the main object of my investigations.

The ethnographic pattern of Humla is characterised by the close proximity of Tibetan-speaking Bhotia communities and Nepali-speaking Hindus, mainly of Tahkuri and Chetri caste. Up to an altitude of about 10,000 feet these population elements are interspersed, but the higher valleys are inhabited exclusively by Bhotias. The majority of villages conform to a pattern which extends over a large part of the Karnali zone, irrespective of ethnic and linguistic boundaries. Thakuris, Chetris and Bhotias live in villages of very similar type. Houses are built wall to wall in such a way that their flat roofs form a large terrace, and in some villages the principle of clustering is taken one step further and houses cling to a slope with each house touching the one below and the one above. Such fort-like villages are found mainly in the narrow, gorge-like valleys, and in the more open country of the higher regions houses stand by themselves or in small groups.

The agricultural activities of the people of Humla extend over a very wide range of different levels, and thus involve a high degree of seasonal mobility. Unlike regions such as Khumbu and Dolpo, Humla consists not only of very high country with a short cultivating season, but comprises also some relatively low valleys, where sheltered from extremes of climate crops such as rice and millet can be grown in limited quantities. At higher elevations these crops recede, and buckwheat, barley, wheat, radishes and potatoes provide the staple food.

Humla is one of the regions of Nepal where there is as yet no acute shortage of land, but since much of arable acreage is marginal there is only limited scope for expansion of cultivation, and the population could not increase agricultural production to any great extent if the income from other sources should decline as a result of a shift in trading patterns.

The importance of animal husbandry increases in proportion to the altitude of settlements. In Lower Humla common cattle and buffaloes are kept in limited numbers as an adjunct to the farming economy, but as one moves to the higher regions one encounters first cross-breeds between yak and common cattle, and above 10,000 feet large herds of sheep and yak. The herding of yak necessitates seasonal moves to high pastures, and this is facilitated by the possession of alternative houses within easy reach of grazing grounds above the tree line.

Sheep and goats are of vital importance as the only pack animals capable of negotiating the very difficult routes which lead from Upper Humla through a series of narrow river gorges to the middle ranges. Only the owners of sizeable flocks of sheep and goats can contemplate engaging in the profitable salt and grain trade.

The whole of Upper Humla is dependent on this trade and it is the recent changes in the trade pattern caused by external factors which threaten the prosperity of the entire region. The people of Humla are aware of the gradual shrinking of their economic base, but neither they themselves nor the administrators concerned about their future can see a solution to the problems resulting from the reorientation of trade both in Tibet and in Nepal.

The traditional trading system of the people of Upper Humla was based on the fact that in Tibet grain is much more valuable than salt, while in the middle ranges of Nepal salt could be exchanged for as much as eight times its volume in grain. At the time when communications between India and the Nepalise lowlands were poor, and a belt of malaria infested jungles separated the Terai from the middle ranges, hardly any Indian salt penetrated into Nepal and the entire need for salt was met by imports from Tibet.

As long as this situation persisted and the whole of the Tibetan border regions were open to traders from Nepal, the people of Humla were assured of good profits and a relatively high standard of living. For in such Tibetan markets as Taklakot they could exchange the grain their animals carried across the passes for several times its volume in salt, and they could obtain by barter unlimited quantities of wool as well as any number of live animals such as sheep and yak. But the coming of the Chinese and the rigid control they imposed on the border trade deprived the Nepalese of the possibility of doing business with individual trading partners. They still take grain to Tibet but must sell it at government trade depots at fixed prices and purchase salt at a rate determined by the Chinese. Thus there is no longer any bargaining: the quantity of wool available to Nepalese is limited and so is the export of livestock. Even more serious, however, is the drop in the value of salt in the middle ranges of Nepal. While old men of Humla remember the days when they bartered salt in the region of Acham, Bajura and Raskot for 7-8 times the volume of rice, today the average exchange rate in these areas is 1:1 and the profits of the Humla people are consequently greatly reduced. The reason for this development is the easy availability of cheap Indian salt in the southern regions. With the improvement of internal communications Indian salt is bound to creep deeper and deeper into the middle ranges of Nepal, and to undercut the Tibetan salt brought there by the people of Humla.

The exact cycle of trade depends on the location of the traders' home village, but an example from the villages in the vicinity of Simikot will serve to demonstrate the pattern of movements involved in the operations of the average traders. Those people who own flocks of carrier-sheep and goats undertake the first trading journey to Taklakot immediately after the harvest of the winter crops at the end of June. They carry partly rice, bartered during the winter in the middle ranges and partly barley grown in their own fields. In Taklakot they exchange grain for salt. In 1972 the rates were about 1:2½ barley: salt, and 1:5 rice:salt. On the way to and from Taklakot the sheep and goats are kept for some time on the rich pastures above Yari. Such trips may be repeated in July and August, until the traders have accumulated a sufficient store of salt for their trading expeditions to the middle ranges. After the end of the monsoon and the harvest of the summer crops, the traders set out with carrier-sheep and goats carrying salt, and move first along the valley of the Humla Karnali and then across one of the passes leading south to such rice growing areas in the middle ranges as Bajang, Acham and Raskot. There they exchange their salt for rice. In 1972 the usual rate was 1:1, or at the most 5 measures of rice for 4 measures of salt. They bring the rice back to Humla, and in November set out for a much longer journey. This time they take all their sheep and goats with them, even ewes and lambs which are not used for the carrying of loads. Again they barter salt for rice and sometimes other grain grown in the valleys of the middle ranges. Such grain is used partly for their own consumption during the journey and partly stored with trading friends in places such as Bajura and Acham. They then move slowly further south letting the animals graze wherever there are pastures, and finally they take their carrier-sheep to Nepalganj or Rajapur in the Terai. There they buy Indian salt, usually for cash which they obtain by selling woollen blankets or disposing of some animals for slaughter. This Indian salt is taken to the middle ranges and bartered there mainly for rice. The reason why the Hindu villagers of Acham and Raskot do not fetch Indian salt themselves is their lack of transport. They have neither carrier-sheep nor other suitable pack-animals.

The Humla people spend the whole winter on these migrations, for in their own villages there is at that time of year no grazing for their flocks, and the needs of animal husbandry thus coincide with those of the grain/salt trade. By the time the herdsmen are ready to return to Humla in April and early May, they have accumulated a store of rice and other grain which they now carry on their sheep and goats to their home villages.

The difference between the exchange rates in Tibet and the middle ranges of Nepal constitutes the profit of the traders, and enables them not only to live themselves during part of the year on grain grown at altitudes much lower than that of Humla, but also to bring back more rice and other grain than that required for their barter transactions in Taklakot. In this way they supplement with the grain obtained by barter their store of home-grown grain.

This rough outline of the pattern of journeys and barter transactions does not account for several other openings for the exchange of Nepalese grain for Tibetan salt. In the Humla region there are several trade-marts where at certain times, usually early in November, Tibetans and men of such border villages as Yari sell salt and wool to people from the lower regions, and before the Chinese had concentrated the trade in Taklakot, there were similar marts at other points of the boundary.

It is obvious that this whole elaborate pattern of movements of people, animals and goods depends on the possibility of selling Tibetan salt to the producers of a surplus of rice and grain occupying the middle ranges of Nepal. If their needs were to be met entirely by supplies of cheap Indian salt, the whole system would break down. The Tibetans could no longer dispose of their salt and the people of Humla would be unable to obtain the grain which they need for supplementing their stores of home-grown grain. For they would have no commodity to offer in exchange.

The construction of roads from the Terai into the middle ranges, while no doubt beneficial to the traders of the lowlands, would thus have disastrous effects on the economy of the high altitude dwellers of the northern borderlands. For these populations cannot subsist solely on the yield of their land, and if deprived of the profits from the salt trade they might be unable to maintain themselves in their present habitat. Even the seasonal migrations of their herds of sheep and goats, necessitated by the lack of winter grazing in Humla, depend on the sale of salt in the middle ranges. For without the possibility of bartering salt for grain, the herdsmen could not feed themselves in an area where they have no other sources of supply.

This leads one to the conclusion that by the improvement of communications in the lower region, rightly deemed advantageous for the economic development of its inhabitants, the economic basis of such zones of high altitude as Humla and Mugu may well be irreparably damaged. This danger, though clearly looming on the horizon, is fortunately not yet imminent. For the terrain is such that considerable time will elapse before motorable roads can be driven into the middle ranges of Western Nepal. Ultimately, however, Tibetan salt will be replaced by the cheaper Indian salt, and the people of Humla will inevitably suffer from the loss of their markets.

A situation very different from that prevailing in Humla has arisen among the Sherpas of Khumbu. Even a generation ago the pattern of life in the two areas had much in common, even though among the Sherpas there were rich merchants engaged in trade with Shigatse and Lhasa who had no comparable counterparts in Humla. Now, however, the economic scene in Khumbu has undergone changes much more profound than those affecting the Bhotias of the Karnali zone. The reasons for the different pace of change are manifold. Firstly the Chinese restrictions on trade with Khumbu seem to be much more severe than those imposed on the flow of goods between Humla and Taklakot. Secondly, the operations of the larger Sherpa merchants were geared to long-distance trade on goods of much greater variety than that of the commodities bartered by the far less ambitious traders of Humla. The fact that traders from Nepal are no longer allowed to travel deep into Tibet or even maintain contacts with Tibetan business partners has hit the Sherpas much more severely than the Bhotias of Humla who had always concentrated on trade with the inhabitants of the nearby border areas. Thirdly, the Sherpas had the possibility of switching their energies from trade to mountaineering and tourism whereas Humla was until very recently an area closed to foreigners, and so far has not attracted any tourists. Thanks to the new possibilities of employment in the tourist industry, the Sherpas' economic prospects for the future are more favourable than those of the Humla people, but against this must be set the far greater disruption of their traditional pattern of life brought about by the influx of tourists and the periodic absence of large numbers of Sherpa men on mountaineering expeditions and trekking tours.

While at the time of the flight of the Dalai Lama from Tibet in 1959 the frontier between Khumbu and the Tingri district was completely closed, later the Chinese allowed a very limited trade in a few basic commodities. But no Tibetan is permitted to cross the frontier, and Nepalese citizens may only travel as far as Tingri, and must sell their goods to an official, Chinese-run trading depot. A few enterprising Sherpas of Khumbu occasionally still carry some loads of grain across the Nangpa La and receive from the Chinese salt and sometimes small quantities of wool in exchange. The goods involved, however, meet only local needs, and the Chinese do not encourage trade on the large scale such as existed before they imposed their rule on Tibet.

The dwindling of the Sherpas' trade with Tibet not only deprived professional traders of their livelihood, but had also an adverse effect on the traditional crafts of Khumbu. As long as Tibetan wool was imported in substantial quantities, weaving flourished, and the Sherpas produced a variety of woollen cloth for their own use as well as for sale in other parts of Nepal. Newly immigrant Khamba women, expert in weaving, were much in demand. They were paid a daily wage and their employers supplied them with food as long as they worked in their houses. Today one; rarely sees women weaving, and the Sherpas are desperately short of warm, woollen cloth. As a result of this shortage standards of clothing have deteriorated, and while women continue to wear their traditional dress of Tibetan style, few men wear the woollen clothes and boots, which as late as 1957 were universal among

Khumbu Sherpas. They have largely been replaced by an assortment of mountaineering dress and other clothes of modern type.

During the past decade there has been a rapid development of tourism, and while previously only organised mountaineering expeditions and a few scholars ventured into the remoter mountain regions of Nepal, trekking has become a sport attracting increasing numbers of foreign tourists. Being experienced in work with foreigners and themselves enterprising and used to long-distance travel, the Sherpas proved excellent guides and camp servants, and today they are employed not only for tours to the Sherpa country, but also for trekking in Western Nepal.

Khumbu itself has seen a spectacular rise in tourist traffic. During the seven months I stayed there in 1957 the area was visited only by one Swiss official of F.A.O. and two mountaineers. In twelve months between July 1969 and June 1970, 642 tourists with trekking permits checked in at the police station of Namche Bazar, and in the nine months from July 1970 until the beginning of April 1971 the number of tourists was 533. Neither of these figures includes the members of organised mountaineering expeditions. In the spring of 1971 three major expeditions were operating in the Khumbu area: an international Mount Everest expedition, a South Korean Lhotse expedition and a Japanese expedition climbing on a minor peak. The Mount Everest expedition alone employed 60 Sherpas, including three *sirdar*, high altitude climbers, cooks, kitchen boys and wood carriers.

The rates of pay commanded by Sherpas employed by mountaineering expeditions are high by Nepalese standards. *Sirdar* are paid an average daily wage of Rs. 25, high altitude climbers and cooks Rs. 15, and porters carrying supplies and wood to the base-camp Rs. 10. These daily wages do not represent the entire income of the more senior mountaineering Sherpas. *Sirdar* often act as contractors for the supply of local produce such as potatoes, fresh meat, eggs, vegetables and even rice, and their profit margin may be considerable. Moreover, the custom has grown up that at the end of an expedition the Sherpas participating in the actual climbing are given their personal equipment, including the valuable down jackets and sleeping sacks. Such items are partly retained for their own and their family's use, and partly sold to tourists either at Namche Bazar or in Kathmandu.

In villages such as Khumjung and Khunde about 70% of the households contain at least one member sometimes engaged in work connected with mountaineering and tourism, and some of the younger men spend as much as eight or nine months of the year away from their village. The fact that nowadays many Sherpas are employed in trekking work in western Nepal makes it impossible for them to return home in between periods of employment, and some of them have secondary establishments in Kathmandu, where they can be joined by their wives. For the past fifteen years some Sherpas have also worked as servants in the houses of Europeans and Americans, and such men tend to bring their whole family to Kathmandu. Even those whose economic base has shifted to the Nepal Valley retain their houses and land-holdings in Khumbu, and intend no doubt, to return there in their old age. No man of Khumjung or Khunde has a yet sold his house and permanently moved to Kathmandu, but three men of Namche Bazar did so. Seeing no prospects for early revival of trade in Khumbu, they left their home and are trying to develop business enterprises in Kathmandu.

Apart from the cash earnings of Sherpas employed by mountaineers, tourists and foreign residents, the economy of Khumbu benefits also from the payments of tourists for supplies and accommodation while they are in Sherpa villages. The tradition of hospitality typical of Sherpas and Tibetans, makes it easy for tourists to find shelter and food in Sherpa houses, and what began as casual *ad hoc* arrangements is in the process of being developed as a regular business. One progressive Sherpa of Khunde has already built an attractive annexeto his house with the express purpose of letting it to tourists, and others are planning to turn whole houses into simple inns.

The influx of cash and the resulting monetization of the Sherpa economy finds expression in the operation of a weekly market in Namche Bazar, where the trading is almost entirely in cash. Although Namche Bazat was always a settlement of traders and a place visited by Tibetans who came there to barter their goods for Nepalese commodities, it was not the site of a regular market. In 1965, however, the local panchayat encouraged the establishment of a weekly market where suppliers of grain and other produce of the middle ranges can sell their commodities to the people of Khumbu. This weekly market is now a well established institution and it is estimated that the usual turnover on a bazaar-day is Rs. 12,000 - 15,000. An average of 200 - 400 people from the regions south of the Sherpa country bring their wares to Namche, and Sherpas from all the villages of Khumbu gather to make their purchases. The sellers, most of whom come from distances of three to six days' journey are known by the generic term of Dakre. Most of them are Rais, but there are also some Chetris and members of other Hindu castes among the men and women who carry supplies to Namche Bazar. Rice, maize and millet are their main wares, but some of the men also bring wheat, flour of various grains, bananas, eggs and chickens. They gather on an open site just outside the village and sit down in rows behind their baskets, calling out the price of their goods.

In April 1972 rice was sold at this market for Rs. 12 per *pathi*, a measure of capacity corresponding roughly to 1 gallon, and knowing that prices tend to go up before the next rice harvest, Sherpas bought large quantities to build up a store for the monsoon. Transactions were in cash, and the large bundles of ten rupee notes produced by some Sherpas were a sight seldom seen in the Khumbu of the 1950s. The amount of cash circulating in Khumbu is so great that people from the lower country jokingly say that "there must be a mint in Khumbu producing all this money.". I have also heard Sherpas say that their people are not used to budgeting, and when they have cash in their hands, they spend it often on non-essentials. Thus while in 1957 sugar was unobtainable in Khumbu, now Sherpas buy considerable amounts, and often drink tea with sugar and milk, rather than the Tibetan salted tea.

The traders from the middle ranges sell all their wares for cash, and do not buy anything from the Sherpas. The era of barter has clearly come to an end, and so has buying on credit. Previously, Rais came to Namche Bazat and exchanged grain for Tibetan salt. The Namche merchants stored the grain and then sold it to Sherpas from other villages, often on credit. Nowadays only people with ready money go to the weekly market and buy grain for cash. However, there is still some scope for credit transactions. Wealthy Sherpas purchase in the weekly market rice and other grain on speculation, and store it in their houses. When the price has risen they sell it to other Sherpas either for cash or on credit. In 1970 the price of rice went up to Rs. 18 per *pathi*, thus enabling men who had stored supplies to make a profit of 33% within less than half a year.

While the old established traders of Namche Bazar undoubtedly engage in such transactions, buying and selling grain is no substitute for the large scale Tibetan trade which was the mainstay of their business. They had therefore to look for new sources of income. Some of them found those in work for tourists, while others developed trade with the Kathmandu valley. Contact with the outside world and in particular with foreigners has given the Sherpas a taste for manufactured goods and such commodities as sugar, biscuits, Indian tea, condensed milk, soap, electric torches, gym shoes, and a variety of clothing. As woollen hand-woven materials are now in short supply, there is a growing demand for cotton textiles, and some of the Namche traders have begun to buy such goods in Kathmandu and to transport them to Khumbu, where they sell them to Sherpas who have cash to spare.

Thus, the north-south axis of the traditional trade has partly been replaced by a flow of trade along a route running roughly from east to west. There is also still some trade with the Terai, but this is diminishing as the Sherpas can no longer produce the Tibetan goods which they used to sell there, and for those buying goods for cash Kathmandu is a more convenient source of supply.

The partial transformation of the economy of Khumbu has had considerable repercussions on the social life of the Sherpas. Two phenomena are immediately apparent to anyone who knew Khumbu before external events disrupted the traditional economic pattern: the composition of village society has become unbalanced because of the absence of a large percentage of the young men during the greater part of the year, and economic power has shifted from the older men of long established Sherpa families to young and middle-aged men who are not necessarily of families enjoying inherited high status.

In my book *The Sherpas of Nepal* I have shown that as late as 1957 the villages of Khumbu were virtually autonomous except for the levy of a very modest land-tax by the government of Nepal. The task of collecting this tax was entrusted to a number of prominent men know as *pembu*, who stood in a - usually hereditary - patron relationship to the men who paid them their land-tax. Other civic tasks and responsibilities, the enforcement of rules laid down by the village assembly, and the control of such natural resources as the village-forests, were allocated according to a system of rotation combined with the informal selection of men suitable for various offices. The system worked well at a time when the village-communities were largely self-contained and contacts with outsiders were slight. Though in theory the laws of the state applied to Khumbu as much as to any other part of the kingdom, in practice no outside agency intervened in the affairs of the Khumbu people, as long as they arranged to pay the annual revenue to the appropriate government office, which was located at Okhaldunga, the district headquarters.

With the improvement of communications and the establishment of a type of grass-root democracy based on the panchayat system throughout Nepal in 1963, the Sherpas were inevitably drawn into a wider political network. Khumbu is now divided into two wards; one consists of Khumjung, Khunde, Phortse, Tengboche, Pangboche and Dingboche, and the other ward consists of Namche Bazar and the entire Thami-Thamote area. Each of these wards has a separate panchayat headed by a chairman *(pradhan panch)*. The ordinary panchayat members who represent the population of the villages, comprised within the ward, are elected informally by a show of hands but a ballot is conducted for the position of chairman. Among the panchayat members there are several women and in the ward including Namche a woman recently won the election in the contest for the chairmanship. This reflects the enhanced position of women resulting at least partly from the frequent absence of men on expedition and trekking business.

The village panchayat levies a small house-tax, ranging from Rs. 2 for a big house to Rs. ¼ for the smallest house, and 50% of this tax is used for village purposes while 50% goes to the district panchayat. The village panchayat may, moreover, apply to the district panchayat for funds for development projects. The chairman of the panchayat acts as a link between the people of the ward and the district panchayat.

The panchayat also mediates in disputes, such as arguments about the boundaries of fields. My Sherpa informants voiced the view that the method of dealing with disputes has basically remained unchanged, and that the panchayat members act in the same way as previously the *pembu* and *naua* did.

The establishment of statutory panchayats has not made the institution of *naua* or 'village guardians' obsolete. Such village guardians are still being appointed, their selection being the result of informal discussion in villages such as Khumjung or Khunde or determined by a system of automatic rotation such as in Phortse. Matters such as the utilisation of pastures are still being dealt with by the village-guardians, but it would seem that their importance is diminishing even though at present the institution co-exists with the new panchayat system.

Sherpa villages used to be characterised by their unity of purpose and the absence of factionalism. The interests of the villagers were seldom in conflict, and disputes between individuals could usually be settled by mediation. The village was the focal point of the aspirations of all inhabitants, and economic advancement and the build-up of prestige was considered in the terms of a man's position within the village community. Now, however, the focus of many Sherpas' interests has shifted to the economic possibilities provided by tourism, and success in this sphere and in business enterprises located in Kathmandu, provides an alternative to the acquisition of influence in local affairs. There are also indications that Sherpa villages are no longer always united in their reaction to events and propositions originating outside the confines of Sherpa society. This became obvious when a consortium dominated by a Japanese group began the building of a hotel on a site considered by the people of Khumjung as being part of their village land. The employment provided by the project was of obvious advantage to the villagers, but there was understandable resentment about the destruction of forest involved in the scheme. In the assessment of the balance of advantages and disadvantages of the hotel project, the village split, and individuals took up positions according to the personal benefits they could expect from the scheme.

There is an obvious conflict between the interests of the older men with considerable holdings of land and herds of cattle, who depend for their farming on hired labour, and younger men, who see their future in the development of tourism and want to sell their labour at the highest possible rate. Such projects as the new hotel near Khumjung impinge on the supply of labour, and are hence frowned upon by the established landowners, while they are welcomed by younger men keen to take advantage of modern developments.

An important factor in the change of the social climate is the education scheme initiated and financed by Sir Edmund Hillary in 1961. At present there are six schools in Khumbu, and 43% of the children of school age are enrolled as pupils of these schools even though they do not necessarily attend throughout the year.

The intellectual and spiritual life of the Sherpas has developed within the framework of Tibetan Buddhism. Monasteries were the centres of all cultural activities, and village rituals were performed according to Buddhist traditions. Lamas provided education both for those preparing for a religious life, and for boys without such aspirations but intent on acquiring the ability to read and write for both practical and religious purposes. Until recently there was no alternative to this type of education, and lamas never lacked pupils anxious to profit from their skill and wisdom.

The first half of the twentieth century saw a great expansion of religious institutions in Khumbu and Solu, and the Sherpa country as a whole was a most fertile soil for the growth of Buddhist culture and ideology. When I visited Khumbu in 1953 and 1957 the monasteries of Tengboche and Thami were thriving institutions, and the number of novices seemed to augur well for their future development.

In 1971, however, the scene had changed. The majority of the

Sherpas were undoubtedly still firm believers in the Buddhist doctrine and there was no sign of the appearance of any rival ideology. But the practical interest in religious institutions and performances had noticeably diminished. This was most clearly apparent in the monastery of Tengboche. In 1957 the monastic community consisted of the reincarnate abbot and 32 monks of all ages. By 1971 the number of monks had dropped to 14, and only two were boys in the early stages of their training as monks. Three monks had recently died, but nine had left to return to secular life. Two of them had joined the Makalu expedition of 1971 as porters without even informing the abbot. The reincarnate lama spoke sadly about the decline in religious fervour and learning. Hardly any of the remaining monks were interested in scholarship, and while they were still keen on such ritual performances as the Mani rimdu, which has become a tourist attraction, they cared little about their deeper content. The outward appearance of the monastery confirmed the waning interest of both monks and laymen.

While in the past Sherpas gave rich donations to religious institutions, the present generation is much less generous. Most of the cash is now in the hands of young men,who, though not outspokenly irreligious, have little interest in gaining merit by devoting their wealth to the support of religion. Previously old men controlled much of the wealth of Khumbu, and many of them spent lavishly to maintain monasteries, build religious monuments such as *chorten* and *mani*-walls and commission ritual performances. It is significant that within the past decade in the whole Khumjung-Khunde area not a single rock inscription has been newly carved, whereas in earlier years many were commissioned to gain merit or to commemorate a deceased relative who would benefit from the acquired merit.

The situation in which the Sherpas find themselves today does not conform to the usual pattern of the integration of ethnic minorities into larger economic and political systems. The termination of their traditional contacts with Tibet through political events outside their control has forced them to reorientate their economy and to seek new sources of income. But unlike many other communities in similar situations, such as for instance some of the tribal minorities of India, they were able to avoid entering into a relationship of dependence with a numerically and politically superior population. They have not had to link their economy with that of any of the dominant castes of Nepal, but have developed their role in the tourist industry of Nepal in the spirit of potential entrepreneurs and not in that of labourers seeking work outside their own homeland. Sherpa climbers and tourist guides consider themselves as professionals and they have been able to establish a monopoly which is not seriously threatened by any other community in Nepal. Thanks to the admiration and affection felt by western mountaineers for their Sherpa companions they have acquired a certain mystique, and western tourists have come to regard Sherpas as indispensable helpers not only in mountain-climbing but also on any trek in area where experience in camping, resourcefulness and reliability are essential qualities in guides and tour-servants. The relatively large wages Sherpas can command reflect the estimation in which they are held, and the ability to earn such wages facilitates the accumulation of capital which the former generation of climbers invested in the traditional way in land and cattle, but which modern Sherpas are prepared to invest in the creation of tourist facilities in their own villages.

The collapse of the trade with Tibet and of many trading contacts assiduously built up and passed on from generation to generation has not led to any despondency or loss of initiative, but has stimulated the Sherpas to enter a new field of enterprise, a field to which they brought all the skill and spirit of adventure they had developed as independent traders.

In the sphere of social relations the transition from a society in which authority and influence is linked to inherited wealth to a situation favouring the young and enterprising is going on smoothly. The Sherpas' inbred courtesy and sense of decorum makes the successful young entrepreneurs respect the dignity of the representatives of the older order, and the trust in the old leaders is still great enough to assure their election to such posts as chairman of the village panchayat. Thus there is no break with the past, and Sherpa villages have preserved the atmosphere of friendliness and cooperation even though sectional interests are sometimes in conflict. Those who knew Khumbu years ago cannot fail to discern, however, a certain deterioration in the quality of life, and this is due to the frequent and prolonged absence of many of the younger men and the unnatural solitary life imposed on their wives.

The recent changes in the fortunes of the Sherpas of Khumbu and the Bhotias of Humla are indicative of a process which for the past fifteen years has affected most of the northern border areas of Nepal. Populations which for centuries acted as the main intermediaries in the trans-Himalayan trade see the basis of their traditional economy shrinking, and have to seek new means of subsistence. There are other areas such as Thak Khola, Dolpo and Manangbhot where similar readjustments are inevitable, but the circumstances are different in each case, and there is an urgent need for research into all the local variants of a development threatening the very existence of many groups of high altitude dwellers. Some of them may cling to their ancestral land despite declining living standards, while others, such as the Thakalis of the Kali Gandaki valley, may abandon their villages and move to area with better prospects for trade. Whatever the outcome of the various local developments may be, there can be no doubt about the seriousness of the problems facing many of Nepal's most resilient and enterprising trading communities.

Christoph von Fürer-Haimendorf

Les Récits Chantés de L'Himalaya et le Contexte Ethnographique

Dans cette communication, j'expose les premiers résultats d'un travail de terrain effectué au Népal occidental et au Kumaon, d'octobre 1969 à février 1970 et d'octobre 1970 à mars 1971. Travaillant avec deux bardes népalais et quatre bardes Kumaoni, j'ai recueilli un corpus de récits chantés (plus de soixante-dix heures d'enregistrements magnétiques); je les ai analysés et classés; j'ai aussi traduit intégralement certains d'entre eux. Après avoir donné rapidement une définition et une classification de ces récits chantés, je me limiterai à la présentation détaillée d'une partie du corpus: prenant un groupe de douze récits d'amour dont j'analyserai la structure narrative, je dégagerai le type de conduite et les valeurs qu'ils glorifient pour les comparer aux normes sociales traditionnelles qui apparaissent lors d'une enquête ethnographique ou du dépouillement des codes de droit.

I DEFINITION ET CLASSIFICATION DES RECITS CHANTES[1]

Dans tout l'Himalaya central, de la vallée de la Karnali dans le Népal occidental jusqu'au Garhwal, on peut entendre des récits chantés qui constituent un répertoire relativement homogène. Ce sont des histoires, de longues histoires, qui peuvent durer d'une ou deux heures jusqu'à huit ou dix heures; elles sont racontées par des bardes, généralement intouchables, qui sont des spécialistes; qui, utilisant une technique de composition orale, tantôt chantent, tantôt déclament, tantôt parlent; et qui s'accompagnent d'un tambour (tambour sablier, *huṛki*; ou tambour à deux peaux, *ḍhol*). Lors de l'exécution, les bardes se font toujours aider par deux ou plus de deux acolytes qui prennent part au chant à la fin des strophes et/ou jouent d'autres instruments à percussion (tambour, timbale ou plat de laiton). Tels sont les caractères communs à tous ces récits chantés. Les folkloristes indiens les appellent *lok-gāthā* (terme savant forgé pour traduire l'anglais: folk ballads); mais les dialectes locaux ne possèdent pas de terme général s'appliquant à tous.

En revanche, on trouve dans le dialecte Kumaoni quatre termes spécifiques; désignant quatre genres distincts de récits chantés; ils peuvent servir de base à une classification.

A. Deux d'entre eux (*bhārat* et *jāgar*) désignent des récits religieux exécutés au cours de cérémonies célébrées soit dans la cour des temples, soit dans des maisons particulières où les fidèles se rassemblent pour voir et entendre les dieux qui se manifestent par la danse et les paroles de médiums en transe; ils concernent des dieux qui peuvent appartenir au panthéon classique ou être purement locaux. Le barde qui les exécute s'adresse non pas aux assistants, mais aux dieux; il prend part à la cérémonie non pas seulement comme musicien, mais surtout comme maître de cérémonie; il peut, selon les régions, appartenir à une caste pure ou à une caste intouchable, et il peut utiliser différentes sortes de tambour. Ces récits religieux se subdivisent en:

a) *bhārat*, qui sont exécutés au début de la cérémonie; le barde y raconte, à la troisième personne, la création du monde, l'histoire des divinités classiques ou de saints (les neuf Nāth).

b) *jāgar*, qui sont exécutés dans la seconde partie de la cérémonie et qui sont destinés à provoquer et à diriger les transes; le barde parle alors à la seconde personne: s'adressant à chaque divinité, il la contraint à venir posséder le médium et lui raconte son histoire dont les épisodes sont mimés par la danse du médium en transe.

B. Deux autres termes (*bhaṛau* et *caitī*) désignent des récits profanes exécutés par des intouchables qui s'accompagnent d'un tambour-sablier.

a) Le plus grand nombre d'entre eux peuvent être classés comme *bhaṛau*, c'est-à-dire récits de héros. Ils sont exécutés devant un auditoire composé essentiellement d'hommes, soit pour les distraire lorsqu'ils sont invités à une cérémonie familiale (naissance, initiation, mariage) ou rassemblés pour passer une veillée d'hiver; soit pour les encourager dans le travail des champs (repiquage et sarclage du riz); à une époque plus ancienne, le barde les chantait sur le champ de bataille pour encourager les soldats au combat. Ces récits sont consacrés à l'histoire des anciennes dynasties, et aux exploits héroïques ou amoureux des héros locaux.

b) Un nombre plus restreint de récits sont appelés *caitī*. Ils sont exécutés par les membres des castes de musiciens intouchables qui vont mendier dans les maisons de leurs patrons au mois de *cait* (mars-avril); s'adressant à un auditoire de femmes, ils racontent les malheurs des femmes mariées résidant chez leur mari et séparées de leurs frères.

II LES RECITS D'AMOUR ET LE CONTEXTE ETHNOGRAPHIQUE

Quand j'ai commencé à étudier ces récits chantés, je pensais y trouver une expression des normes traditionnellement approuvées par la société. Est-ce que les résultats de ce travail ont répondu à mon attente? Il n'est pas possible ici de tester cette hypothèse sur l'ensemble du corpus; je me limiterai à un groupe de douze récits d'amour du genre *bhaṛau* (B, a), que j'ai choisis pour deux raisons: je les connais mieux que le reste du corpus car j'ai traduit intégralement l'un d'eux, Mālū Shāhī d'après un enregistrement d'une durée de douze heures fait auprès d'un premier barde[2] et j'ai eu l'occasion d'étudier en détail un autre enregistrement du même récit fait auprès d'un autre barde.[3] En second lieu, je dispose d'un matériel ethnographique et historique plus abondant sur ce sujet que pour le reste du corpus; il m'est ainsi plus facile de confronter ces douze récits aux réalités sociales.

A) Analyse des recits

Voici la méthode employée. Les bardes utilisent une technique de composition orale; leurs récits peuvent être analysés à trois niveaux: ce sont, pour reprendre la terminologie de A. B. Lord (1964, pp. 30-123), les 'formules' utilsées par le barde pour composer les vers; les 'thèmes' tout prêts qu'il emploie pour développer les différentes parties du récit; et enfin le 'chant' c'est-à-dire l'argument de l'histoire racontée. Comme formules et thèmes sont pratiquement identiques sur l'ensemble du corpus, c'est seulement au niveau du chant que l'on peut découvrir des traits spécifiques communs permettant de regrouper ensemble certains récits et de les distinguer d'autres groupes de récits. C'est ainsi que j'ai pu isoler un groupe de douze récits d'amour. En les comparant j'ai pu dégager une structure narrative commune à dix d'entre eux qui seront désormais désignés comme 'récits sérieux': utilisant une méthode inspirée de V. Propp (1970, pp. 28-34), je définis cette structure comme une série de 'fonctions' ou événements qui apparaissent dans le même ordre dans tous les récits. Les deux autres récits, que j'appellerai 'comiques', présentent une altération de cette structure de base.

a) les recits serieux.

Présentons d'abord un exemple:

RECIT I: Mālū Shāhī

Sunapati Shauka, *Bhoṭyā* de Jauhar dans le nord-est du Kumaon, et sa femme Gangulī n'ont pas d'enfant. Ils vont en pélerinage dans le sud du Kumaon pour demander au dieu Shiva la faveur d'avoir un enfant. Ils y rencontrent Ajaya Pāl, roi du pays Huṇa (i.e, Tibet occidental) qui est venu avec sa femme dans le même but. Ils prennent l'engagement solennel de marier les deux enfants à naître s'ils sont de sexe différent. Sunapati Shauka obtient une fille qu'il appelle Rājulī; Ajaya Pāl, un fils qu'il nomme Chandra. Rājulī grandit et devient une belle jeune fille; un automne, elle accompagne son père dans une expédition commerciale vers le Sud; conduisant une caravane de moutons et de chèvres chargés de sel, ils arrivent à Bairāṭh (Kumaon central), capitale d'un roi Katyuri, Mālū Shāhī. Un jour, pendant que son père est parti troquer son sel contre du riz dans les villages avoisinants, Rājulī garde son troupeau près du temple de la déesse Agneri, sur le bord du Ram Ganga. Mālū Shāhī vient se baigner sur l'autre rive du fleuve et voit son image reflétée dans l'eau bleue; croyant d'abord qu'il s'agit de la déesse, il en tombe éperdument amoureux. Dès lors ils se rencontrent tous les jours en cachette, jusqu'au moment où le père de Rājulī en est informé; il la contraint alors de revenir à Jauhar et à épouser immédiatement Chandra Pāl. Emmenée au Tibet chez son mari, Rājulī parvient bientôt à s'échapper, revient à pied à Bairāṭh au prix de bien des dangers et, une nuit, rejoint Mālū Shāhī dans son palais. Mais elle repart très tôt le lendemain matin, avant que le roi ne s'éveille, laissant derrière elle la lettre suivante: "Je crains qu'un jour tu ne te lasses de moi et ne me reproches d'être venue de ma propre initiative, sans que tu ne m'aies appelée. Si tu es vraiment un homme, viens, reprends-moi de force à mes parents et à mon mari." Le lendemain matin, quand il découvre la lettre, Mālū Shāhī devient fou de chagrin; se désintéressant de ses devoirs de chef de famille et de roi, il abandonne tout pour aller conquérir Rājulī; sa mère, ses soeurs, ses femmes, ses sujets essaient en vain de le retenir; il se fait initier comme *kān-phaṭṭā yogi* par le *pīr* du monastère de son royaume; il part accompagné de Keka Dās, son *guru* magicien et musicien et la troupe de ses sujets déguisés aussi en Yogis. En passant un col élevé, ils sont empoisonnés par des herbes vénéneuses, puis ressuscités par Keka Dās. Quand ils atteignent Jauhar, Mālū Shāhī se querelle avec son *guru* et ses sujets qui l'abandonnent et rentrent chez eux. Resté seul, il s'introduit près de Rājulī qui est revenue chez ses parents; il vit avec elle dans leur maison pendant quelques semaines. Mais Sunapati Shauka n'aime pas cette situation; il a peur de représailles de la part de Chandra Pāl. Un jour que Rājulī est absente, il met du poison dans la nourriture de Mālū Shāhī et jette son cadavre dans un ravin. L'âme du roi apparaît en rêve à sa mère pour lui demander son aide. Elle dépêche à Jauhar le *guru* Keka Dās qui retrouve le cadavre du roi et le ressuscite. Chandra Pāl, ayant eu vent de la présence de Mālū Shāhī à Jauhar arrive avec son armée pour le tuer. Il s'ensuit un furieux combat entre le roi tibétain et son armée, d'un côté; et Mālū Shāhī, de l'autre, aidé de son *guru* qui met à sa disposition toutes les ressources de son savoir magique. Chandra Pāl est tué; Mālū Shāhī ramène triomphalement Rājulī à Bairaṭh; leur mariage est célébré au milieu de grandes réjouissances; ils vivent heureux mais n'ont pas d'enfant.

Si nous comparons maintenant ce récit aux neuf autres du sous-groupe des récits sérieux, nous trouvons des fonctions qui se présentent toujours dans le même ordre; je vais analyser en détail six d'entre elles qui sont communes aux dix récits, mentionnant seulement en passant les six autres qui n'apparaissent que dans quelques-uns d'entre eux.

1. Le père d'une jeune fille (B) l'a mariée ou va la marier à un homme (C): ici Sunapati Shauka fiance puis marie Rājulī à Chandra Pāl.

2. Un autre homme (A) et cette jeune femme (B), ici Mālū Shāhī et Rājulī, sont amoureux l'un de l'autre. La combinaison de ces deux fonctions constitue la situation initiale dont découle fatalement l'ensemble du récit.

3. L'amant (A) est informé du mariage. Le message peut être transmis de bien des façons différentes: ici Rājulī vient elle-même porter la nouvelle; c'est le seul cas où la héroîne (B) se déplace elle-même; dans les autres récits, elle envoie un message oral ou une lettre, ou bien apparaît en rêve; ou une tierce personne prend l'initiative d'informer l'amant.

4. L'amant (A) prend la décision d'abandonner tout autre souci pour aller arracher la jeune femme (B) à ses parents et à son mari.

Ici s'insèrent de nombreuses péripéties qui constituent la plus longue partie du récit; elles peuvent s'analyser en six fonctions dont aucune n'est commune à tous les récits, mais dont chacune est illustrée dans plusieurs d'entre eux; la série complète étant présente dans trois récits, dont Mālū Shāhī:

5. L'amant (A) se déguiser en Yogi: ici Mālū Shāhī non seulement prend l'habit du Yogi mais se fait initier.

6. Il rencontre des obstacles en chemin: herbes vénéneuses, démons, ogresses. Mālū Shāhī est empoisonné par des herbes vénéneuses.

7. Il rencontre secrètement la jeune femme (B): Mālū Shāhī s'introduit chez Rājulī.

8. Il est tué soit par le mari (C), soit par le père de la jeune femme: Mālū Shāhī est empoisonné par le père de Rājulī. Lorsque cette fonction est présente, elle entraîne nécessairement les deux suivantes:

9. L'amant (A) apparaît en rêve à sa mère pour l'avertir de sa mort.

10. La mère envoie un magicien qui le ressuscite.

Nous arrivons maintenant aux deux dernières fonctions qui sont communes à tous les récits.

11. L'amant (A) doit affronter le mari (C) en un combat singulier ou en une bataille rangée entre deux armées, le héros utilisant soit des armes ordinaires, soit des armes magiques.

12. L'issue de ce combat doit être fatale pour le mari (C) ou pour l'amant (A) ou pour les deux. Cette fonction détermine non seulement les dénouements possibles, mais aussi les conséquences impliquées par chacun d'eux:

a) Si l'amant (A) est victorieux et le mari (C) tué, le premier ramène triomphalement chez lui la jeune femme et l'épouse: ainsi Mālū Shāhī revient victorieux à Bairāṭh avec Rājulī.

b) Si l'amant (A) est tué (ou si le mari (C) et l'amant (A) sont tués tous les deux) la jeune femme (B) se brûle sur le bûcher de son amant (ou le bûcher commun de son amant et de son mari).

Présentons un autre exemple de ce sous-groupe:

RECIT II: Kālā Bhaṇḍārī

1. Udaimālā (B) est fiancée par son père à Rupu Gangsara (C).

2. Kālā Bhaṇḍārī (A) voit en rêve Udaimālā (B) dont il tombe amoureux; il va demander sa main à son père qui promet de la lui donner s'il lui apporte un van plein de roupies d'or. Pendant que Kālā est parti gagner cet argent, le père d'Udaimālā oublie sa promesse et décide de la marier à Rupu (C).

3. Udaimālā (B) avertit Kālā (A) en lui apparaissant en rêve que la date du mariage est fixée.

4. Kālā (A) décide de partir arracher Udaimālā (B) à ses parents et à Rupu (C).

5. Il se déguise en Yogi.

7. Il rencontre secrètement Udaimālā.

11. Le jour du mariage, Kālā (A) attaque Rupu (C) et ses amis.

12b Rupu (C) est tué ainsi que tous ses amis, sauf un qui parvient à s'enfuir et tue ensuite Kālā (A) par traîtrise. Udaimālā (B) prépare un bûcher sur lequel elle s'assied: ayant posé la tête de Kālā sur son genou droit et celle de Rupu sur son genou gauche, elle allume le feu et meurt dans les flammes.

Ce récit présente bien, dans le même ordre que Mālū Shāhī, les six fonctions communes: n°1 à 4, 11 et 12; mais deux seulement des fonctions intermédiaires sont représentées, les n°5 et 7; alors que dans l'exemple précédent l'amant (A) était victorieux (12a), le présent récit illustre l'autre dénouement possible (12b) où l'amant est vaincu.

Cette série de fonctions apparaissant dans le même ordre constitue un schéma que le barde doit respecter s'il veut raconter une histoire sérieuse, et les dix récits analysés jusqu'ici sont bien sérieux pour l'auditoire.

b) les récits comiques

La contre-épreuve en est fournie par les deux récits restant dans la nature et/ou l'enchaînement des fonctions sont altérés, ce qui fait rire l'auditoire.

RECIT III: Ranu Rāvat.

1. Bimla (B) est mariée à Ranu (C).

2. Elle tombe amoureuse de Jhankru (A).

3. Ranu doit partir pour la plaine. Bimla en avertit Jhankru et lui demande de venir la rejoindre.

4. Jhankru vient vivre avec Bimla.

11. Ranu (C), averti par un rêve, revient. Jhankru (A) a d'abord peur de combattre et se cache dans un grand panier; démasqué, il est finalement obligé d'affronter Ranu.

12. L'issue de ce combat n'est fatale ni pour l'amant, ni pour le mari car la mère de ce dernier intervient pour les séparer. Ranu (C) renonce à sa femme (B) qu'il donne à Jankru (A).

Les fonctions apparaissent dans le même ordre que dans les

dix récits sérieux; mais la nature de certaines d'entre elles est modifiées. A partir du n°4, l'amant ne montre pas le courage qu'on attend de lui: au lieu des exploits héroïques qui s'insèrent généralement entre cette fonction et le n°11 le barde raconte les péripéties comiques qui amène à la découverte de Jhankru caché dans son panier. Enfin le dénouement n'est pas régulier, car ni l'amant, ni le mari ne meurent.

RECIT IV: Jairāj Dhuniyā̃

1. Lālī Jaitulā (B) est mariée à Jairāj Dhuniyā̃ (C).

3. Elle demande à son mari de l'emmener à une foire. Il finit par accepter à la condition qu'elle ne sourie à aucun des hommes qu'elle rencontrera; si elle sourit à l'un d'eux, il l'abandonnera à lui.

4. Quand elle arrive à la foire, les hommes ont entendu parler de la condition posée par le mari; ils essaient de la faire rire; aucun n'y parvient. Un mendiant appelé Suniyā Kaṭhāyat (A) décide d'obtenir Lālī Jaitulā.

5. Suniyā (A) se déguise en bouffon.

7. Il s'approche de Lālī Jaitulā et fait des grimaces; elle éclate de rire.

11. Jairāj (C) donne Lālī Jaitulā (B) à Suniyā (A) sans combat.

12. Jaitulā écrit à son père pour lui demander de venger l'affront que lui a fait son mari.

Dans ce récit, la série des fonctions est perturbée dès le début. Il manque le n°1 (amour réciproque de A et de B) qui généralement met en place la situation initiale. La narration ne se déclenche que par la fonction n°3 dont la nature est altérée: la femme demande à son mari (C) et non à un amant (A) de l'emmener. Dès lors, toutes les fonctions sont altérées. Si Suniyā (A) conquiert Lālī Jaitulā (B) (n°4 à 11), il n'est qu'une caricature d'amant car il ne court aucun risque et n'a pas à combattre: c'est pourquoi il se déguise non en Yogi, mais en bouffon (n°5). Jairāj (C) ne défend pas ses droits sur sa femme et la livre sans combattre: il n'est qu'une caricature de mari (n°11). Le dénouement est irrégulier (n°12): le récit ne s'arrête pas là et va se prolonger sur un conflit entre le mari et son beau-père.

Ces récits dans lesquels la nature et/ou l'enchaînement des fonctions qui définissent le rôle des principaux protagonistes sont altérés, font rire l'auditoire.

c) caractères généraux des récits d'amour

Nous allons revenir sur ces rôles tels qu'ils apparaissent dans les récits sérieux. Premier trait frappant: l'importance accordée à l'amour réciproque de A et de B(n°2). Il est toujours désigné par le mot *dhoko* qui revient sans cesse sur les lèvres du barde tout au long du récit pour justifier les actions de ces deux protagonistes; le sens de ce terme oscille entre "désir intense" et "erreur, illusion, tromperie". C'est toujours, pour l'héroïne (B), un amour adultère: l'amant peut être ou non marié, cela n'a pas d'importance dans ce contexte social. Cet amour naît soudainement par une sorte de coup de foudre lors de la première rencontre (récit I) ou par une vision en rêve (récit II). Les amoureux se désintéressent alors de tout: ils en oublient de manger et de boire, renoncent à toutes leurs obligations familiales et sociales. Le *dhoko* justifie tout et est décrit en termes qui évoque soit la folie (l'amoureux est alors *baulo*, "fou"), soit le renoncement au monde *(udāsī, bairāgī)*: si dans plusieurs récits l'amant (A) prend l'habit du Yogi (récits I et II, n°5), ce n'est pas seulement un artifice de narration, la valeur religieuse de la passion est soulignée dans le récit I où Mālū Shāhī se soumet à une véritable initiation; par contraste, celui qui n'est pas amoureux n'aura droit qu'au déguisement de bouffon (récit IV, n°5). L'amour est donc idéalisé comme dans notre légende de Tristan et Yseut.

En tant que passion individuelle, il entre alors en conflit avec les obligations sociales. Les liens familiaux ne comptent plus: l'héroïne refuse de se soumettre à ses parents et à l'homme à qui ils l'ont mariée; le héros aussi abandonne sa famille: Mālū Shāhī refuse d'écouter sa mère et ses sept femmes qui veulent le retenir. Lorsqu'il est roi, il délaisse aussi toutes ses responsabilités politiques. Il n'a d'autre souci que de conquérir sa bien-aimée.

Aller jusqu'au bout de cette passion est pour les protagonistes un point d'honneur: Rājulī risque plusieurs fois sa vie pour aller rejoindre Mālū Shāhī. Mais ce point est particulièrement mis en relief dans le cas du héros, avec la fonction n°4 d'abord qui est commune à tous les récits: l'héroïne utilise pour le mettre au défi des termes identiques à ceux qui apparaissent dans d'autres groupes de récits héroïques pour encourager au combat: "Si tu es réellement un homme ...". Dès lors le héros doit risquer sa vie: c'est ce thème que développent les fonctions optionnelles insérées au milieu des récits:

n°6 et surtout les n°8 à 10 (mort et renaissance); il culmine avec la fonction n°11, présente dans tous les récits sérieux où l'amant doit engager un combat à mort avec le mari. Au rebours, Jhankru qui refuse de combattre (récit III) et Suniyā qui obtient Lālī Jaitulā sans risque (récit IV) sont des anti-héros. Cette obstination à aller jusqu'au bout de la passion ne peut se comparer qu'à celle des protagonistes de certains récits héroïques qui vont jusqu'à la mort ou au suicide pour un point d'honneur.

La glorification de la passion est poursuivie jusque dans les deux issues possibles: est considéré comme heureux, dans l'optique des dix récits sérieux, le dénouement par lequel l'amant obtient la victoire, tuant le mari et épousant la jeune femme (n°12a, récit I). Si l'amant a perdu la partie, c'est-à-dire s'il meurt car il ne peut transiger (12b, récit II), l'issue est malheureuse non seulement pour lui, mais aussi pour la jeune femme qui refuse de survivre. Les dix récits sérieux reflètent ainsi avant tout le point de vue du couple d'amant qui mettent leur point d'honneur à s'enfermer dans une alternative: le triomphe de la passion ou la mort.

Les autres protagonistes principaux sont les parents de la jeune femme et son mari (C): les premiers délèguent au second leurs droits sur la jeune femme (n°1) et c'est lui qui les défendra dans le combat final (n°11). Les dix récits sérieux présentent ces protagonistes comme des adversaires; ils portent comme titre le nom de l'amant et la jeune femme ne suivent pas cette logique de la passion portent comme titre le nom du mari.

B) Rapport au contexte ethnographique

a) presentation du contexte

Il nous faut retrouver la situation conflictuelle illustrée par les récits et les règles traditionnellement édictées pour la résoudre.

La situation est bien connue: c'est le *jārī*, i.e. le détournement d'une femme mariée. On peut le décrire, comme dans les récits, par un enchaînement de fonctions:

1. Une jeune fille (B) est mariée par ses parents à un homme (C).

2. Un autre homme (A) tombe amoureux d'elle.

3. Avec le consentement de la jeune femme,
4. l'amant (A) décide de l'enlever à son mari et de l'emmener vivre avec lui.

Il s'ensuit une série de péripéties correspondant à nos fonctions n°5 à 10.

En ce qui concerne le dénouement du conflit, il faut distinguer entre les règles traditionnelles en vigueur jusque dans la première moitié du dix-neuvième siècle, et celles qui résultent de la législation moderne. Traditionnellement, pour certaines hautes castes du moins,[4] le mari avait le droit officiellement reconnu de se faire justice lui-même en tuant l'amant de sa femme: *jār hānnu*. Bien attesté au Kumaon avant l'annexion par les britanniques (Atkinson, 1886), ce droit a fait l'objet de descriptions précises par les observateurs anglais travaillant au Népal. La première en date est celle de Hamilton (1819, p.23): "Ils se font un point d'honneur de ne jamais prendre de repos tant qu'il n'ont pas répandu le sang de l'homme soupçonné d'avoir des rapports criminels avec leur femme (...). Cette attitude est considérée comme si louable qu'à Kathmandou la police, par ailleurs si stricte, n'intervient pas". L'amant mettait aussi son point d'honneur à affronter le mari: comme le notait D. Wright (1968, p.19), il pouvait refuser le combat pour sauver sa vie, "mais une telle attitude était considérée comme si ignominieuse qu'il préférait généralement la mort." Nous retrouvons ainsi la fonction n°11: l'amant devait affronter le mari.

Et comme dans la fonction n°12, ce combat devait entraîner la mort: pour le mari, "le déhonneur subi devait être lavé dans le sang; la mort étant le sort réservé à ceux qui commettent l'adultère avec les femmes des *Parbattias*" (Hodgson, 1880, p.242).

Au Kumaon, le droit du mari à punir l'amant de sa femme a été aboli par les britanniques après 1816; sur le territoire népalais, il a été soumis à un contrôle judiciaire préalable par Jang Bahadur (Wright, p.19; code de 1853, pp.605-612), pour être finalement aboli au début de ce siècle: le mari n'a plus droit désormais qu'à une compensation en argent *(jārī khat* ou *bihā kharcā)*. Mais j'ai pu observer au Népal central une survivance du droit du mari à venger son honneur: même si en fait il se désintéresse de sa femme, il se doit de se battre avec l'amant de celle-ci; combat plutôt symbolique d'ailleurs, avec des bâtons ou à mains nues, auquel les témoins mettent rapidement fin. Ce n'est qu'après avoir ainsi satisfait son point d'honneur que le mari acceptera de négocier le montant de la compensation en argent; lorsqu'il l'aura reçue, il renoncera par écrit à tous ses droits sur sa femme.

Ce qu'on peut observer aujourd'hui correspond donc à un récit comique comme celui de Ranu Rāvat (Récit III); les dix récits sérieux, eux-mêmes un leg du passé, ne peuvent se comparer à un état de fait présent; on doit les rapporter à l'époque héroïque, antérieure au milieu de XIXème siècle, où l'ancienne coutume, sanctionnée par la loi, était encore en vigueur.

b) rapport des récits à ce contexte

Comme dans les récits, les parents de la jeune femme et le mari faisaient cause commune contre le couple d'amoureux; on avait donc la même rèpartition des protagonistes. Mais alors que les récits présentent le point de vue des amants, développant une sorte de logique de la passion, les sources juridiques qui nous renseignent sur l'ancienne coutume nous présentent le point de vue opposé, fait de droits et de devoirs, c'est-à-dire une certaine norme sociale. C'était le droit des parents de marier leur fille à qui ils voulaient, et celle-ci était tenue de se soumettre au mari qu'ils avaient choisi. Le mari de son côté, avait le droit d'exiger la soumission de sa femme et de venger de ses propres mains l'affront qui lui avait été fait; il n'était pas tenu d'avertir préalablement les autorités judiciaires, et il en était quitté avec la loi s'il pouvait, après coup, prouver la culpalité de l'amant: "Il peut s'adonner à sa vengeance sans avoir une pensée pour le juge. Mais bien qu'il n'ait rien à prouver avant, il doit être prêt à fournir des preuves légalement valables par la suite au cas où sa femme nierait les faits et l'assignerait devant les tribunaux." (Hodgson, 1880, p.243). La terminologie juridique reflète d'ailleurs ce point de vue: le mari offensé est appelé *sādhu*, littéralement: droit, pur, terme qui dans la langue courante s'applique à un renonçant; et il est remarquable que dans les récits au contraire ce soit l'amant qui soit comparé au renonçant.

Se faire justice était aussi pour le mari un point d'honneur. Alors que les récits mettent l'accent sur le sens de l'honneur de l'amant, les textes juridiques détaillent le point de vue du mari: "Tout mari trompé peut, s'il le veut, avoir recours aux tribunaux au lieu de faire usage de sa propre épée; mais toute personne (sauf un brahmane instruit ou un garçon sans force), qui agirait ainsi se couvrirait de honte pour toujours." (Hodgson, 1880, p.242).

En ce qui concerne le dénouement, les sources juridiques ne nous parlent guère que du cas où le mari était victorieux, ce qui correspond à notre fonction 12b: il peut alors punir sa femme: "Il n'épargne pas alors la femme infidèle: il doit lui couper le nez, la chasser avec ignominie de sa maison; sa caste et son rang étant pour toujours perdu." (Hodgson, 1880, p.243). On comprend alors que dans nos récits, où ce dénouement est considéré comme malheureux, la femme préfère la mort et se brûle sur le bûcher de son amant; elle est alors considérée comme *satī*; les récits, sur ce point, s'écartent de la tradition qui réservent ce terme à la femme qui se brûle avec le cadavre de son mari.

Les sources juridiques, au rebours, sont muettes sur ce qui se passait dans le cas où l'amant était victorieux; sans doute la famille du mari portait-elle plainte auprès des tribunaux. En l'absence de documentation précise, contentons-nous de juger de la plausibilité de ce que les récits présentent comme issue heureuse (12a): la victoire de l'amant est assurée par les armes, ce qui est une solution sans appel s'il est roi; mais par contre, s'il s'agit d'un simple noble, il refuse toute autorité judiciaire au-dessus de lui, ce qui supposerait un état d'anarchie où le héros serait son propre législateur; or, d'après ce que nous savons de l'Himalaya central avant son annexion par la dynastie de Gorkha, un tel état n'a jamais existé (Hamilton, 1819, pp.101-117); les récits en idéalisant leurs héros, nient donc certains aspects de la réalité historique. D'autre part, pour ce même dénouement, ils décrivent un retour triomphal de l'amant victorieux ramenant la jeune femme et l'épousant solennellement avec tous les rites: or, selon la tradition hindoue, une femme qui a déjà mariée peut certes se remarier mais selon un rituel simplifié différent du grand rituel solennel qu'elle ne peut célébrer qu'une fois dans sa vie.

Conclusion

Analysant les récits d'amour, nous avons montré que le barde, s'il veut raconter une histoire sérieuse, doit suivre une séquence narrative relativement stricte. Le modèle ainsi dégagé peut-être rapporté à un certain contexte ethnographique: les coutumes et les lois suivies en matière d'adultère par les membres des hautes castes de l'Himalaya central jusque dans la première moitié du XIXème siècle. Ces récits se réfèrent donc à un état de fait passé.

Celui-ci peut être reconstitué à partir de sources historiques et juridiques qui nous en donnent une image fidèle quoiqu'incomplète, d'un certain point de vue, essentiellement celui des parents de la jeune femme et du mari. Les récits présentent le point de vue opposé, celui de la passion du couple d'amoureux qui refuse toute obligation et s'enferme dans l'alternative: succès ou mort; les récits, emportés par leur propre logique idéalisant certainement ce second point de vue, car certaines de leur conclusions sont incompatibles avec ce que nous savons de l'histoire et des coutumes de la région considérée.

Il est néanmoins remarquable que ces récits qui vont à l'encontre des normes traditionnelles soit si populaires: cherchant une expression de ces normes, j'ai en fait trouvé une apologie de la transgression.

Marc Gaborieau

NOTES

1. Pour les matèriaux et la bibliographie concernant cette définition et cette classification, voir: GABORIEAU, a).

2. Enregistrement effectué auprès du barde Yoga Ram, du village de Patiya, près d'Almora en 1960 par Mme M. T. Datta: une édition et une traduction commentée de ce texte sont en préparation.

3. Enregistrement effectué en 1965 par le Dr. Konrad Meissner, de Francfort sur le Main, qui prépare une édition de ce texte. Je le remercie de m'avoir montré son travail avant la publication.

4. Ce droit étaient essentiellement reconnu pour les membres de la caste royale et pour les *Khas* (appelés aujourd'hui *Chetri* sur le territoire népalais et *Rajput* au Kumaon). Selon Hodgson (1880, p.242), ceux des brahmanes qui exerçaient le métier de soldats en usaient aussi. Ce droit était aussi reconnu aux membres de certaines tribus (Hodgson, 1880, p.242) et à certaines castes intouchables (Code de 1853, p.608, § 18), mais nous n'en parlons pas ici car ils ne figurent pas comme personnages de nos récits.

BIBLIOGRAPHIE

ATKINSON (Ed. T.) — *The Himalayan Districts of the North-Western Provinces*, vol.III, Allahabad, 1886.

CODE DE 1853 — édité à Kathmandou par le Ministère de la Justice, en V.S. 2022, sous le titre: *sri 5 surendra vikram shaha deva kā shāsan kāl mā baneko mulukī ain.*

GABORIEAU (Marc) — a) *Sur quelques critères de classification des récits chantés: recherche sur la littérature orale des populations hindoues de l'Himalaya*, à paraître dans POETIQUE, Paris, 1974.
b) en collaboration avec HELFFER (M). *A propos d'un tambour-sablier de l'Himalaya Central ...*, sous presse dans FESTSCHRIFT EMSHEIMER, Kungl. Musikalika Akademien, Stockholm, 1974.

HAMILTON (Fr.) — *An account of the Kingdom of Nepal*, Edinburgh, 1819.

HODGSON (B.H.) — Some account of the System of Law and Police as recognized in the State of Nepal, *Miscellaneous Essays relating to Indian Subjects*, Vol.II, London, 1880.

LORD (Albert B.) — *The Singer of Tales*, Harvard University Press, 1964.

PROPP (Vladimir) — *Morphologie du conte*, 2ème édition, Paris 1970.

WRIGHT (Daniel) — *History of Nepal*, réimpression, Calcutta, 1958.

Monkhood versus Priesthood in Newar Buddhism

No other institution of Newar society[1] has aroused the scorn and condemnation of Western scholars more than that of the hereditary caste of priests, the Bare, who have come to replace Buddhist monks as the inhabitants of what have ceased to be monasteries *(vihara)* in anything but name. Indeed most scholars who have written about Buddhism among the Newars of the Kathmandu Valley have condemned as corrupt, degenerate or decadent the institutional structures of Newar Buddhism. Brian Hodgson, who spent a total of twenty-seven years in Nepal and was a man of extraordinary talent and perspicacity, wrote in the early nineteenth century:

> *Genuine Buddhism* proclaims the equality of all followers of Buddha - seems to deny to them the privilege of pursuing worldly avocations, and abhors the distinction of clergy and laity. *All proper Bauddhas are Bandyas;* and all Bandyas are equal as breathren in the faith. They are properly all ascetics or monks - some solitary, mostly coenobitical. Their convents are called viharas. The rule of the viharas is a rule of freedom; and the door of every vihara is always open ... (Emphasis is mine). (Hodgson 1971: 63).

Having set forth his view of genuine Buddhism, Hodgson goes on to describe as "corrupt" the actual form of the then present day Newar Buddhism:

> Nepaul is still covered with viharas; but these ample and comfortable abodes have long resounded with the hum of industry and the pleasant voices of women and children. The superior ministery of religion is now in the hands of the Bandyas, entitled, *Vajra-Acharya* in Sanskrit; *Gūbhāl* in Newari: the inferior ministery, such Bhikshus as still follow religion as a lucrative and learned profession, are competent to discharge. And these professions of the Vajra-Acharya, and of the Bhikshus, have become by usage hereditary, as have all other avocation and pursuits, whether civil or religious, in Nepaul. And as in modern corrupt Buddhism of Nepaul there are exclusive ministers of religion or priests, so there are many Bauddhas who retain the lock on the crown of the head, and are not Bandyas.

This same attitude that the central core of Buddhism lies in the institution of celibate monks who form a religious elite and who comprise the only pure practitioners of Buddhism is held by the great French Indologist Sylvain Lévi, who like Hodgson saw Newar Buddhism as lacking such a monastic system and thus as decadent and moribund. But whereas for Hodgson Newar viharas "resound with the hum and industry and the pleasant voices of women and children" (Hodgson: 63) for Lévi

> The population of the viharas has sadly changed: the ancient community of celibate monks, learned and studious, has disappeared; it has given way to unworthy heirs, the Banras. If they (the viharas) had been sanctuaries of meditation and of prayer, they now serve as dwellings for a swarming, noisy multitude of men, women and children crowded together in defiance of hygiene in small, low-ceilinged rooms where they pursue occupations completely mundane, gold- or silver-smithing, sculpturing, decorative arts; others amongst the Banras are employed outside as carpenters, casters, plasterers. (All religious) expertise is dead, or mostly dead: a miserable pujari, charged by the community with the daily worship, comes each day to mutter in front of a statue of Shakyamuni hymns (stotras) in adulterated Sanskrit (a language) which he doesn't understand, or to recite a section of the *Prajnāpāramitā* in Eight Thousand stanzas (Astasahasrike) of which he understands even less ... (Lévi; 1905: 26).

Henry Oldfield, a British writer of the mid-nineteenth century, condemned Newar Buddhism in precisely the same manner as Hodgson and Levi: a condemnation of caste and the view that early Buddhist texts (non-Tantric) are the proper spiritual basis of Buddhism.

> Buddhism in Nipal has sadly degenerated from the high standard of doctrine and of discipline which was established by the Buddhist Church. Theoretically the religion is unchanged. ... but the Church itself has become corrupt, its discipline is totally destroyed, and its social practices at the present day are in direct defiance both of the letter and spirit of Buddhist law. Its monastic institutions, with their fraternities of learned and pious monks, have long since disappeared; the priesthood has become hereditary in certain families, and the system of caste, which was denounced by Sakya and the early Church as utterly repugnant to their ideas of social equality, has been borrowed from the Hindus, and is recognised

> as binding by all classes of Buddhists in the country ... The reign of Buddhism is now over in Nipal. Though still nominally the national faith of the majority of the Niwaris, yet it is slowly but steadily being supplanted by Hinduism, and before another century shall have passed away, the religion of Buddha, will have died a natural death, from the effects of its own internal corruption and decay. (Oldfield 1880, Vol. II: 72).

A hundred years after Oldfield's judgement David Snellgrove proclaimed the fulfillment of Oldfield's prediction. For Snellgrove Buddhism in Nepal "...has been forced into conformity with other traditions, which represent the negation of all its higher strivings, so that it has died of atrophy, leaving outward forms that have long ceased to be Buddhist in anything but name." (Snellgrove, 1957: 112). Snellgrove links this state of degeneracy to the decline of the traditional monastic structure and quotes Oldfield's statement that "Nothing has contributed so much to the decline of Buddhism in Nipal as the adoption of caste by the Buddhist Niwaris and the consequent decay of all the monastic institutions of the country" (Oldfield; Vol. II: 131) (Snellgrove; 1957: 6).

The observations made by all these scholars that Newar Buddhism is no longer characterised by a separate body of celibate monks or nuns is correct. The belief that this transformation is to be faulted is an opinion which can only be upheld when Newar Buddhism is judged according to the precepts and institutions of orthodox Buddhism and thus found to be "aberrant" and "corrupt". Another, and perhaps more fruitful, area of inquiry is the attempt to understand Newar Buddhism within the context of the changes that have occurred within Newar society and in terms of its own ideology and institutions.

The Replacement of Renunciation by Reversal and Caste

Today among the Newars there is a caste of hereditary priests called the Bare whose members claim the status of 'pure' Buddhists as they alone are the inhabitants of Newar Vajrayana monasteries and as they alone have been ritually purified and ordained as monks. The Bare are men who become monks only later to return to the world of ordinary men, though retaining the status of being sanctified. Bare is the shortened form of *Bande* or *Banra* (honourable), a term designating persons entitled to reverence because of their extraordinary spirituality. Thus the very name of Bare signifies the special sanctity of men who though householders retain the right to have their heads completely shaven, a symbol of celibacy and renunciation. This right thereby continues to give them the sacred aura of the renouncer. Indeed it is the ideology and symbolism of renunciation that permits the Bare to enter into relations with the world of the untonsured without impairing or losing their status of ritual purity.[2]

The term *sangha* usually means a community of celibate Buddhist monks or nuns but in the Newar context refers to an ecclesiastical corporation of adult male Bare who have been ordained as monks in a common monastery and who though they are married constitute that monastery's personnel. Moreover, this transformation of the traditionally open Buddhist *sangha* into a closed caste-delimited corporation has been concomitant with the development of an elaborate corpus of Tantric rituals based upon esoteric doctrines known only to the specially initiated, that is, only to the Bare. Thus it is the Bare, the only Newars eligible for initiation and membership in the *sangha*, who are empowered to employ advanced Buddhist meditative practices, to perform special tantric rites and to serve the special tantric deities housed within their monasteries.

The Newar monastery (*vihara*) is the centre of the religious life of Newar Vajrayana Buddhism, and through their control of these institutions the Bare are able to maintain their monopoly of the spiritual and secular benefits which accrue to them. Just as the traditional Buddhist monk is thought to stand in a special relation to the Buddha and his teachings by virtue of his immediate or forthcoming attainment of Enlightenment, so the Bare, by virtue of their control of the *vihara* and its deities and shrines, lay claim to and validate their common status as an assembly (*sangha*) of the elect.

All members of a monastery's *sangha* belong to a common assocation, the *Bare guthi* or *Vihara bhojan guthi*, which meets at least once a year at which time a *puja* (religious ceremony or act during which an offering is made) to the monastery's major shrine is performed, followed by a communal feast. The *Bare guthi* also is responsible for providing a guardian *(dyo pala)* who has the duty of opening the monastery's shrines, worshipping its images and serving as an attendant during that period of time which the shrine is open to public worship. The responsibility of serving as guardian of the monastery's major shrine passes on a rotational basis to all members of the *Bare guthi*. This group's leadership is provided by an executive committee usually ranging in number from four to twelve. The basis for membership on the governing committee is seniority. Membership in a monastery's *sangha* and thus in its *Bare guthi* automatically follows after the performance of the rite of ordination into the monkhood. Seniority within the monastery is judged not by one's age but according to the length of time one has been a member of the *sangha*.

All functions of the monstery are regulated and executed through various *guthis*, and hence it is these caste associations which organize and control the duties that devolve upon the Bare by virtue of their monopoly of the Buddhist priesthood. These duties include the carrying out of acts of image worship, elaborate festivals and numerous communal feasts, as in present day Newar monasteries Buddhism is no longer primarily a matter of individual activity on the part of monks each of whom is seeking his own salvation but is intimately tied to an endless series of festivals and feasts. Each festival, feast or ceremony is the responsibility of a particular *guthi* and membership in that *guthi* entails the obligation of assisting in the execution of these duties. Thus, the privilege of undergoing ordination as a monk entangles one in a web of binding responsibilities.

Often a monastery will possess an endowment of land or money to provide crops and/or cash to support the vihara's activities, including the numerous feasts. However, if expenses should be greater than the amount secured through the endowment, the *guthi* committee responsible for that particular activity will have to cover the deficit. On the other hand, any surplus is the organizing committee's members' personal gain. The endowment of land or money is also know as *guthi*, so that this term refers to both any organization or association that is responsible for the observance of religious or charitable duties and/or the form of ownership under which such corporations hold property in trust.

The Bare sees the world as governed by a condition of dependency: children are dependent upon parents; the individual upon the family; the family upon the caste; the caste upon the community; and the community upon the gods. Human life then is viewed as involving inescapable relationships of dependence and of reciprocal obligations. To be human is to fulfil them. To fail to fulfil such obligations is to cease to be a man. But to cease to be a man does not lead to the attainment of the Absolute. For the Newar Buddhist when one severs social obligations one becomes like an animal, not like a god.

According to Newar Buddhism he who pursues the most sublime goal is the one who undergoes a special series of ceremonies of consecrations and purification, who follows a special series of ritual observances, and who thereby gains knowledge of a mystic and magical nature. Thus the world of the Absolute is intelligible only to those who have been initiated into special mysterious practices. Only those who pursue such mysterious rituals attain experience of the Absolute. And only the specially initiated may participate in such mysteries.

The goal of deliverance is the same as is found in other Buddhist sects. The difference lies in the respective attitudes toward the process whereby liberation is achieved. In Newar Buddhism there no longer is the demand that one abandon the social world. Rather than by withdrawing from all that is distinctively human and social in order to overcome the limitations of physical existence, the Bare reject escetic renunciation, and become supra-human beings who have passed beyond the impotence and suffering of ordinary existence through the adoption of the opposite of renunciation, namely the celebration of earthly pleasures and through the sacrificial enjoyment of all that is normally rejected and condemned by Buddhist monks: alcohol, meat, fish, and ritual copulation.

Although in addition to their own salvation, the Bare seek to achieve magical powers. Like deliverance, this is a goal which the Bare share with traditional Buddhist monks. Once again we find a divergence in the manner in which the monk and the Bare attain such powers. The monks attempt to attain supra-human powers by disengaging himself from all that is human, social and physical and by supressing and extinguishing all passions, emotion, and human attachments. The Bare attempt to attain supra-human powers by the ritual use of tantric reversals. The magical powers of the monk come through his rejection of the social world and its rules and conventions. His is the power of the unstructured, of the anti-social, of the liminal. Moreover, the magical power and sacredness of the monk are personally attained and spontaneous. The magical powers of the Bare come through the celebration of earthly pleasures. The Bare reject the concept of ascetic renunciation as well as the exaltation of the unstructured and the liminal.

The Bare form a caste which has a fixed position in a highly structured and highly hierarchical social system. In spite of their use of reversals, the ritual use of such symbols of ecstasy, sexuality and aggression is strictly controlled. There is absolutely no response or action that is not dictated and carefully defined. During the rite there is no possibility of individual innovation and spontaneity. The ritual procedures are elaborate and complicated. Therefore they are difficult to master and to perform. Yet one cannot deviate from what is prescribed in so great detail without suffering severe penalty: one who does not perform the rituals as required is thought to go mad or even to die. Moreover, the charismatic attainment of magical potency, rather than being highly personal and individualistic adheres specifically to all members of the Bare caste.

Ordination as a Rite of Passage

The Bare are men joined together in *sangha* to whom various ritual services and rights are allotted by virtue of their *birth* and conferred through *initiation*. The Bare as a corporation is defined by virtue of its relationship to and control over certain central rituals, and this control is based upon hereditary rights. Only one born of a Bare mother and fathered by a Bare male can be ordained as a monk and initiated as a Bare. This is justified in terms of *karma:* those who led lives guided by honesty and righteousness win the right to be born not only as mortals but as Bare. But proper birth alone is not sufficient. Heredity must be coupled with initiation.[3] All male Bare must be incorporated into the caste of Bare, and this is accomplished when the boys are made into symbolic monks. This ceremony of ordination is called *Bare chhuyigu* and literally means the making into Bare. A male who is born of Bare parents but who has not been initiated as a Bare loses for himself the ritual and social status of being a Bare.[4] He cannot marry a girl of that caste; he cannot freely interdine with members of that caste; he cannot take part in any of the religious or secular activities of that caste. He is not a Bare but drops down to the level of the next highest Buddhist caste, that of Urha. He is freely accepted into this caste but then so are all the offspring of Bare fathers and high caste non-Bare mothers (such as Shrestha, Jyapu or Urha) or Tibetan mothers.

A Bare boy must be initiated in the monastery where his father was ordained and where his father is a member of its *sangha*. One cannot change monasteries. Thus the Newar vihara is a patrilineal descent group. Each monastery is said to have been founded by a single 'monk' so that all members of a single monastery claim to be descendants of a common ancestor. This descent from one man, however, is merely assumed.

The ritual status of the Bare is conceptualized not as an inherent attribute but as ritually derived, *Bare chhuyigu*, is a rite of purification, as are all Newar life crisis ceremonies. All are thought to be born impure, but only some men are then purified through a series of special ceremonies *(samskara)*.

Purity therefore is seen as being derivative of purificatory ceremonies and not as a natural state. Failure to perform such rites is said to precipitate low caste status because one remains thereby in an impure state. The ultimate goal of such purificatory and initiatory ceremonies is the attainment of deliverance and hence escape from the physical and "natural". The Bare claim high caste rank because they undergo the largest number of such rites among the Buddhist Newars and thus they alone have removed the taint and impurities of the natural and physical and they alone have been rendered fit for the pursuit of the sacred.

Bare chhuyigu is a rather complex series of ceremonies. The most important phase of the rite consists in the initiation of the boy, symbolically, into the life of the ascetic mendicant. The boy promises to uphold the Five Precepts of Buddhism and to seek refuge in the *Tri-Ratna:* the Buddha, the Dharma and the Sangha. The boy's body is ritually purified and consecrated. His father's sister's husband fastens a gold ring about the hair on the crown of the boy's head thereby making a top-knot. His head is then shaved, by a man of the barbering caste of Nau, except for the hairs bound by the ring. The top-knot is cut off by the boy's father's sister's husband. The cut hairs are caught in a bronze plate held by the boy's father's sister. She will keep this cut hair for the four days of his ritual monkhood, worshipping it each day through the offering of beaten rice moistened with curds. After four days she will throw it in the river.

After his head has been completely shaved the boy receives a special sacred consecration *(Pancha abhisheka):* water from a conch shell and from four holy vessels is poured over him. The eldest member of the monastery pours water from the conch shell while the four holy vessels are held by the next four oldest members. The boy receives a new name. The initiator reads out the ten principles which should govern and guide the behaviour of monks, and the boy promises to follow these precepts. He then dons the garb of the monk: red or saffron robes, golden earrings, necklaces and bracelets of silver or gold; begging bowl (which though made of wood may be decorated with silver or gold overlays), a wooden walking staff and a water pot.

The boy is then said to follow the life of a Buddhist monk for four days. This role, however, is merely one of pretence. Although the boy assumes the external signs of monkhood for these few days, he does not lead the actual life of a mendicant or monk. Nor is initiation into the monkhood with its open egalitarian ethos but into the Newar caste hierarchy. The very essence of the ceremony is incorporation into caste and agnate descent group. Thus at no time are there acts that express reversal of the principles governing these social institutions, which would be the case if the boy were in fact to actually live the life of a Buddhist monk. Monkhood involves rejection of homelife, of caste and of hierarchy. The monk goes forth, leaving behind all ties of family and kinship. But the boy never lives in a homeless state nor in a monastery. Indeed rather he continues to reside in the house of his father. The monk is oblivious to the normal societal rules of social distance and pollution: he begs for his food, accepting anything offered. The boy never wanders about accepting alms of whatever food is given to him by any and all who wish to gain merit through such donations. Rather he continues to limit the pattern of food exchanges to that followed by all members of his caste. The boy at no time begs from individuals of low caste status. Indeed, he only accepts unhusked rice or beaten rice when begging and both of these are items which can freely be exchanged by members of all Newar castes of clean status. Moreover, when he does beg he goes at most to only four or five houses which usually are those of affinal relatives.

There are some restrictions of the boy's diet: he cannot eat meat, alcohol, garlic, tomatoes, salt or foods classified as salty. He cannot take drugs. He cannot touch men or animals such as dogs or chickens that are considered unclean. These restrictions are meant to express and to protect the boy's state of ritual purity and are in no way symbolic of the renunciation of caste restrictions on commensality. They are the same restrictions which would apply any time a Bare is considered to be in a state of special sacredness such as when he is serving as temple priest.

All Hindus must retain a tuft of sacred hair. When the Hindu ascetic *(sannyasin)* cuts this tuft it is symbolic of his "having gone forth"; of his having rejected the entire system of Hindu social practice. His shaven head is also expressive of his celibate state. The Bare also shaves off the tuft of hair on the crown of his head. The first time that this occurs is during his ordination as a monk. However, henceforth whenever he undergoes a rite of purification he will bathe, his nails will be cut and his head will be shaven, sacred tuft and all. His shaven head then is not symbolic of his renunciation or of celibacy but merely of his status as a "pure" Buddhist. In the Newar context Hindus and "impure" Buddhists, that is, Buddhists of castes lower in the ritual hierarchy than that of the Bare, retain a tuft on the crowns of their heads while the Bare do not.

When other Newar boys of clean caste status, i.e. of castes for whom either a Buddhist Vajracharya (a subcaste of Bare) or a Hindu Brahman will act as domestic priest *(purohita)*, are initiated into their castes their heads are shaven (except for the tuft of sacred hair); they don a loincloth; they are given a deerskin as protection from the cold and the rain and as a prayer mat; they are given a bow and arrow for protection from physical harm; and they received a symbolic gift of alms. That is, they assume the symbolic role of ascetic. They act as if they are about to run off into the jungle and to follow the actual life of the *Brahmacharin*, the student of the Vedas and the first of the four Hindu stages of life, but they are prevented from running off by their maternal uncles. And so ends their ritual role of student ascetic. The boys then receive new clothing and are feasted. They are now free, indeed impelled to marry.

Thus, all Newar boys impersonate world renouncers. The difference between the Bare and other Newar castes of clean status is that the former become Buddhist monks *(bhikshu)*, the latter *brahmacharin;* the former have their heads completely shaved, the latter retain the sacred tuft; the former play the part of monks for four days, the latter for an hour or so; and the former, having once become monks retain an aura of sacredness so that they claim that they are not mere householders while the latter pass onto the third stage, that of *grahastha*, householder.

Within the structure of all of these rites of initiation, the role of ascetic and of monk expresses the fact that the boy who is undergoing the rite has entered a sacred ritual category. Van Gennep, and more recently Victor Turner, have forcefully demonstrated that all rites of passage are characterized by three phases: separation, liminality or marginality and aggregation. The phase of separation comprises symbolic behaviour signifying the separation of the initiate from either an earlier fixed point in the social structure or a set of cultural conditions. Aggregation is the phase when the transition is consummated and the initiate is re-incorporated into the social structure (Turner; 1969: 93). The period of transition between the point of separation and re-incorporation is one where the initiate is in an ambiguous status which has none of the characteristics of the past or coming state. Persons within this transitional phase are 'betwixt and between' societal positions assigned by social convention and as such are indeterminate and ambiguous entities. (Ibid: 95). Moreover, Turner notes that novices undergoing life-crises rites are often during this liminal period secluded from the sphere of everyday life, are levelled and stripped of all secular distinctions of status and rights over property, are subjected to acts that teach them humility and obedience as though it is necessary for an individual to first be lowered on the status ladder before he can be elevated in status (Ibid: 169 - 70).

Here Turner gives us two keys by which we can understand why the Bare's monkhood as well as the *brahmacharin* status of other Newar initiates is assumed. The role of ascetic and homeless wanderer provides a powerful set of symbols that establish and express the liminality of the novice during his phase of ambiguous indeterminant status. In addition, both the role of monk and that of *brahmacharin* entail the stripping off of all secular distinction of social status so that the novice is first divested of status and rank before he is elevated to a new and higher rank.

What more potent symbol of separation is there than that of the monk: the individual who renounces the social world; who shaves off all his hair including the sacred tuft; who dons the red or yellow robes of the mendicant; who sets forth from home with begging bowl and walking staff in hand and who wanders about seeking alms? As the monk leaves the world of family and caste and enters that of the homeless wanderer so the Bare boy is separated from his old identity as a child and assumes for a short period that of the monk, searching after sacred knowledge. His old identity is shed, his old self dies. After having his head shaved and after receiving the consecration of holy water the Bare boy is given a new name. In addition, his re-birth is symbolized by the act of taking seven steps, an action replicating the seven steps that the Buddha took after issuing forth from his mother's side.

Who possess a greater set of symbols of institutionalized liminality than the monks? Symbolically they have nothing: no status, property, insignia, secular clothing, kinship position, nothing to demarcate them structurally from their fellow initiates. Their condition is the very proto-type of sacred poverty and as such is most appropriate to express the temporal liminality of the Bare boys during the betwixt and between phase in the rite of passage from casteless childhood to rigidly defined and hierarchical adult roles.

Ordination and the Affirmation of Caste and Kin Ties

Because *Bare chhuyigu* establishes membership in a caste it is not surprising to find that the rite of passage expresses and re-enforces ties of kinship and stresses the importance of marriage. The boy's head, except for the tuft of sacred hair, is shaved by a member of the caste of barbers (Nau). The barber is tied to the family of the novice by a relationship of jajmaniship. Here we see expressed the need for a ritual specialization which is hereditary and caste determined. The tuft of hair on the crown of the boy's head is cut by the novice's father's sister's husband *(jichā-paju)*.[5] That is by one to whom the boy is related because someone born within his descent group has married out.

The *Thapaju*, eldest member of the vihara, is stated to be the one "who really should cut the tuft of hair" but he "isn't used to cutting hair" and so he asks the boy's *jichā-paju* to do it for him. This is a very interesting substitution and one that parallels Dumont's example of the role of ZH or FZH in the funeral rites among the Brahmans of Gorakhpur district in eastern U.P. This Brahman community has no purohits. In the funeral rites the role of the purohit's impersonation of the dead relative is performed by the sister's husband or father's sister's husband.

> "The reason of the identification of father's sister's husband and sister's husband is here proclaimed; they are wife-receivers, in two different and successive generations ... We are in a hypergamous milieu. Wife-takers are higher in status than Ego, and each of them is therefore fit 'to be worshipped' *(pujyā)* by having his feet bathed ..." (Dumont, 1966: 94).

With the Newar Vajracharya and Bare we have a comparable situation. The father's sister's husband lies within the category of wife-takers. This is a separate distinct kinship category designated by a separate kinship term, *jichā* or *jilā*. The father's sister's husband can act as a substitute for the *Thapaju* because he is of the category of wife-taker and thus of a higher status. Being of a higher status he is fit to replace the high status elder of the vihara. Moreover, his position as one related by marriage expresses the benefit obtained through the establishment of marriage ties.

Indeed three important roles in the rite are played by people whose relations to ego are all ones which exemplify the need to marry and to thereby enter into ritual exchange relationships. These roles are that of *jichā-paju*, FZH, who cuts the top-knot; father's sister (who is the person connecting the boy's agnate descent group with that of her husband), who catches the boy's hair as it is shaved and worships it during the four days he is a monk; and mother's brother who holds the boy at various times during the ceremony. Not only do all three have responsibilities to perform during the ceremony, but they must also observe the same dietary restrictions as the novice himself and for the same length of time.

Although *Bare chhuyigu* is on one level a ceremony of going forth, of renouncing the life of the householder, of taking a vow of celibacy, it is also a rite which expresses the benefits of going forth into marriage and of establishing a network of reciprocal relations with one's affinal relatives. This fact has not gone unnoticed by the Newars themselves. A short time before her marriage a young Bare friend wrote the following:

> When the marriage feast ends the ceremony of *gwe ka bhoy* occurs. This is a special feast to which all the husband's paternal relatives *(phuki)* must be invited. If the groom's family does not give this feast, their paternal relatives will never come to assist in major rituals where their attendance is required. The most important of these are childbirth, *Bare chhuyigu*, and death. These are significant events in the human life cycle, and people cannot carry out our wonderful social customs without the help of others. In *gwe ka bhoy* the new bride offers betel nut to all her husband's paternal relatives. By accepting the offering they say "She has become one of us". Because she becomes a member of a new family, this family of her husband will now help her own parents and brothers in carrying out their rituals.

An exchange of betel nuts also occurs in *Bare chhuyigu* and marks the acceptance of the boy into the monastery and caste of his father. This exchange occurs four days prior to the actual performance of the rite.

The Use of the Monkhood to establish the Ritual Status of the Bare

I began with the theme that all Western scholars who have written about Newar Buddhism have chosen to judge Newar institutions in the light of orthodox Buddhist monastic practice. When viewed from this perspective Newar Buddhism, of course, is found deviant: orthodox monastic institutions no longer are to be found; the orthodox monkhood has been replaced by a caste of hereditary and married priests; this caste of priests forms one of the component units in a Buddhist societal structure which replicates the Hindu caste system. However, by labelling it as degenerate or corrupt one is not analyzing or understanding Newar religion but only dismissing it. Whereas monasticism is central to most Buddhist sects and hence must be dealt with if one is to understand such forms of Buddhism, the priest is essential to Newar Buddhism, and his role must be understood if one is to understand anything at all about Newar Buddhism.

Yet the problem is not that simple. The reason that western scholars have judged Newar Buddhism by orthodox Buddhist doctrine is that this is what the Newars do themselves. In 1823 Hodgson was told by a Vajracharya pandit:

> According to our Puranas, whoever adopted the tenets of Buddha, and has cut off the lock from the crown of his head, of whatever tribe or nation he be, becomes thereby a Bandya ... Besides this distinction into monastic and secular orders, the Bandyas are again divided, according to the scriptures into five classes: first, Arhat; second, Bhikshu; third, Sravaka; fourth, Chailaka; fifth, Vajra Acharya ... Such is the account of the five classes found in the scriptures; but there are no traces of them in Nepaul. No one follows the rules of that class to which he nominally belongs. Among the Bhotiyas there are many Bhikshus, who never marry; and the Bhotiya Lamas are properly Arhats. But all the Nepaulese Buddhamargis are married men, who pursue the business of the world, and seldom think of the injunctions of their religion. The Tantras and Dharanis, which ought to be read for their own salvation, they read only for the increase of their stipend and from a greedy desire of money. (Hodgson, 1971: 51 - 52).

It is little wonder then that Hodgson interpreted Newar Buddhism in terms of its deviation from orthodox practice. I too was continually told of how Newar Buddhism was corrupt; of how it has degenerated from an earlier pristine form. When I asked about Newar monasteries I was told that at one time these structures housed "real" monks but now only married men lived there. Often some comment about how in fact Bare should not be married would be added. When I asked about the use of flesh and/or blood sacrifice I was told that in Buddhist tantra actual animal sacrifice was never performed but that now in Newar Buddhism it was necessary, in spite of the fact that it is in direct opposition to the principles of Buddhism and their injunction against the taking of life. When I asked about the significance of the shaven head I was told that only Buddhists had shaven heads without any tuft of sacred hair. The Bare continue to have completely shaven heads to show that they are Buddhist, in spite of the fact that the shaven head is also a symbol of celibacy and renunciation neither of which are practised by present day Bare. When I asked about Buddhist belief I was told that usually Buddhists did not believe in the existence of a permanent, unchanging soul but this was often not the case among Newar Buddhists. When I asked about the existence of the Bare caste and its exclusive control of the Buddhist priesthood, I was told that formerly those who were true Buddhists did become monks and that anyone from any caste could and did become a monk, but that now Newar Buddhism was corrupt and that now there was a married clergy instead of the usual celibate monkhood. When I asked about the rules governing the interchange of food between men of different castes I was told that according to the Buddha there should be no restrictions on commensal relations but that now people did in fact bother about such matters.

Although Newar Buddhists acknowledge that their customs are corrupt, it should not be inferred that they necessarily regret or feel ashamed of their 'degeneracy'. Apart from those Newar Buddhists who in the last quarter century have been influenced by Theravadian doctrine or who have had contact with Tibetan immigrants and who may in fact regret such deviations, the vast majority of Newar Buddhists see changes in their religious structure in terms of the harmony that now exists between Buddhism and Hinduism. Nepal, one is told, is a land where Buddhism and Hinduism live side by side in perfect harmony: the Buddhists regard the Hindu gods as different manifestations of the supreme godhead, the Adi-Buddha; while Hindus regard the Buddha as one of the avatars of Vishnu. Thus, it is said that to worship Shiva is to worship the Buddha and to worship the Buddha is to worship Shiva.

A question then arises: why do the Bare continue to recognize and employ a body of symbols relating to the traditional Buddhist monastic apparatus, and which, in point of fact, are inconsistent with the actual Newar institutions of caste and priesthood? The answer is that the Bare need to justify ideologically their superior ritual and caste status and this justification must be rooted in a non-Hindu religious tradition. The Bare need to validate their position as a priestly caste and to do this they need to retain their identity as Buddhists. Their position as a religious elite is based upon their control of 'Buddhist' temples and shrines, upon the performance of 'Buddhist' rites, and upon the worship of 'Buddhist' deities. To abandon the distinction between Buddhist and Hindu would mean the Bare's replacement as priest by the Brahman. However, because the Bare want to remain identified as Buddhist, they, unlike the Brahman, are faced with a lack of traditional and sacred literature which justifies and validates their exclusive right to function as a sacred caste of priests. Consequently the Bare continue to accept and exploit the orthodox Buddhist institutional structure while at the same time acknowledging their deviation. The Bare claim that they alone have a right to reside in and to control the religious apparatus of present-day Newar monasteries because they are the descendants of their former inhabitants, orthodox Buddhist monks. The Bare claim that they should be at the top of the caste hierarchy because they are the ones who come closest to approximately the life of the Buddhist monk: they alone among present-day Newars have the shaven head; they alone among present-day Newars are the occupants of monasteries; they alone attempt to follow the path of the Buddha; and they alone have earned a degree of spirituality because they alone have been ordained as Buddhist monks.

The paradox of the Bare accepting the validity of monkhood while at the same time rejecting the institution of celibate monks has not gone unnoticed by the Newars themselves. In order to explain this paradox there is the myth of the defeat of Buddhism in Nepal by the great Hindu reformer, philosopher and mystic, Shankara Acharya. This myth is well known to most Newars and is often referred to in order to explain how Newar Buddhism came to deviate from orthodox practices. The following passage is from a translation of a late Newar *vamshavali*, or 'history', translated for Daniel Wright by Munshi Shew Shunker Singh and Pandit Sri Gunanand.

> At this time the incarnation Shankarāchārya was born in the Deccan of an immaculate Brahmanī widow. This Shankara in his six former incarnations had been defeated in religious discussions by the Bauddhamārgīs, and had been cast into the fire. At the time of his seventh incarnation there were no learned Bauddhamārgīs there, but only sixteen Bōdhisatwas (or novices), who, hearing of the advent of this great reformer, fled to the North, seeking refuge, wherever they could find it, and there they died. Shankarāchārya, finding no clever Bauddhamārgīs with whom to argue, and hearing that the sixteen Bōdhisatwas had fled to Nepāl, pursued them, but could not find them ...Shankara found that of the three Bauddhamārgī sects, two had no clever men to argue with him. Therefore some of the Grihastha Achāryas, when preparing to argue with him, brought a jar of water, in which they invoked Saraswatī (the goddess of speech) to aid them. While contending with them, Shankara somehow became aware that Saraswatī had been invoked to help against him. He therefore entered the

> temple at the southern door and dismissed her, after which the Bauddhamārgīs were soon defeated. Some of them fled, and some were put to death. Some, who would not allow that they were defeated, were also killed; wherefore many confessed that they were vanquished, though in reality not convinced that they were in error. These he ordered to do *himsa* (i.e. to sacrifice animals), which is in direct opposition to the tenets of the Buddhist religion. He likewise compelled the Bhikshunīs, or nuns, to marry, and forced the Grihasthas (Grihastha, or alternatively grahastha, means householder or family man) to shave the knot of hair on the crown of their heads, when performing *chūrā-karma*, or first shaving of the head. Thus he placed the Banaprasthas (ascetics) and Grihasthas on the same footing. He also put a stop to many of their religious ceremonies, and cut their Brahmanical threads. (Wright, 1877: 118-119).

In this portion of the myth one clearly sees that the contradiction of the monk who is not a monk and of the priest/monk who is also a *grahastha*, or man with a family, is not covered over or ignored, but explained by appeal to "historical" circumstance. 'We are what we are because we were defeated by the great Hindu reformer Shankara Acharys.' The monks were made into householders, and the householders into monks (as they were forced to shave their heads). Blood sacrifices were introduced. However, the myth goes on to state that Buddhists were left as priests in those temples founded by Buddhists:

> Shankarāchārya thus destroyed the Buddhist religion, and allowed none to follow it; but he was obliged to leave Bauddhamārgis in some places as priests of temples, where he found that no other persons would be able to propitiate the gods placed in them by great Bauddhamārgīs. (Ibid:119).

The myth also explains what happened to life in the Buddhist monasteries. The descendants of monks who were forced to marry ask:

> How then can we leave these deities and relinquish our former creed? If we remain in our former creed, however, we cannot discharge the duties of Achāryas without performing the *chūrā-karma* as ordered by Shankarāchārya. Our fathers died, leaving us as infants, unable to perform any action ourselves. There is no image of a god here, without which *chūrā-karma* cannot be performed.

The problem is clear. They must worship their old Buddhist gods, and they must do so under *chūrā-karma* or *Bare chhuyigu*. But how are they to do so as they have no one to make them Bare nor have they a god before whom they can be made into priests? The solution to this dilemma is that they go to their uncles, the Bhiksu of Charumati Bihar, and ask their advice. Their uncles reply that they will come to their monastery and make them Bare:

> They then went to Pingalā Bahāl, and worshipped with great ceremonies the Iswarī Nairatmā. Then they made a chaitya for Swayambhu and an image of Sākya Sinha Buddha; and to keep up the worship of these, they took bhikshus (living now as grihasthas), the descendants of those who had followed Sakya Sinha into Nepāl, and appointed them as priests. (Ibid: 122-3).

And so were established the traditions that are followed today. *Bare chhuyigu* is done in the monastery of one's father but with the help of one's paternal aunt and her husband. The rite itself makes one a member of the monastery and thus eligible to serve as a priest in that monastery's shrine.

Summary

Newar Buddhism no longer maintains the traditional monastic structure. The Kathmandu Valley is still covered with viharas but these now house married priests and their families rather than celibate monks. Heredity has come to be the sole criterion for selection for the priesthood. Only those born within the Bare caste are eligible for membership in present-day Newar viharas. Those with the proper credentials may then be ordained as monks. This rite of initiation marks the incorporation of Bare boys into the descent group of their fathers, the Bare guthi of a particular monastery. The act of ordination then is a rite of passage and as such shares many of the same features as other non-Bare cast initiations. All Newar boys of clean caste status are made to impersonate ascetics. This role of the renouncer expresses the fact that these boys have withdrawn from the normal state of social relations and have entered a sacred ritual category. Moreover, this role permits expression of the liminal status of the boy during the period of his initiation.

There are three basic contradictions entailed in the use of the Buddhist ceremony of initiation into the monkhood to initiate Bare boys into their caste and of the continued use of the ideology of renunciation to validate the superior ritual status of a priestly caste. (1) The novice seems to assume the ritual role of monk, but in fact even during the period of his symbolic impersonation he never leads the life of an actual monk in a monastery though it is claimed that all Bare are monks for four days. (2) The Bare equate their religious role with that of the monk in order to justify their caste function of priest and yet their actual role of priest repudiates and stands in opposition to the traditional role of the monk. (3) The ideology of monkhood is used to justify a caste position. Yet the Buddhist monastic structure embodies principles of equality, egalitarianism, and renunciation. Moreover, these principles are in direct contradiction to the principles of hierarchy, pollution and caste which underlie the present-day Newar Buddhist institutions.

These contradictions have led most western scholars who have written about Newar Buddhism to condemn the contemporary Newar practices as corrupt and decadent. The Newars themselves are aware of these contradictions. The Bare do not want to abandon the distinction between monk, one who pursues a higher and purer religious life, and lay-man, one who is not a true Buddhist. The important gesture of the Bare's continuing to be tonsured in spite of their status as family men must be viewed in this perspective. Hindus retain a top-knot. Improper Buddhists retain a top-knot. But those Buddhists who truly follow the Dharma are men who have shaven heads. Because the Bare also have shaven heads they symbolically state that they, like traditional Buddhist monks, constitute a religious elite. The Bare continue to call themselves *Bandya*, a term directly related to the notion of monkhood and directly related to the Chinese and Japanese term *bonze*, or monk. Moreover, the Bare continue to reside in compounds called *vihara* (or *bahal* in colloquial Newari), a term meaning monastery.

The Bare are not true monks however, but *grahastha*, householders. On the religious level, they view the state of monkhood as merely an elementary religious stage and one that must be passed through as one progresses toward Enlightenment. Thus, they become monks only to repudiate the state of monkhood, and pass on to that of married cleric who is adept in the ways of tantra. On the secular level they are men who are married, as are most other Newar men, and who are a priestly caste who also traditionally follow the occupations of gold and silver smithing, or of tailoring.

Thus the Bare are both "monks" and "householders". They are *bhikshu-grahastha*, although this, of course, entails a contradiction in terms. The Bare continue to utilize, in a new context, symbols related to and only consistent within the context of the orthodox Buddhist monastery which in point of fact are in direct opposition to actual Newar religious institutions. Renunciation and asceticism are rejected and replaced by the role of hereditrary priest, and yet the idealogy of the Buddhist monkhood is still used to validate the new institution of a priestly caste.

Stephen M. Greenwold

NOTES

1. The Newars are a Tibeto-Burman speaking people found in villages and towns throughout Nepal as well as in Northern India, Sikkim, and Bhutan. However, their initial home was the Kathmandu Valley of Nepal. It is here that the vast majority of the Newars live. And it is here that one finds the centre of Newar civilisation.

2. See Heesterman 1964 for an account of how the Hindu Brahman's ritual purity is found in the ideology of renunciation.

3. The need for initiation as well as credentials of proper birth would seem to be a pecularariarity of the Buddhist Bare and, as such, be a characteristic that distinguishes them from Hindu castes. Yet, in fact, there is a parallel to this in Hinduism. As Hocart so correctly points out:

> The son of a brahman is not really a brahman till he has been initiated into the caste of his father. In a good family he will be initiated as a matter of course, and so he is thought of as a brahman before he really is one, just as our king is thought of as a king before his coronation, though, strictly speaking, he should still not be, and cannot wear the crown. Our coronation ceremony however has travelled much further on the road to survival than the Indian initiation. If it were omitted it would make no difference. If the Indian initiation is omitted, the brahmanic youth fall to the status of vratya; at least it was so when and where Manu's laws were written. A nobleman's, a priest's and a farmer's rank thus still depends not only on birth, but on initiation. Birth itself is inadequate..... (Hocart, 1950: 55-56).

Whether Manu's dictum is actually followed, or indeed, if it has been followed for some time amongst Hindu castes in India, is a matter of considerable doubt. But among the Newar Bare although not the sole criterion, initiation is of extreme importance.

4. During my twenty-two months in Nepal I personally came across no actual instance of such a loss of caste rank and privilege but was continually told that in the not too distant past loss of Bare caste membership was not unheard of because of failure to be properly initiated. However, during my stay there was one case of which I am personally aware where a Bare whose family had moved outside the Kathmandu Valley to a rather remote market hill town and

who had never received the proper initiation, though his father had, returned to the monastery of his ancestors and requested that his sons be initiated. This man was told that this would be impossible for although his own father had been initiated he himself had not, so he was not a Bare by caste nor were his sons. However, he was also told that once he himself had been initiated, then his sons could be initiated. Thus the father first was made into a Bare and then his sons. If the father had died before receiving initiation his sons would have been denied access to the Bare caste.

5. *Jichā* (or alternatively *jilā*) is the Newari term used to denote a person related to oneself by having taken a wife from one's descent group. It does not just mean "in-law", i.e. one related by marriage. For this the word *sasa* is used as a prefix: *maju* is mother, *sasa-maju* is mother-in-law; *baju* is father, *sasa-baju* is father-in-law. *Jichā* or *jilā* appears only in the following three terms: *jichā-paju*, father's sister's husband, formed by adding *jichā* to *paju*, the latter also being the Newar word for mother's brother; *jichā-bhāju* or *jilanja*, daughter's husband (son-in-law) and younger sister's husband; *jichā-dhaju*, elder sister's husband.

REFERENCES

Dumont, L. 1966. North India in relation to South India. *Contributions to Indian Sociology*. Vol. IX, pp. 90-114.

Hocart, A.M. 1950. *Caste, A comparative Study*. London: Methuen.

Hodgson, B.H. 1971. *Essays on the Languages, Literature and Religion of Nepal and Tibet*. Varanasi: Bharat-Bharati.

Lévi, S. 1905. *Le Nepal: etude historique d'un royaume hindou*. 2 vols. Paris: Ernest Leroux. (Unpubl. trans. by L.S. Greenwold, 1972).

Oldfield, H.A. 1880. *Sketches from Nipal: historical and descriptive*. 2 vols. London: W.H. Allen & Co.

Snellgrove, D.L. 1957. *Buddhist Himalaya*. Oxford: Clarendon Press.

Turner, V.W. 1969. *The Ritual Process: structure and anti-structure*. London: Routledge and Kegan Paul.

Wright, E., ed. 1877. *History of Nepal*. Cambridge: The University Press.

A Shaman's Song and some Implications for Himalayan Research

In December 1972 at the meetings of the American Anthropological Association held in Toronto, Canada, a symposium was held on the topic: The Hindu-Tibetan Interface. By its very title the symposium to some extent has committed itself to a diffusionary research strategy. By the term strategy I mean an approach to a phenomenon - in this case a sociocultural phenomenon - with certain questions or hypotheses in mind. Unless the strategy is doctrinaire, unless, that is, the answers already are contained in its questions, or the questions are regarded as the only ones (or the only worthwhile ones) to be asked about a phenomenon, a strategy is adopted in order to see what it will yield; and the implication is that every strategy is suppositious. Science, any science, is in this sense like the children's game:

> We dance round in a ring and suppose
> The secret sits in the centre and knows.[1]

If this is true, a suggestion that the strategy of interface, and other basically diffusionary strategies for understanding the Nepal Himalaya, is partial, and encourages blindness to some aspects of our topic, is a gentle impeachment indeed. And if I suggest only one of a number of possible counter-strategies, it is in full realization that for some purposes and to meet some scholarly interests these other approaches, including the diffusionary, are of value.

The approach to Nepal as a diffusionary cultural interface has had a long history and during the late 18th and early 19th centuries is associated with the names of British officials such as Kirkpatrick, Hamilton and Hodgson.[2] The continuing vitality of the approach was shown not only by the Toronto symposium but by its choice as a topic for a session at the IXth International Congress of Anthropological and Ethnological Sciences held in the summer of 1973.[3] This is not surprising, for as Berreman has noted, some peoples of the Nepal Himalaya do "share many cultural traits with Tibetans" and "others have been thoroughly Hinduized."[4]

A weakness in this perspective is its omission of other traditions, including the one I am concerned with in this essay, a form of shamanism which may be termed Dhaulagiri Shamanism, because it flourishes on the southern and western slopes of the Dhaulagiri range. If one is mainly interested in Nepal, and in particular this region, as an interweaving of Indian and Tibetan cultural strands, much of this religious phenomenon simply fails to register. It is of interest from the Indianists' point of view that the First (and mythical) Shaman is called Rāmā, and from the Tibetanists', that contemporary shamans in their chants invoke powerful lamas. But from a different perspective these and many other diffusionary features are peripheral and relatively insignificant.

One moves easily from a conception of Dhaulagiri Shamanism as a reflection of two civilizations to an approach associated with Redfield[5] and his followers. From this perspective one's focus is on textual materials deriving from the Tibetan and Indian cultural traditions, and the questions asked have to do with whether or not the complex reflects ideas of the Great Tradition and is a vehicle through which these ideas operate in the lives of ordinary people.[6] Or one might ask whether some of its ideas have been received into either Great Tradition, there to be reworked and preserved in the writings of the learned.[7] A danger of this approach is a tendency to treat as derivative ideas that may be internally generated, and as parochial ideas that despite their non-literate nexus possess both depth and universality.

The same problem may arise however, even when one concentrates on Dhaulagiri Shamanism as part of a separate non-Indian, and non-Tibetan tradition. A possible perspective and one I myself, and also Ter Ellingson, have used,[8] asks about its relation to the shamanism of Inner Asia.[9] Instead of beginning with Tibetan or Indian textual materials, one may turn to Eliade's reconstruction of what he terms the "classic" Inner Asian tradition; and to what he regards as the Golden Age of the phenomenon, because it corresponds more closely to what he conceives of as "true" shamanism. An upshot is the conclusion that Dhaulagiri Shamanism in important respects is neither very "true" nor very "classic". It is, in short, derivative and somehow diminished.

I want to suggest that in our attempt to understand the Nepal Himalaya, and I am speaking especially of religious phenomena that basically may be neither Buddhist nor Hindu, that we begin of course by analyzing them in their own psychological and social contexts, and as symbolic systems having their own internal coherence. But it is important I think that having done this we not overlook the possibility that though local and unwritten these religions have high potential - both for generating within themselves and for representing dramatically a number of insights that have human depth and universality, not unworthy of comparison with valued religious ideas found in textual materials from India and Tibet.

As an example let me take a shaman's song from the Dhaulagiri Complex. Approaching the song from four different points of view, I will begin with consideration of its social context and note how it mirrors ambiguities found first in a system of connubium or generalized exchange, and second in the status of shaman. At a more general level I will suggest that it embodies reference to deep-seated sexual anxieties, and finally that the song by means of its alchemy has converted all previous levels into a dramatic representation of an ultimate metaphysical paradox.

Although Dhaulagiri Shamanism is shared by a number of ethnic groups, for simplicity I will speak of it as the possession of Magars, a middle caste group in this region. A focal aspect of Magar social structure, found also among the other ethnic groups most involved in the religion, is generalized exchange[10] among localized patrilineages.[11] Any given patrilineage is flanked by patrilineages it regards as wife-givers, and by other patrilineages it regards as wife-receivers. To state it differently any localized patrilineage exists in dual relationship involving reciprocal obligations: it is either wife-giver to wife-receivers or wife-receiver from wife-givers. Patrilineages hold some land in common and this is a major factor reinforcing their sense of separate identity. In the marriage relation, which links patrilineages but does not obliterate their separateness, the wife-givers have a somewhat superior position. This is evidenced by their power to give or withhold a sister or daughter; to be supportive or to reprimand a daughter's or sister's husband if he does not come up to expectations; and either to exert strong pressure to keep a marriage together, or to provide a haven for a dissatisfied daughter or sister who wishes to terminate a marriage - a power that often includes assistance in finding a new spouse. Because of these powers a wife-giving lineage is a source of anxiety to its wife-receivers.

The shaman is a recognized status filled by men who are self-selected, usually on the basis of a supernormal experience. They serve an apprenticeship to a practising shaman, learning spells, rituals and a long song cycle. Some of the help a shaman provides a client is neutral with respect to the community. His spells, rituals and songs are directed against supernatural beings. However, when a client is being bothered by an enemy, an opponent in a court case, for example, and as often happens, the shaman provides assistance, his powers are directed at individuals within the community. What is good from his clients' point of view is bad from theirs. With respect to good and evil therefore the shaman's status is ambiguously coloured.

We have then as two aspects of the social context opposites whose distinctness is blurred by ambiguity. In the kinship domain of generalized exchange localized patrilineages having separate identities and interests are linked in marital alliances; and wife-givers, who can be beneficent also can be punishing and therefore a source of anxiety. In the domain of shamanism we find a status which similarly is ambiguous, because like the status of wife-giver, it also is associated with power that can be either beneficent or punishing.

Before turning to the Shaman's Song let us glance very briefly at other cultural expressions of these ambiguities. Opening marriage negotiations by carrying off a resisting girl without prior consultation with her, or her parents, is a dramatic enactment of lineage opposition. The subsequent negotiation, on the other hand, becomes a medley both of this theme and a theme emphasizing the necessity, if society is to continue, of overcoming opposition by alliance. In one instance the theme of alliance in the context of opposition was nicely epitomized by a boy's post-capture emissary to the captured girl's parents, for the emissary was a man who had received the boy's sister as a wife and whose own sister was the captured girl's mother.[12]

In a supernatural context we watch the playing out of the same themes. For the biennial offering to its stipulated supernatural founder and his continuing spirit, a patrilineage asks its wife-givers to come and help. On a platform that stands for the whole lineage and its backward extension in time, they erect a number of smaller shrines, one for each contemporary lineage family head and his wife. At each of these shrines they make a blood offering; a cock for the man and a hen for his wife. But in addition the offering is made to the supernatural founder of the lineage and to all descendant men, plus their wives. Thus the lineage god is conceived of as a materialization from generation to generation, not only through the agnatic line of descent but through the necessary series of matrimonial alliances. These alliances are symbolized "on the ground" by the presence of wife-receivers and their wife-givers. The opposition between this patriline and all the separate but necessary wife-giving patrilines is symbolized during the ritual by rough horseplay between the men of the wife-receiving lineage and the younger women of the wife-giving lineage.

I have mentioned the anxiety associated with powers of a wife-giving lineage. We often find one expression of this during the early part of a shaman's all-night séance. Before the shaman dons his complete costume and undertakes the major rituals, he answers questions about matters bothering some of those present. Those who are seeking answers place a rolled up piece of birch bark between the shaman's toes. They do not verbalize their question and the shaman must learn by supernormal means what is on their minds. In a high proportion of cases the shaman, when answering men, will refer to evil influence from the direction of the in-laws.

The ambiguity inherent in the shaman's status is openly discussed, not infrequently by shamans themselves. Among its many ritual and dramatic expressions probably none is more central and explicit than the act of possession itself. During a séance the shaman plays host with his own body to spirits whose evil potential is known and feared. Thus although he is helper and champion of his client, he has become at the same time dangerous and an embodiment of evil.[13]

Let us turn now to the Shaman's Song and note how these themes, as well as the two others mentioned above, are mirrored in it. The song is one of a number that accompany various rituals during a séance. Of all the songs, it is the most frequently sung, partly because it legitimizes the shaman's transcendental persona, but also because it is used to rid the client of witch-evil, a most common source of human ills.

The story tells of happenings in the First Age of the world's present era. Nine Witch Sisters, the gift of God to an aging childless couple, have grown up and have begun to do evil. For help, the king calls Rāmā, The First Shaman. After inviting them to take a journey with him, Rama by various means, some magical and some not, kills all but the youngest and most beautiful sister. Obviously attracted by her, Rāmā nevertheless is trying to bring himself to kill her when she reminds him that if he does he will be out of a job. Appreciating the cogency of her argument he refrains and she in turn agrees to stop tormenting any client of his whenever in the future he ritually offers her the proper food, consisting in part of a ball of ashes. Although she wishes to share his house with his faithful wife and his village with his lineage brothers, Rāmā fears the evil she might do, and as the song ends, he persuades her that she must live at the crossroads outside the village.

When we seek to interpret this song, first with respect to connubium or generalized exchange, we must look to the role of the wife, because it is around this role that the inherent ambiguity of the system clusters. As a member of a different lineage than her husband, and often of another village, the wife occupies a somewhat anomalous position. This is reflected symbolically when a wife dies. Not only her husband and his lineage but also her natal lineage refrain for a period from certain foods. The anomalous position of the wife is apt to appear with special sharpness during the early years of a marriage. Prior to the birth of a child it is not uncommon, even for older girls, to return for quite lengthy periods to their natal homes. The reason given by the in-laws is need for the girl's domestic services. I knew of two young men whose childless wives had been living in their natal homes for over two years during which time they had been trying fruitlessly to persuade the father-in-law to send them back. It would be unusual for a wife with a baby to stay away for so long in this phase of the marriage. But while their wives are still young, many husbands fear divorce, which can be obtained without much difficulty. Structurally the fear stems from the opposition between the wife-giving and wife-receiving lineages, and the incomplete incorporation of the wife in the latter. In a wife's character, it is reflected as the contrast between faithfulness and faithlessness. In the song we see a representation and an apparent resolution of the problem of the husband's fear. Two aspects of women's character are represented: on the one hand, Jammu, the faithful wife, and on the other, the Witch, to whom faithlessness and all other evils would not be foreign. At the close of the song, Rama banishes the Witch and is reunited with Jammu. Faithfulness and a happy and secure marriage apparently win the day. Yet this is not the final meaning. For Rāmā has allied himself with the Witch as well as with Jammu. Rāmā, flanked by two kinds of women, divided in loyalty, symbolizes, though in male guise, the opposition of two lineages allied in marriage, and the anomalous position of wives. He represents the persistent social context in which are nourished the husband's fears.

Again, if we look at the story for reflections of ambiguities inherent in the shaman's status, we find it beautifully exemplified in the pact. The shaman's power against evil comes both from his knowledge of it and his implication in it. At this level, Rāmā, as presented in the song, represents the community's attitude toward the shaman, and the reasons for it.

Moving to the third perspective, it is noteworthy that the song has strong erotic overtones. The physical beauty of the youngest witch is described at length and because of this the song seems to suggest that loss of his occupation was not the only reason Rāmā did not kill her. He also refrained because he found her very attractive. Earlier in the song a different sexual theme is stated. Before setting out with the Nine Witches Rāmā climbs a pole and watches them dance round beneath him. When they turn themselves uspide down, exposing their genitals, the pole topples over. Rāmā lies on the ground in a faint, and the Witches try to eat him, a fate from which he is spared by his magic apparel. In these two themes we see mirrored deep-seated, universal and conflicting feelings about women. Are the Witches - in particular the youngest Witch - Rāmā's sisters or his potential wives? No version of the song was completely unambiguous on this point, though when interpreting the song one shaman said Rāmā was a Pun Magar, and the Sisters Budhāthoki, and hence marriageable. If the Witches are lineage sisters and unmarriageable, Rāmā's banishing of the Witch represents his allegiance to the rule of exogamy. All the evil he feared the Witch would cause if he allowed her to enter his home and village is a description of the socially disruptive effects of incest; and it mirrors also the attraction that must be repressed if incestuous desires are to be overcome. But if the Witch is marriageable we see in Rāmā's desire for an abhorrence of the youngest sister the apparently universal human ambivalence derived from the child's earliest associations with the mother. (The mother is nuturant, a benevolent goddess and the child is omnipotent; the mother is absent, she appears destructive and the child is abject and terrified.)[14]

Although this last interpretation of the song lifts it from a particular social and psychological context, it is not this I had in mind when proposing it as an example from an oral and parochial tradition that generated insights of intrinsic profundity and broad human implication. Without insisting that the song be equated with Greek drama and Biblical parable,[15] I do find it impressive from a metaphysical point of view. This is because it maintains awareness of opposites, their interpenetration and the never-ending tension between them. The song of the Nine Witch Sisters becomes a symbol of ambiguity - as well as distinctness - inherent in relations between mother and child, men and women, groups of maritally allied kinsmen, and finally good and evil. Clearly this is no "hymn the Brahman sings",[16] where all opposites are dissolved in the One. Evil is ever-present and in his nightlong séances Rāmā, Champion of the Good, provides only a series of temporary stays against the Witch. He prevails, but just barely and only briefly, and he prevails at the cost of an alliance with evil, possibly even at the cost of "knowing" the Witch, with the dual implication carried by the word.

As Niebuhr so clearly realized,[17] these two adversaries, especially in contexts having to do with power and its exercise, are not easily separable; and among the many perceptions the symbols of this myth subsume, is that while the moralist in polities may promise what is literally attainable "and while he may do everything he says he will do, he can never - simply because he must operate in a real, hard, amoral world - act with the constant moral courage of his pretensions."[18]

John Hitchcock

NOTES

1. Frost, Robert. "The Secret Sits".

2. Kirkpatrick, William. 1811. *An Account of The Kingdom of Nepal, Being the Substance of Observations Made during a Mission to that Country in 1793.* London: Miller; Buchanan, Francis, 1819. *An Account of The Kingdom of Nepal, and of The Territories Annexed to this Domain by the House of Gorkha.* Edinburgh: Constable; Hodgson, Brian M., 1874, *Tibet, Together with 12 Further Papers on the Geography, Ethnology, and Commerce of Those Countries.* London: Trubner.

3. At the IXth International Congress of Anthropological and Ethnological Sciences a session will consider the Himalayas as "an interface" between "The South Asian and Chinese culture areas".

4. Berreman, Gerald D., 1963. "Peoples and Cultures of The Himalayas". *Asian Survey.* Vol. III, No. 6, 297-298.

5. Redfield, Robert. 1956. *Peasant Society and Culture.* Chicago: University of Chicago Press.

6. Singer, Milton. 1961. "Text and Context in The Study of Contemporary Hinduism". *The Adyar Library Bulletin.* Vol. XXV, Part 1-4, 274-303. See also Jones, Rex L., 1968. "Shamanism in South Asia: A Preliminary Survey". *History of Religion.* Vol. 7, No. 4, 330-347. He sees the Shaman's loss of the art of Ecstasy (ascent and descent of the Shaman's soul) in parts of South Asia as in line with Buddhist and Hindu ideas of rebirth and Karma.

7. Marriott, McKim. 1955. "Little Communities in an Indigenous Civilization". McKim Marriott (ed.) *Village India: Studies in the Little Community.* Chicago: University of Chicago Press.

8. Hitchcock, John T. 1967. "A Nepalese Shamanism and the Classic Inner Asian Tradition". *History of Religion,* Vol. 7, No. 2, 149-158. Ter Ellison. Illustrated talk at the 1971 Association for Asian Studies Meetings.

9. Eliade, Mircea. 1964. *Shamanism, Archaic Techniques of Ecstasy.* New York: Bollingen Foundation.

10. Lévi-Strauss. 1969. (Original 1949). *The Elementary Structures of Kinship.* Boston: Beacon Press.

11. Hitchcock, John T. *ms.* Chapters VII - IX. *Sickle and Khuhuri.*

12. Hitchcock, John T. *ms.* "A Magar Social Drama".

13. "For whatever the true personality and inner feelings of the shaman it is society which regards him ambivalently as at once a healer and, potentially at least, a witch". I.M. Lewis. 1971. *Ecstatic Religion.* Harmondsworth: Penguin Books. p. 201.

14. Klein, Melanie. 1955. *New Directions in Psychoanalysis.* London: Tavistock.
La Barre, Weston. 1970. *The Ghost Dance.* New York: Dell Books.

15. Fortes, Meyer. 1954. *Oedipus and Job in West African Religion.* Cambridge: Cambridge University Press.

16. Emerson, Ralph Waldo. "Brahma".

17. Niebuhr, Rinehold. 1941. *The Nature and Destiny of Man.* New York: Charles Scribner's Sons.

18. Anson, Robert Sam. 1972. "Just Plain George". *Harper's,* November, 76.

A Note on Possession in South Asia

These preliminary remarks are an attempt to contrast some ethnic groups of the central and eastern Himalayas with parts of the Hindu population of the Indian subcontinent. The discussion is focused on the following question: Why is it that among the former groups the ecstatic communication with the superhuman is a privilege of certain specialists, while among the latter not only specialists but also laity (the clients of a specialist) can be possessed by a superhuman being? The reader will rightly find some of the conclusions premature and speculative, and all I can hope is to draw attention to a problem.

In another paper (cf. in this volume) I have stated that possession is not a "dramatic" event in the rituals of the Tamang shaman in Central Nepal. If it occurs, as it has to at every seance, the Tamang shaman is not a passive vessel of the possessing agent. A state of possession is rather controlled than simply "endured" by him. A second characteristic of possession among the Tamang is that it never befalls laity. As a matter of fact,laity is excluded from every kind of ecstatic communication, be it by possession or by other ritual techniques.

A similar situation seems to prevail among some other non-Hindu, or partly and recently Hinduized, ethnic groups of the Himalayas, such as the Gurung, Magarm Limbu, Rai, Lepcha, etc. Especially, possession of laics has not been reported among these groups, as far as I can see.[1]

In contrast to these ethnic minorities, among the Hindu population of both India and Nepal possession in its various forms is characterized by a) a high grade identification of the possessed person with the agent possessing him, i.e. a state which closely reminds one of a "suffering" (Dumont 1959: 68, Elwin 1955: 216), and b) the fact that often also laics can, or must, attain a state of possession at certain rituals.

Such possessions of laics can be of many types. From the viewpoint of the possessing agent, it can be caused by gods or by the ghosts of the dead. As far as possession by gods is concerned, one has to differentiate, because often the person possessed is neither a laic nor a specialist stricto sensu but someone who is known for his ability to become "easily" possessed. Such a medium is resorted to mainly at periodic rites involving the community or larger kin groups and territorial units, e.g.

among the Pahari in North West India (Berreman 1963: 92), the Coorg (Srinivas 1965: 193 - 200) and the Pramalai Kallar of South India (Dumont 1957: 347 - 354). These media mainly serve as oracles, and their possession is regarded as auspicious.

In numerous other cases, virtually anybody can become possessed by gods or ghosts. This possession is episodic; it happens either spontaneously or is induced by a specialist upon the client. *Spontaneous* possessions have been reported, i.a., by Harper (1963) and Dumont (1957: 405; 1959: 69) in South India, and by Stanley and Freed (1967) and Opler (1958) in North India. In these instances, ancestors or ghosts of those who died a premature (or violent) death manifest themselves in their close relatives or friends, chiefly in women. With regard to the *induced* type of possession, only a few examples should be cited here. Among the Pahari of North West India, when a god or an ancestor is suspected of troubling somebody, the former is made to possess the latter with the help of a specialist. Through the victim the god or ancestor will tell about the cause of his anger and prescribe how he should be appeased (Berreman 1964; 1963: 87 - 94 ff, 369-387). Among the Jaisi Brahmans of Central Nepal, a similar pattern is to be found. The dead can possess their male relatives belonging to the same patrilineal descent group *(kul)* as themselves, and it is a specialist who induces them to do so. (This specialist can be possessed only by gods, mainly by his tutelaries, but never by the dead). Often a long series of all-night seances are needed to invoke the dead and make them speak through their relatives in order to find out the cause of a trouble, such as illness, accidents, etc. (Höfer and Shrestha 1972; cf. also Sharma 1970). For Far Western Nepal, Gaborieau notes some cases in which laics, men or women, are possessed by gods or ghosts in the presence of a professional oracle (Gaborieau 1969: 37, 39). Some further instances of induced possession of laics have been described by Dumont (1957: 406 - 410) among the Pramalai Kallar (mainly women, possessed by ghosts and demons), by Rose (1919: 199) (possession by ancestors) and Crooke (1896: 251 - 252) in North West India.

Possession in general, and possession of laics in particular, is also present in some "tribal" groups of Middle and North East India. Both, possession by gods and possession by the dead, occur. The dead possess the laics (their relatives?) mainly at certain ceremonies concluding the funeral rites. Among the Santal, e.g. it is through such possessions that the dead reveal their last wishes and inform the living about the cause of their death (Bodding 1942: 179f, 183; cf. also Rahmann 1959: 749). In other cases, we have possession by gods either at periodic rites, such as village festivals (Santal, Gond, Bhumia), or at death ceremonies (Gond) or in connection with exorcism (Bodding 1942: 150 - 157; Fuchs 1960: 345 - 346, 460 - 463; Elwin 1939: 300f,

388, 394). The *barua* or *barwa*, a man who easily goes into trance, closely resembles the media among the Hindus proper (cf. above). He too seems to be a person who, in contrast to the specialist par excellence, is acting due to a certain predisposition rather than by virtue of a training and initiation.

Seen apart from the case of media and generalizing somewhat, the characteristics of the possession of *laity* may be summarized as follows: 1) Possession of laity occurs in any major strata of the caste hierarchy; the sources quoted above prove its presence among Brahmans (Harper, Hofer and Shrestha, Sharma), in castes which might be classified as Kshatria or Shudra (Berreman, Dumont), in tribal groups (Elwin, Bodding, Fuchs) and among Untouchables (Stanley and Freed). 2) It involves both, possession by gods and possession by the dead. In the latter case, the dead often belong to the same kin group as the person(s) possessed by them. 3) It is confined to small kin groups, i.e. it concerns, and happens in, the extended family or a segment of a descent group. 4) Its believed cause is often connected with some evil, e.g. a failure entailing the malevolence of gods or ghosts. 5) In most cases, it serves as a particularly intense and rapid way of communication with the superhuman, and its main purpose is to solve acute problems which emerge in connection with life-cycle crises, such as death or marriage. Being connected with the life-cycle and/or having its cause in some conflicts between the individual and his group (which is particularly true in cases where women are likely to be possessed), it occurs episodically, i.e. independently of feasts and other periodic rites. (The Santal are one of the exceptions). 7) The persons possessed are in some cases only women (Harper), in others only men (Höfer and Shrestha, Sharma), and in others again both men and women (Stanley and Freed, Gaborieau). 8) In most instances (Rose 1919 seems to be an exception), a specialist is needed who either induces or at least analyses the possession of his clients in order to satisfy the possessing agent. This specialist may be of the same caste as the client (Höfer and Shrestha, Sharma) or of a lower caste than the latter (Berreman) but obviously never a Brahman priest as such. In the Nepalese case (Höfer and Shrestha) he is a Jaisi, i.e. a low-ranking Brahman who is (theoretically at least) excluded from serving as priest (purohit).

The question, why the possession of laics is such a widespread phenomenon among Hindus and - to a certain extent - among more or less Hinduized tribal groups, cannot be answered without analysing the problem of possession as a whole in India.

Possession in its various forms is a pervading feature throughout India and, as Dumont (1959: 56) states, "an institutionalized function complementing priesthood." At the present state of our knowledge it would be fruitless to ask whether or not it is of pre-Aryan or non-Aryan origin; it would be easy to cite arguments both, *pro* and *contra*.[2] Yet one is certainly allowed to hypothesize that the present spread and importance of possession in general derive from some socio-cultural factors specific to India. In the following, an attempt is made to elaborate on these factors.

To a certain extent, possession may be considered a logical alternative to the shamanistic journey to the Other World. (Both, possession and journey aim at a direct contact with the superhuman. While, in a journey, man goes to the gods, in a state of possession, the gods come to man - to put it in the simplest terms). In Indian culture, such an ecstatic journey, e.g. in connection with psychopompism or curing, does not seem to be as pre-eminent as possession.[3] Why this is so is a puzzling question. Jones (1967) assumes that it is the emergence of a specific form of the ancestor's cult which led to confusing eschatological ideas and altered the ecstatic experience.

But there seems to be more involved. A factor which might have favoured the spread of possession to the detriment of the journey-like access to the sacred is that in India, with the emergence of a religious elite, the distance between humans and superhumans has been, so to speak, reduced by the development of a) the figural and verbal representation of gods in sculpture, painting and literature, b) mysticism, such as Tantrism, Yoga and other techniques of meditation,[4] and c) the concept according to which gods may temporarily be incarnated in humans.

Iconography in particular brought the gods "on to the earth"; it made them visible and palpable (one is tempted to say that it made them emerge out of the diffusity of "animism"), while philosophical speculation elaborated their functions, attributes, etc. This might have enhanced the possibility for humans to represent superhumans in drama or through possession. But, in fact, all these distance-reducing techniques were developed by a religious elite (including the renouncers) and have remained its privilege. In other words, while the distance between humans and superhumans is reduced, at the same time, the distance between the religious elite and the laity increases. The question is, whether the spread of possession in India may be seen also as a response to this situation, i.e., whether it was a process which took place in defiance *and* in default of the religious elite. In defiance, because possession represents an alternative access to the sacred and as such, an alternative to the distance-reducing techniques of meditation and asceticism. In default, because, firstly, the intellectualism and other-worldliness of the elite could not satisfy all the religious needs of laity and/or because, secondly, a specific concept of status debars parts of this elite from serving as priests among certain groups of the population or on certain occasions during the life-cycle, from which impurity accrues.

Possibly, the specific pattern, namely the possession of laics, was just a by-product of this general development. It might have emerged either as an ultimate means of conflict solution for under-privileged individuals, or as a particularly intense, cathartic process reinforcing kinship ties, or yet again as the expression of a "democratized" access to the sacred, i.e. an intensified devotion connecting the *individual* as such with the superhuman. The first case is well illustrated by the possession of women[5] (Harper, Stanley and Freed), the second by the ghost exorcism of the Jaisi in Nepal (Höfer and Shrestha) and the third, to a certain extent, by the "shamanism" among the Pahari (Berreman).

To return to our initial question: Why is possession of laics absent among the ethnic groups of the Himalayas? A comparison with the Indian background discussed above may offer an indication as to where the answer lies. Until the last century, most of the ethnic groups in question lived in marginal zones in-between the high cultures of India, Tibet, etc. In spite of being influenced by the latter, the cultural history of these ethnic groups lacks a development of specific distance-reducing techniques which could have constituted an alternative to the traditional forms of ecstatic experience. The authority of the traditional religious specialists remained more or less uncontested, and their concepts and techniques continued to be regarded as part of the ethnic tradition of each group. Although in most cases we find a clear-cut division of tasks between the ecstatic and non-ecstatic specialists (roughly, *priest* versus *shaman*), this division does not involve superiority or inferiority of one of these categories of specialists, and it does not stem from a discrepancy between an "elitarian" and a "popular" tradition, as in India. To sum up, the traditional worldview of these ethnic groups with its emphasis on the distance between the human and superhuman was not, as a whole, perturbed by a new soteriology, and the traditional distance between the specialists and the laity was not altered by the emergence of a new religious elite. The capability of ecstatic communication could perhaps continue to be a privilege of some specialists all the more because it was, and still is, primarily a *religious* privilege rather than, at the same time, a social or even political one.

Two questions remain unanswered. The one is, how far our Indian model would apply to Tibet where, within certain limits, a similar development took place with the advent of Buddhism and Tantrism. It is interesting to note that according to Hoffman (1972: 95), evidences of possession in post-Buddhist Tibet are more numerous than those of a shamanistic journey.

The second question relates to the presence of possession - especially, possession of specialists - among the "tribal" groups of Middle and North East India. To what extent can it be attributed to the impact of "popular" Hinduism? Undeniably, these tribals have been exposed to its influence for a far longer time than the Himalayan ethnic groups. Yet the complexity of the problem requires careful interpretation. To mention just one example: As far as I can see, there is one feature which clearly distinguishes the "tribal pattern" from the "Hindu pattern" of possession. That is that, among Hindus, the dead possess the living only incidentally and outside the regular death ritual, while, among the tribals, they regularly do so within the framework of the funeral ceremonies (cf. Rahmann 1959: 748 - 750). Among the latter, the dead can possess laics or, more frequently, certain specialists, as is the case with the Saora (Elwin 1955: 339 - 400). Now, the Saora shaman closely reminds us of the *mun* of the Lepcha (Nebesky-Wojkowitz 1951-52; Gorer 1967: 357 - 360). The *mun* has two tasks, namely psychopompism and possession. He first accompanies the decesased to the abode of the dead and then, just as the Saora Shaman, becomes possessed by him and narrates why his client had to die, etc. Is this a "missing link" indicating that at least the possession by the dead among the tribals in question is older than the influence that Hinduism has had upon their religions? Rahmann (1959: 750) states that in the present funeral practices of the tribals, there is no evidence of psychopompism or journey. Can we thus conclude that the effect of Hinduism consisted merely in favouring the spread of possession among the tribals - to the detriment of psychopompism, which might have existed in former times and, perhaps, side by side with possession? Furthermore: Is the possession of laity, as it occurs, e.g. at the funeral ceremonies of the Santal, to be regarded as a survival of an active role which relatives originally played at death rituals and which has ultimately been intensified, i.e. developed to a state of possession, under Hindu influence?

Further research is needed to elucidate these questions. I am aware of the porblems this interpretation raises, such as, e.g., the "Hindu/non-Hindu" or the "tribal/non-tribal" dichotomies, or yet again the wide range of meanings the term 'possession' conveys. It should also be emphasised that this paper does not claim to offer a model but is just an attempt to point out some of the possible factors favouring the spread of a phenomenon within a certain area.[6]

Andras Höfer

NOTES

1. It would be necessary, of course, to show the distribution of this pattern more systematically and also with reference to the western Himalayas. In her thesis, Friedl (1965) does not mention the existence of possession of laics in the Hindukush and Karakorum.

2. cf. also our concluding paragraphs.

3. Quite in contrast to India, ritual journeys of ecstatic and non-ecstatic character are a pervasive feature in "the culture of the Bodic speaking area" (Allen 1973); cf. also Gaborieau 1969: 45, who aptly contrasts the experience of possession with that of a shamanistic journey.

4. This is not to deny that there is a certain continuity between these new techniques of mysticism and some more archaic patterns of ecstatic experience (cf. Eliade 1957: 384 - 401).

5. Harper (1963: 166 - 167) calls this type of possession (of women) "a culturally acceptable pattern whereby individuals attempt to gain some control over their environment through *temporary hallucinations that they are themselves a supernatural"* (italics mine).

6. I wish to thank M. Gaborieau, J. Reinhard and Ph. Sagant for their comments.

BIBLIOGRAPHY

Allen, N.J. 1973: Notes of some Categories of Ritual Journey. (Mimeogr. Paper read at the Symposium on the Anthropology of Nepal, London, SOAS).

Berreman, G.D. 1963: *Hindus of the Himalayas*. Berkeley, Los Angeles: University of California Press.

Berreman, G.D. 1964: Brahmins and Shamans in Pahari Religion, in *Religion in South Asia*. Ed. by E.B. Harper, pp 53 - 69. Seattle: University of Washington Press.

Bodding, P.O. (and Sten Konow) 1942: Traditions and Institutions of the Santals. *Oslo Etnografiske Museum Bulletin* 6.

Crooke, W. 1896: *The Tribes and Castes of the North-Western Provinces and Oudh.* vol. III. Calcutta: Govt. Printing.

Dumont, L. 1957: *Une sous-caste de l'Inde du Sud. Organisation sociale et religion des Pramalai Kallar.* Paris, The Hague: Mouton.

Dumont, L. 1959: Possession and Priesthood. *Contributions to Indian Sociology*, 3: 55 - 74.

Eliade, M. 1957: Schamanismus und archaische Ekstasetechnik. Zurich, Stuttgart: Rascher.

Elwin, V. 1939: *The Baiga*. London: John Murray.

Elwin, V. 1955: *The religion of an Indian Tribe.* Bombay: G. Cumberlege, Oxford University Press.

Friedl, E. 1965: *Trager medialer Begabung im Hindukusch und Karakorum.* Wien: Osterreichische Ethnologische Gesellschaft.

Fuchs, St. 1960: *The Gond and Bhumia of Eastern Mandla.* London: Asia Publishing House.

Gaborieau, M. 1969: Note preliminaire sur le dieu Masta. *Objets et Mondes*, 9,1: 19 - 58.

Gorer, G. 1967: *Himalayan Village. An Account of the Lepchas of Sikkim.* London etc.: Th. Nelson & Sons. 2nd edition.

Harper, E.B. 1963: Spirit Possession and Social Structure, in *Anthropology on the March.* Ed. by B. Ratnam, pp. 165 - 177. Madras: Social Sciences Association, The Book Centre.

Hoffman, H. 1972: Erscheinungsformen des tibetischen Schamanismus, in *Ergriffenheit und Besessenheit, ein interdisziplinäres Gespräch über transkulturell-anthropologische und - psychiatrische Fragen.* Ed. by J. Zutt, pp. 95 - 104. Bern: Francke.

Höfer, A. and B.P. Shrestha 1972: Ghost Exorcism among the Brahmans of Central Nepal. *Central Asiatic Journal* (in press).

Jones, Rex L. 1967: Shamanism in South Asia: A Preliminary Survey. *History of Religions* 7: 330 - 347.

Nebesky-Wojkowitz, R. de 1951-52: Ancient Funeral Ceremonies of the Lepchas. *The Eastern Anthropologist* 5,1: 27 - 40.

Opler, M.E. 1958: Spirit Possession in a Rural Area of Northern India, in *Reader in Comparative Religion.* Ed. by Lessa, W. and E. Vogt, Evanston. Quoted by Stanley and Freed 1967.

Rahmann, R. 1959: Shamanistic and Related Phenomena in Northern and Middle India. *Anthropos* 54: 681 - 760.

Rose, H.A. 1919: *A Glossary of the Tribes and Castes of the Punjab and the North-West Frontier Province.* vol. 1. Lahore: Government Printing.

Sharma, P.R. 1970: A Study of the Vayu Cult in a Village of Central Nepal. *Vasudha* 13,8: 31 - 35. (Kathmandu).

Srinivas, M.N. 1965: *Religion and Society among the Coorgs of South India.* 2nd edition. London: Asia Publishing House.

Stanley, A. and R.S. Freed 1967: Spirit Possession as Illness in a North Indian Village, in *Magic, Witchcraft, and Curing.* (American Museum Sourcebooks in Anthropology). Ed. by J. Middleton, pp. 295 - 320. New York: The Natural History Press.

Is the *bombo* an Ecstatic? Some Ritual Techniques of Tamang Shamanism[1]

> "I take it to be an analytic truth about language that whatever can be meant can be said." (Searle 1970: 17).

If we speak of shaman we always automatically associate with this notion the attribute 'ecstatic'. A shaman is in a fit, is possessed, enters a trance, etc. Such statements are based either on our informants' comments or simply on visual and acoustic observation. But, since many ecstatic specialists have to recite ritual texts preceding or during an ecstatic state, one may wonder how such a state is reflected and/or described by the texts in question.

The present paper is an attempt to throw some light on this problem. In part II the question of the shaman's personal identity will be examined, while part III is concerned with the shamanistic "journey". But first some introductory notes on the Tamang shaman and his ritual are necessary.

I

The term *shaman* is used here in a restricted sense, and it should be considered a provisional translation of the Tamang word *bombo*.[2] The *bombo* is a ritual specialist who establishes his contact to the superhuman mainly by means of some ecstatic techniques. With regard to his role, the data on the Tamang *bombo* almost fully cover the admirable definition which Macdonald (1962) gave of the *jhā̃kri* in and around Darjeeling. It suffices, therefore, to specify only the following points:

The *bombo* is always a man. Essentially, he is a healer whom one consults whenever the illness of man or the cattle is believed to be connected with the intervention of the superhuman. This superhuman can be a personalized agent, e.g. some gods of the Hindu or the Tamang pantheon, on the one hand, or the dead who died a premature or violent death or whose funeral rites were not performed in the prescribed manner, on the other. In other cases, -he superhuman is not the direct cause of the trouble; it rather acts through certain "vehicles", e.g. through a witch or through a self-efficient curse formula cast by a (human) enemy. The *bombo* is also specialized in profilaxy, and can be requested, i.a., to act as mediator for a small child whom the parents want to place under the particular protection of a certain god.[3]

Besides the tasks of a healer, the *bombo* can also recover stolen property or ward off the influence emanating from a bad constellation of stars. His casual intervention in the purification ceremonies after childbirth or in some rites of communal importance seems to be a recent development, having its cause in the decay of Tamang lamaism.

The *bombo* is independent of any organisation. Because he is a healer, his clients are (seen apart from the communal ceremonies) individuals or households. Often, the specialist-client relationship tends to be hereditary; on the clients' side it is transmitted from father to son(s), and on the specialists' side from teacher to adept or from father to son (if they are both *bombo*). The fact that the *bombo* mainly deals with individuals and that his tradition is not based on written sources accounts for a considerable flexibility of Tamang shamanism with which it could always integrate elements from other religions, e.g. nowadays from Hinduism.

In spite of this flexibility, the tradition of the *bombo* is esoteric. This is true in the sense at least, that the primary ritual techniques are only known to certain individuals privileged by a particular predisposition and a training. In many instances, the *bombo's* profession may be regarded as hereditary. More exactly, the *bombo's* teacher may be his father, his father's brother or another male agnate, or yet again the *bombo's* tutelaries may be the same as those of one of his ancestors on his father's or mother's side. But this is a statistical frequency rather than a rule. Practically speaking, any Tamang can become a shaman, provided he has had a vocation experience and is prepared to undergo training.

To experience a vocation is called *phamo neppa*, lit. 'tutelary + to become sick'. The symptoms of this "sickness" are virtually identical with what has been described in connection with classical shamanism (cf. Eliade 1957: 22 ff, 43 - 76). Besides certain dreams and visions, temporary and uncontrolled trembling[4] in the whole body is an unmistakeable sign of vocation, and the person affected will soon seek the advice of a *bombo*. The choice of the teacher (*guru*) is often influenced by some practical considerations. Preference can be given, e.g., to a *bombo* among one's own relatives because it is easier to come to terms with a relative about the expenses involved (nRs. 50 - 200 and gifts, mainly cloths). Whomever the candidate has chosen, his request to be taught must not be refused by the *bombo* whom he approaches.

The teaching lasts several months and is done partly at some remote place and partly at night. The *guru's* task consists of three main steps: a) teaching the ritual texts and techniques, b) presenting his adept with some ritual implements, at least with a drum, and c) performing the adept's initiation. It is at the initiation ceremony that the *guru* chooses a tutelary for his adept, by a sort of divination. For this, he enumerates a long series of names - until the adept starts shivering. The tutelary whose name preceded this shivering is the one sought after. - Even after the initiation, the adept's relationship to his *guru* continues to be marked by reverence.

The *bombo's* most important ritual implement is a drum (*ṅa*, cf. Tib. *rṅa*) which closely resembles the drums used by Tamang and Tibetan lamas.[5] It consists of a round-shaped wooden frame covered on both sides with a membrane; of a carved handle, the one end of which is fixed in the frame and the other is pointed; and of a curved drum-stick. For the membrane the leather of the wild goat (Nep. *ghoral*) is used; the frame and the handle are of the wood of a particular tree, and the stick of a particular species of cane. The drum is mostly beaten from the front, i.e. towards body of the *bombo*, or from the side. While reciting a blessing or another text of a "mild" type (*šiway*, cf. Tib. *ži-ba*), the face carved on the upper part of the handle is turned towards the *bombo*. While fighting with the spirits, the *bombo* turns this face towards the same direction in which he himself is looking. Doubtless the main function of the drum is to provide the recitation with an accompaniment. The sound of the membranes is believed to summon or terrify the beings with which the *bombo* deals, while the handle with its pointed end also serves as a weapon to 'pierce' or to 'fix' the evil to be exorcised.

During the seance, the *bombo* does not wear any headdress. His long hair tuft[6] is uncoiled and let hang down his back. He dons a white skirt-like garment which is fastened to his hips with a cloth-belt and reaches to his ankles. This skirt is called *jāmā* (Nep.). On the *bombo's* chest and back, two strings of the Eleocarpus fruit (Nep. *rudrācche*) and two straps (or chains) with small bells attached to it are worn crosswise and in such a way that one string and one strap reach from the left shoulder to the right hip, while the other pair from the right shoulder to the left hip. The strings are called *rudrācche mālā* (Nep.) and the straps *šyaṅšyaṅ rolmo*.[7]

A number of other implements, which cannot be detailed here, are well-known and widely used in lamaist and Hindu rituals, e.g. the ritual dagger (*phurba*, Tib. *phur-bu*), the thigh-bone trumpet (*kaṅliṅ*, Tib. *rkaṅ-gliṅ*), the dough-figures (*tormo*, Tib. *gtor-ma*) representing superhuman or human beings, the trident of Śiva (Nep. *triśul*), etc. Furthermore, all Tamang *bombo* seem to possess the beak and skull of a horn-bill, representing a mythical bird[8] called *khyuṅ* which is believed to be one of their most important helpers while fighting with the spirits.

The seances always take place at night and on the ground floor of the client's house. The *bombo* occupies the side opposite the window, i.e. the "male side", while the other side (which is under normal circumstances the "female side") is reserved for the client's family; the rest of the room is filled by neighbours and onlookers. In front of the *bombo* an altar is erected, the shape and size of which varies according to the occasion. This altar seems to fulfil two functions simultaneously: it is a materialization of, and a bridge to, the Other World. It contains the symbols and attributes of the gods (the *khyuṅ*, the *tormo*, etc.) as well as the offerings and the implements of divination.

For the most part of the seance, the shaman acts in front of the altar. Seen apart from the divination, when he is often standing, and from the more ecstatic parts, during which he is dancing, he sits most of the time cross-legged, with the upper part of his body swinging to the rhythm of the drum and thus making the bells on the strap tinkle. He only leaves the house while expelling the evil or while erecting the symbol of the patient's "life-tree" (cf. below) in the courtyard.

Even though the ritual of the seance is focused on the patient, neighbours and onlookers can also benefit from it. For example, those who want the *bombo* to make a divination for them bring some rice from their homes and deposit it in a leaf-cup on the altar. The shaman, who does not know in advance whose leaf-cup it is, smells or counts the rice-grains from each client in order to identify the latter and to find out the cause of his trouble. As far as humans are concerned, he does not mention any names, neither that of the client nor that of a witch or an enemy. The message of the divination, conveyed by him, has to be deciphered on the basis of approximate indications, such as the direction of the house or place, the sex, etc.

Every Tamang shaman has a répertoire of certain ritual texts which he learnt by heart at the time of his initiation. Different kinds of seánces require different texts. In fact, the texts differ only slightly from each other. While certain syntactic and rhetoric patterns remain more or less unaltered, some sections and some deities' names can be omitted or added according to which kind of ceremony the *bombo* is to perform.[9] The bulk of each text is in the Tamang language and a minor part in Nepali. With few exceptions, both parts are independent from each other. The sections in Nepali are addressed to Mahādew, Kāli (Mai), etc. and to the deities of the Newar pantheon which, nowadays, even Tamang laity know and worship. The sections in Tamang, however, abound with names and places which the average Tamang has "just heard of". Many deities, cult places and Tibetan monasteries cannot be identified or described even by the shamans.

The Tamang shaman's texts pose many problems for an adequate interpretation. They are, first of all, part of an oral tradition and contain a large amount of obsolete vocabulary. Derivations of Tamang words from their correspondants in Tibetan are often hampered by semantic shifts and phonetic changes. Another problem of interpretation arises from the structure of the texts. Sometimes there seems to be no order in them, and rhapsodic "leaps" lead to the interchanging of certain sections or to the confounding of names and events. Often such riddles cannot be solved even by confronting the *bombo* with the tape-recorded text of his own seance. Partly at least, these difficulties may be seen in connection with the shaman's role. He is not only a magician but a poet too - and thus sometimes a swaggerer. He not only heals but also entertains and has in both functions the privilege of enjoying a certain individual freedom for disorder. Furthermore, he is supposed to be a ritual specialist of the "wild" type, *ťhoway* (cf. Tib. *khro-ba*). Thus, when he is intensely dancing or drumming, the people attending the séance often say: *"bombo myoǰi"*, literally 'the shaman has become mad'. A *bombo's* reputation is not only gauged by his success in curing but also by the artistic quality of his performance. He is expected to sing "much" and "nicely". That is, his all-night seances should contain a great variety of text sections, and he should sing with a good voice having a wide range of expressive timbres. There is a saying which compares the lama's work with that of the shaman and which runs in free translation as follows: "The lama proceeds step by step i.e. following a prescribed liturgy , the *bombo* proceeds by his voice i.e. following spontaneous inspiration ."

II

There are two ways of transposing the *bombo* to a higher level of reality (non-ordinary reality) where he is enabled to communicate with the superhuman. One of these ways the shaman shares with other, non-ecstatic ritual specialists; it consists of reciting the *thunrap* or *kerap*.[10] These are stories narrating i.a. the miraculous birth of a deity who is expected to help the shaman or who is believed to be one of the mythical founders of the shaman's institution.

One of these mythical founders is Padmasambhava, the legendary Buddhist missionary in Tibet. By the techniques of *damla tāba*[11] he compelled all evil beings, *noččen*,[12] to content themselves with a scape-goat[13] of the sick, instead of taking the soul of the latter. Today, whenever the shaman presents such a scape-goat for his patient, he has to remind the *noččen* of this obligation. Padmasambhava also "tamed" *(dulba)* the First Shaman, Tũsur Bon, and the present division of ritual tasks between the lama and the *bombo* is a result of Padmasambhava's victory over Tũsur Bon. Tũsur Bon's descendants or disciples (?) are the spiritual ancestors and tutelaries of the Tamang shamans. They are called *phamo* or *gyüpa mēme*, and the spiritual descent line connecting them with the present shamans is denoted by the term *kawa*.[14]

On the conception of *kawa* is based the second way of transposing the shaman to the level of non-ordinary reality. At the beginning of the seance, the shaman severs the ties to this real ancestors by declaring:

> "I am not a shaman born on the earth, but my body was born from [created by] my spiritual mother and my mind was born from [created by] my guru."[15]

It is not the aim of this paper to provide a definition of ecstasy. Suffice it to refer to the etymology of the term and to state that 'ecstasy' necessarily connotes a change of personal identity, on the one hand, and a certain intensification of action by which this change can be attained, on the other. The change of identity consists of, i.a., a widening of sensorial capacities and thus entails a "break-through" from the level of ordinary reality to that of non-ordinary reality.

For the Tamang shaman, this break-through is impossible without a particular energy or will. Consequently, he bids his *phamo*:

> "Descend upon the *bombo* and increase his *ṅargyel* and *ṅoitup*, let blaze his *šerap*."

In modern Tamang, *ṅargyel* means 'pride', 'strong will', and *šerap* something like 'dynamic intellect', as manifested e.g. in quick-wittedness. The word *ṅoitup* seems to be identical with Tibetan *dṅos-grub*, 'value', 'talent'.[16] The use of these terms may be seen in connection with the shaman's "wild" character mentioned above.

A complete change of personal identity, i.e. possession, occurs when the shaman proceeds to divination.[17] Then (though without any obvious sign of being in a somnambulistic state or hypnotically absorbed) he addresses his clients as if a deity spoke through him by declaring:

"Oh you humans, we are [I am] the goddess/god X."

But, as a whole, possession does not play a crucial role in the seances, and seen apart from the divination no evidence of it can be inferred from the text itself. There is no trace of the shaman's personality being fused with, or supplanted by, a deity or another superhuman being. Instead, we find other passages which might be interpreted as indicating a "partial" change of the *bombo's* personal identity.

Let us consider the imagery of the texts:

Repeatedly the shaman promises by turn, to his divine helpers, to the *noččen* and even to his patient:

"gyabla lī̌je khurla, ṅonna čhā̌je teṅla",

literally:

"at the back, [I] will carry [you] on the body,
ahead, [I] will toss [you] with the hands"

The verb *teṅba* means 'to toss in the air and catch a small child' (affectionately). The expression *lǐje khurba*, 'to carry on the body (back)' is reminiscent of the following idioms in modern Tamang: a) 'to carry *(nāba)* an evil spirit', that is, to be closely associated with, or exposed to the influence of, such a spirit, and b) 'to descend on to somebody's back' *(kori yuba)*,[18] i.e. 'to possess'. But to my knowledge, the *bombo* is usually not possessed by a *noččen* or by his patient during the seance. Thus, the metaphor *lǐje khurba/čhā̌je teṅba* seems merely to express an intimate relationship between the shaman and his counterparts. From the viewpoint of physical proximity ("on the back", "with the hands"), this relationship is somewhat similar to possession, while from the viewpoint of the agents, it is different from the latter because the shaman is at the same time a passive "carrier" and an active "player". In difference to possession, here none of the agents gives up his identity, or, in other words, there is no continuity but rather contiguity between them.

Another request or command the *bombo* frequently addresses to his divine helpers and to the *noccen* is:

> *"bondeṅ kha brelkho, lī nolkho, šyaǰik seṅo"*,

literally:

> "come, with the shaman exchange mouth, come join body, make one flesh"

Again, the passage does not express possession. The verbs *brelba* and *nolba* do not mean 'to fuse into a single one' but rather 'to integrate complementary parts into a functioning whole'. Thus, the expression *ñen brelba*[19] denotes the relationship between the exogamous clans which "exchange" wives. The idioms *lī nolba* and *kha nolba* are used for a couple or for friends between whom there is a harmonious relationship characterized by common opinions and interests. (An interpretation of *šyaǰik* is problematic, the expression being not Tamang but Tibetan *ša* + *gčig*).

In sum, this passage seems to describe a particularly intense communication in that the distance between sender and receiver is reduced to a minimum - almost to the point where both of them are identical. This quasi-identity is also demonstrated by the exhortation of a *bir*:[20]

> *"ekkai sāth khelāũ bir"* (Nep.),

literally:

> "let us make play together, bir"

Here the causative *khelāunu* ('to cause to play') appears to be paradoxical because it is the shaman who should make a *bir* "play", i.e. compel it to obey his will - and not the shaman and the *bir* make a third one play. There is cooperation between two agents (subjects), one of whom is simultaneously the object of the action. Practically, we have to do with a zeugma because the verb *khelāũ* shows an incorrect reference to the subject of the sentence.

From other verb forms, again, it clearly emerges that the *bombo* is not acting "in the person" of his divine helpers but as an ally of them. This is the case when he starts fighting against the *noččen* which he has previously identified and localised.

To show some examples of the fighting techniques as reflected by the vocabulary:

- *šyāba*, 'to remove' (a hindrance);
- *dulba*, 'to tame', 'to impose one's will';
- *nemba*, 'to trample down';
- *gelba*, 'to destroy';
- *derkūba*, 'to bring back by chasing', which implies that one goes towards the enemy but attacks him from the rear. This is done e.g. when the *noččen* should be sent into their dough effigies[21] and thus, rendered harmless or paralysed. The term *derkūba* is also used with reference to wild animals in prayers for successful hunting.
- *seṅkulba/seṅkhulba*, lit. 'to make make', i.e. 'to compel to carry out', 'to make happen'.

For each of these tasks the shaman invokes the help of his *phamo* or of the *mābon*[22], a class of fierce deities. The invocation contains either a verb in the imperative second person or, more frequently, a verb form which is equivalent to English 'let us', e.g.:

"šyāni mābon", 'let us go and remove, *mābon*'
"neññi", 'let us go and trample down', etc.

III

An essential component of Eliade's "archaic techniques of ecstasy" is the shaman's journey to the celestial regions or to the underworld (Eliade 1957: 13 -118, 443, i.a.). In the Tamang *bombo's* texts, both, heaven and underworld, are only sporadically mentioned, e.g.:

"pātāl phoriāu māi", 'burst through the underworld and come, *Māi*'

Or:

> *"barkap nañri lungi khorlo nomñi"*, 'let us go and take [the form of] the wind wheel in the atmosphere'

The motif of a shamanistic journey is not lacking, but its destination is not in the heaven or in the underworld.

A considerable part of the texts consists of repeated enumerations of various deities and of the places where the latter are believed to "reside" *(čhāba)* or to "move around" *(tiṅba)*. The names of deities and their places always follow in a certain order: the *bombo* starts from the village where he actually performs the seance and moves then towards the north, to the peaks and lakes of the Himalayas ..., and stops in South Tibet, roughly speaking, in the area around the town Kirong. According to tradition, it is from this area that most of the Western Tamang clans emigrated to Nepal. In the *bombo's* texts, this part of South Tibet and the Himalayas (i.e. parts of the Ganesh and Langtang Himal) are sometimes called *beyül*, 'the hidden country'.[23] It is in this country that Padmasambhava defeated Tũsur Bon and where the first shamans, i.e. the *phamo* of the present ones, have their "residences" or cult places.

At an advanced stage of the seance, the same itinerary is repeated for the third or fourth time but now, when the shaman arrives in *beyül*, he suddenly collapses as if he had fainted. This stage is called *lhari ñiba*, lit. 'to go into the god(s)' or *neri ñiba*, 'to go to the other world'.[24] During *lhari ñiba* the shaman is believed to meet his own *phamo* in a dream-like state. Although the purpose of this meeting could not be exactly explained by the informants, *lhari ñiba* seems to be a culmination of the seance. It confirms the results of what has previously been done by the shaman. In other words, the text sections preceding *lhari ñiba* can be subsumed under the heading "to seek and find", namely the cause of the trouble, while the sections following it are concerned with actions such as the "banning back" of the *noččen* to their places of origin and "blessing" the patient by conferring upon him a sort of vital energy.[25]

There is another pattern of enumeration which reminds one of a journey-like movement in space. This pattern occurs in connection with one of the principal tasks of the *bombo*, namely to search for a) the soul *(pla)* and b) the "life-tree" *(roduṅma)*[26] of the patient; in case the patient is a woman, he has also to search for her c) flower *(mendo)*.

The search must extend over a totality of possibilities within a totality of space and time. Evidently, these totalities can only be represented by economizing synecdoches and metonymies. Thus the space is indicated by the four corners which stand for 'every possible direction', or by polar oppositions, such as

valley - ridege; water - stone; earth - atmosphere.

Time is indicated by, e.g.

"ñemey ñeser naṅri", lit. 'within the light of the sun',
"daway hoser naṅri", lit. 'within the light of the moon'.

The dimension of kinship is indicated by, e.g.,

"phōǰe noppa?", 'does the harm come from the male side?'.
"šyaṅǰe noppa?", 'does the harm come from the female side?' (from the women married in).

The following verbs are used in connection with a search:

- *salba*, 'to look for one thing in an assemblage of others inside a container' (sack, box);
- *pheba*, 'to sort out', 'to find the right one';
- *soysoy-damdam cūba*, 'to sort out' (gradually, e.g. by examining the whole assortment in a shop).

To illustrate these techniques let us take the example of the search for the flower (cf. above).

The word for 'flower' is a euphemism for the genitals of a female. If a woman is barren or has menstruation troubles she is said to suffer from *mendo noṅba*, lit. 'flower' + 'to be spoiled'. The concept underlying the shaman's search for the "flower" is this: There is a mystic linkage between the "flower" of an individual, a particular kind of flower and a particular fairy-like female being called *cen*[27] which (the *cen*) is believed to have caused the trouble. Each (botanical) species of flower is inhabited by, or closely associated with, a certain *cen*. Thus, once the *bombo* has found out the flower corresponding to his patient's "flower", he is able to identify and render harmless the *cen* responsible for the ailment.

To search for one's flower consists of long enumerations of flower names, interspersed with lyrical descriptions of them and of the places where they grow. Often, these enumerations have to be repeated several times - until the shaman feels a slight quivering inside his body: the flower name that precedes this quivering is the flower corresponding to the patient's "flower". The quivering means that the *phamo* or another deity has "grasped" *(cuṅba)* the shaman, signalling the right one from among the many possibilities enumerated.

To what extent are such journeys ecstatic? Evidently, there are ritual journeys which do not require an ecstatic state of those who undertake them.[28] In Tamang religion, for example, similar pars-pro-toto indications and enumerations of deities and places are common to other, non-ecstatic ritual specialists. But what distinguishes them from the *bombo's* journey is, that they are not in connection with a search and do not entail a face-to-face contact with the superhuman, comparable to *lhari ñiba*. Only the shaman is enabled to transcend the level of "the purely verbal" by virtue of his particular energies, such as *ṅoitup* or *ṅargyel* (cf. above).

IV

Only two aspects of the Tamang shaman's ritual techniques have been dealt with in this preliminary paper, namely the question of the personal identity and that of the journey. Because ritual techniques too are actions, the attention has been focused on the verbs. The verbs are the principal components of the imagery in the texts, a great part of which is made up of metaphors and other semantic, or even grammatical, anomalies. These anomalies seem to be an attempt to describe what is essentially "undescribable" in terms of "ordinary" language, namely the ecstatic experience in non-ordinary reality.

Such a study of ritual texts and their imageries is a study in synesthetics too, because we have to do with sensorial descriptions by analogies. But analogies of what? Of what are these descriptions analogies? What is ecstasy or, at least, what does the shaman really experience while reciting? Furthermore, does the use of these descriptions help to induce an ecstatic state in the shaman? The answer lies beyond the scope of this paper but, anyhow, the shaman's texts are neither a series of performative speech acts nor a mere object of esthetic contemplation.

András Höfer

BIBLIOGRAPHY

Allen, N.J. 1974: *The Ritual Journey*. (Paper read at the Symposium on the Anthropology of Nepal, London, SOAS.

Eliade, M. 1957: *Schamanismus und archaische ekstasetechnik*. Zürich, Stuttgart: Rascher.

Jäschke, H.A. 1949: *A Tibetan-English Dictionary*. London: Routledge and Kegan Paul (reprint).

Macdonald, A.W. 1962: Notes prelinaires sur quelques *jhā̃kri* du Muglān. *Journal Asiatique* 250: 107 - 139.

Macdonald, A.W. 1966: Les Tamang vus par l'un d'eux. *L'Homme* janvier-mars: 27 - 58.

Nebesky-Wojkowitz, R. de 1956: *Oracles and Demons of Tibet. The Cult and Iconography of the Tibetan Protective Deities*. The Hague: Mouton.

Searle, J.R. 1970: *Speech Acts. An Essay in the Philosophy of Language*. Cambridge: Cambridge University Press (reprint).

Turner, R.L. 1965: *A Comparative and Etymological Dictionary of the Nepali Language*. London: Routledge and Kegan Paul (2nd ed.).

NOTES

1. The material was collected in 1970-72 in the central part of Dhading district, Bagmati zone. The group studied belongs to the Western Tamang which are linguistically and culturally somewhat different from the Tamang living to the east and north-east of the Kathmandu Valley. The field work was generously sponsored by the Deutsche Forschungsgemeinschaft. - For Nepali and Tibetan, the methods by Turner and, resp., Pelliot are used. Tamang is rendered in a simplified transcription. ť and ď = alveolo-retroflex, č [tʃ], c [ts], š [ʃ], ǰ [dʒ], ṅ [ŋ], ñ [ɲ], ā [a:], / [a:], i [i:], ū [u:], ō [o:], ē [e:].

2. cf. Tib. *bon-po*.

3. Nep. *phulmā rākhnu*, a ceremony which is connected with a vow.

4. *čhekpa*. This verb seems to be restricted in its use to "holy" trembling, in difference to "profane" trembling (cold, fever).

5. cf. Nebesky-Wojkowitz 1956: plate IX. - The meaning of the carvings on the handle could not be adequately explained by the informants.

6. *ralbo*, (cf. Tib. *ral-pa*, 'long hair', 'mane'), Nep. *laṭṭa/laṭṭo*.

7. cf. Tib. *gšaṅ*, which is the name of a low, broad bell carried by Bon deities (Nebesky-Wojkowitz 1956: 19); *rolmo* Tib. *rol-mo*, 'music', 'musical instrument'.

8. Tib. *khyuṅ*, often identified with the Garuda bird of Indian mythology. cf. Nebesky-Wojkowitz 1956: 13, 256 - 258.

9. The textual differences seem to be greater between the repertoires of the various "schools".

10. *ťhuṅrap*, *kerap*, cf. Tib. *'khruṅ-ba*, resp. *skye-ba*, 'to be born and *rabs*, 'series', 'succession'.

11. Tib. *dam*, 'solemn promise', 'oath', and *'debs-pa*, 'to cast'; cf. also Tib. *dam-čan*, 'bound by oath' (i.a. Nebesky-Wojkowitz 1956: 155).

12. Tib. *gnod-čan*, 'harmful'.

13. *lud*, Tib. *glud*.

14. ? <Tib. *ka-ba*, 'pillar' (symbolically). - With regard to *phamo*, cf. Tib. *pha-mes*, 'ancestors' or *pha-ma*, 'parents'; *gyüpa*, Tib. *brgyud*, 'lineage', etc.

15. The terms 'spiritual mother' and *'guru'* refer here to the *phamo*.

16. For *dṅos-grub* Jäschke (1949: 474) also gives 'the supernatural powers of a saint'. - *ṅargyel*, Tib. *ṅa-rgyal; šerap*, Tib. *šes-rab* 'wisdom', etc.

17. called *saldap*, Tib. *gsal btab-pa*, 'to meditate', etc.

18. cf. Nep. *āṅmā caṛhnu*, 'to possess', lit. 'to climb on the back.

19. cf. Tib. *gñen* + *'brel-ba; ñen brelba* was rendered by Nep. *ohar-dohar garnu;* Turner (1965: 63) gives for *ohar-dohar* 'coming and going', 'trade', 'commerce'.

20. According to Turner's Dictionary the term *bir* has two meanings: 1) wild boar, 2) brave man or hero.

21. *linga*, Tib. *liṅ-ga*.

22. ? < Tib. *dmag-dpon*, 'commander', etc.

23. Tib. *sbas-yul*, cf. also Macdonald 1966: 46.

24. The term *ne* is also used with reference to the abode of the dead. - About collapse and unconsciousness *after* the journey in classical shamanism cf. e.g. Eliade 1957: 185 - 203.

25. The "blessing" is called *che wangur*, from Tib. *che*, 'life' + *dbaṅ skur-ba*, 'to confer power'.

26. Every individual is linked with a particular kind of tree which symbolizes, so to speak, his spiritual backbone. This belief resembles the concept of the *bla-šin*, lit. 'soul' + 'tree', in Tibet (cf. Nebesky-Wojkowitz 1956: 481; Jäschke 1949: 383).

27. *cen*, etymologically identical, but conceptually somewhat different from Tib. *bcan* (cf. Nebesky-Wojkowitz 1956: 627 Index).

28. Allen (1974), for example, distinguishes between verbal journeys (which are chanted), danced ("ecstatic') and actually travelled ones.

La Fête des Clans chez les Thākālis. Spre-lo (1968)

(avec prèsentation d'un film)

On ne peut manquer d'être frappé par le dynamisme qui est le propre de l'ethnie Thākāli. Les Thākāli ont su depuis plus de 100 ans s'adapter aux conditions politiques et économiques tout en conservant leur forte individualité.

Si le milieu naturel paraît accueillant lorsqu'on pénètre dans la zone qu'ils occupent au-dessus de 2000m d'altitude dans la vallée de la Kali Gandaki, on ne peut prétendre en même temps qu'il soit riche; cultures de sarrasin et d'orge à faible rendement ne permettant pas de vivre l'année durant. Mais les Thākāli avaient à leur portée un moyen qu'ils ont su exploiter à fond: leur situation géographique, entre le haut plateau tibétain avec le sel des lacs du Changthang, et la production de laine des ovins élevés par les Drogpa, en aval les vallées népalaises productives de grain dont les populations tibétaines manquaient.

Ils ont aussi tiré partie de la situation politique. Les rois du Népal, aprés l'unification du pays, avaient certes des problémes pour assurer un contrôle effectif de l'ensemble du pays (il fallait quinze jours pour se rendre par la piste de Kathmandu à Tukucha); les notables Thākāli ont su capter leur confiance et devenir responsable du contrôle des échanges dans la Haute Kali Gandaki.

Ce dynamisme se traduit aujourd'hui par une scolarisation trés poussée, une émigration vers les centres commerciaux les plus importants et une prise de conscience des problèmes de la nation népalaise; D.B. Bista a mis en valeur ce fait dans une analyse en 1970.

A côté de ce "modernisme" et au fur et à mesure de ma connaissance de la culture des Thākāli, j'ai pu me rendre compte de l'importance, dans la vie de tous les jours, de la complexité de leurs croyances et de leurs légendes.

C'est lors de mon premier séjour en pays Thāk, en 1960, que, tout à fait fortuitement, j'assistais à une réunion au cours de laquelle il était question de la "fête des quatre clans". Elle avait lieu tous les douze ans, l'année du singe, *spre-lo*, dans le cycle tibétain (les Thākāli utilisaient encore en 1960 le calendrier lunaire tibétain qui a été vite abandonné au profit du calendrier népalais.[1] Cette fête s'échelonnait sur une longue période et, pour l'organiser, les membres des clans devaient contribuer, par une somme d'argent, à un dépôt de type bancaire, *dhikur*, géré par les responsables du culte des divinités protectrices du clan.[2]

Mais tout cela apparaissait très complexe et marginal par rapport aux pratiques religieuses "classiques et visibles" en pays Thāk, c'est-à-dire le Lamaïsme essentiellement dans la forme de l'ordre non réformé Nyingmapa.

Au cours de missions successives, les données se sont précisées, d'une part grâce à l'amitié d'un intercesseur (appelé *drom* en Thākāli le *drom* du village de Khanti, d'autre part par l'observation de rituels dédiés aux divinités ancêtres auxquels j'ai pu assister.[3]

En 1967, au cours d'une nouvelle réunion, j'ai pu prendre connaissance de l'organisation de la fête; l'inquiétude était grande car de nombreux Thākāli avaient émigré à Pokhara, Bhairava et Kathmandu: allaient-ils venir? Une décision ancienne précisait bien que tous les Thākāli devaient obligatoirement participer au *spre-lo*. Une bonne nouvelle vint de Kathmandu: dans la capitale, un Comité de fête, *samiti*, s'était constitué qui, non seulement collectait des fonds, mais se proposait de prendre en charge une partie de la responsabilité matérielle.

C'est en mai 1968 que je reçus l'invitation pour participer à la fête du *spre-lo* fixée au mois de Pus du calendrier népalese, c'est-à-dire à la fin du mois de décembre 1968 de notre calendrier.

L'ethnie Thākāli se compose de quatre clans exogames, chacun se subdivisant en un certain nombre de lignées; chaque clan a une divinité tutélaire appelée *lha* en thākāli,[4] et un intercesseur, le *drom*, responsable du culte de cette divinité. En outre, chaque divinité a un prêtre, *panre*,[5] qui va jouer un rôle primordial au *spre-lo*. Ce sont ces quatre divinités qui se manifestent tous les douze ans, s'éjournant pendant 18 jours avec les vivants qui les vénèrent.

L'origine des Thākāli et de leurs clans est relatée dans des mythes et légendes dont nous donnons ici un résumé.[6]

"Dans le royaume de Sinja[7] se dressait un arbre sur lequel quatre oiseaux avaient l'habitude de se percher. Un jour, l'arbre fut abattu et les quatre oiseaux s'envolèrent.

L'un d'eux partit vers le Nord, au Tibet, et devint un yak; les trois autres s'envolèrent vers le Sud et devinrent "l'éléphant joyau", "le monstre marin" et "la lionne blanche des glaciers". Ils se cherchèrent pendant de nombreuses années et se retrouvèrent enfin dans la vallée de la Kali Gandaki, au pied du Dhaulagiri.

Les ancêtres des quatre clans Thākāli sont les incarnations de ces animaux mythiques".

Un autre mythe précise:

"Quatre oiseaux venus de Nubtsen[8] se posèrent à Sinjapati sur an arbre à quatre cimes. Un jour, en plein été, l'une des cimes se dessecha et l'oiseau noir qui y était perché s'envola en direction du Nord. A partir de ce jour là, les vaches ne donnèrent plus de lait, le lait ne caillait plus, le beurre rancissait.

Les hommes se demandèrent pourquoi les vaches ne donnaient plus de lait: l'arbre dont la cime était morte en était-il la cause? Vexés et furieux, les hommes abattirent l'arbre et les trois oiseaux s'envolèrent vers l'Est, le Sud et l'Ouest. Du tronc de l'arbre jaillit du lait. Par divination, les hommes apprirent que les oiseaux étaient les divinités protectrices de leur clan et qu'ils les retrouveraient en allant en direction de l'Est, au pied de la montagne sacrée de Muligang".[9]

"De la racine d'un arbre à quatre troncs, le tronc du côté Nord se dessecha et l'oiseau qui était perché sur l'une de ses branches s'envola en direction du Nord.

Près du Mont Kailas, à côté du lac Mapham, une nonne était en train de tisser une pièce de laine. Il faisait très chaud et la nonne avait soif; tout à coup, trois grelons tombèrent du ciel: elle les avala et se trouve bientôt enceinte....Se cachant de ses amies, ell mit au monde un petit yak qu'elle jeta dans le lac Mapham. Les divinités *lha* et *klu* qui y résidaient nourrirent le yak qui, en un jour, eut des cornes d'un mois et, en un mois, des cornes d'un an, tant il devenait grand et fort.

Le yak partit vers le Nord, jusqu'aux lacs, réserves de sel, puis à Lhasa, enfin, rendit visite à la divinité Lha-yak Kongpo dans la région éloignée du Kongpo.[10] A la fin de son voyage, il revint en pays Thāk pour y rencontrer ses trois frères près de la cascade de *Yom-gyü*.[11] A mesure qi'il descendait dans la vallée, la route devint difficile et dangereuse, il dut s'aider d'un pic pour couper les arbres et amènager la piste. C'est alors qu'un incident provoqua la mort du yak: les habitants de Marpha, village situé en amont de pays Thāk, décidèrent de le tuer. C'est pourquoi ceux de Marpha doivent offrir tous les douze ans la tête d'un yak de 3 ans aux Thākāli".

"Après s'être envolé de Sinja, l'oiseau qui donna naissance à la lionne blanche des glaciers vint se percher sur un arbre à proximité du Muligang. Le masque de cette divinité est fait du bois de cet arbre.

L'oiseau, qui devint plus tard "l'éléphant joyau", vint tout d'abord à Dolpo-Charka puis s'aventura vers le Sud, mais il se perdit dans la jungle de Palati où les habitants, des Magar, ne lui vinrent pas en aide; devenu éléphant, il revint vers le pays Thak.

Les quatre divinités se sont retrouvées à *Yom-gyü*, à l'entrée du pays Thak".

La légende du monstre marin est identique à celle de l'éléphant, mais comprend en outre le récit de la tentative d'extermination de ce clan par les trois autres et l'aventure de Mom Lasarpi et de son petit-fils, Kontso Prum.

"Le clan *sal-qui* était tout puissant et les trois autres clans décidèrent de tuer tous les membres du clan souverain. Par ruse, ils capturèrent les *sal-qui* et les précipitèrent dans la Kali Gandaki. Il n'y eut que deux rescapés, une vieille grand-mère, Mom Lasarpi et son petit-fils Kontso Prum. Tous deux se réfugièrent dans la forêt voisine. Les clans prirent la statue de la divinité tutélaire pour y mettre le feu. Cette divinité, gravement offensée, bloqua la Kali Gandaki prés de Gopang, au lieu dit Gyanbar, au Sud du confluent de la Kali Gandaki et du torrent de Gura Sangphug. Toute la vallée Thak fut inondée. "Les clans, réalisant leur mauvaise action, supplièrent Mom Lasarpi de sauver la vallée.

La vieille exigea alors un grand territoire pour son clan, puis elle chanta un chant en appelant sa divinité tutélaire. Le masque apparût à la surface de l'eau qui s'écoula à nouveau". Ce masque en bois de genévrier est présenté tous les douze ans lors de la fête du *spre-lo.*"

Les clans Thakali et les divinites tutelaires

Nom de clan (Thākāli)	Nom du clan actuel	Nom de l'ancêtre	Animal associé au clan	Ancêtre mythique	Couleur associée	Orient élément associé
čhös-gi	*gau-can*	*Aniram*	"éléphant joyau" *Langba norbu*	mâle frère aîné *ajo*	rouge épée	Ouest[13] feu *me*
phur-gi	*bhaṭṭa-can*	*Damchen Tamdru*	"yak mâle produit par lui-même" *yawa rangchön*	mâle frère cadet *ale*	noir pic	Nord vent *rlün*
sal-gi	*tula-can*	*Samle-cham*	"monstre marin" *Chusing gyalmo*	femelle soeur cadette *phijang*	vert bident	Sud eau *chu*
thin-can	*šer-can*	*Tragpa Gyaltsen*	"lionne blanche des glaciers" *Ganyla Senga Karmo*	femelle soeur cadette *phijang*	blanc hache	Est terre *sa*

L'éléphant joyau est maître du feu.
Le yak mâle est maître du vent.
Le monstre marin est maître de l'eau.
La lionne blanche des glaciers est maître des avalanches.

Le culte aux divinités des quatre clans

La fête qui a lieu tous les douze ans s'inscrit dans un calendrier au cours duquel plusiers rites doivent être accomplis.

Ainsi, dès que la fête *spre-lo* est terminée, les responsables des quatre clans préparent la fête suivante en précisant le montant des contributions en argent à verser par chaque famille Thakali (il avait été prévu une somme de 12,000 roupies pour la fête de 1968).

Tous les ans, au mois de *to-ren-la* (le 1° mois du calendrier religieux Thakali), le 3ème jour (*tsa be som*), jour où furent édifiés les temples des quatre divinités, les *panre*, accompagnés d'un assistant portant le vase sacré *bumpa*, se rendent au sactuaire et y offrant des lampes à beurre.

Trois ans avant l'année du singe, dans l'année du cheval (en 1966, Bikram Samvat 2022) mois de *to-ren-la*, les quatre *panre* se rendent au Martsangyü[14] pour se purifier, puis font le tour des 13 villages Thakali, passant de maison en maison; c'est le *sö-sö lawa*. Le *panre* qui représente le yak et qui porte un collier des cloches, pénètre dans la maison par le toit terrasse sur lequel on a tracé un carré avec de la terre rouge et placé à proximité un récipient de bière. Par trois fois, il donne un coup de pic sur le toit et sur la poutre maîtresse, signe de bénédiction; il a le droit de prendre les victuailles qu'il veut en les frappant de son pic. On considère cette visite des *panre* comme un acte de bon augure.

C'est à ce moment là que les habitants de Marpha sont obligés, selon la coutume, d'envoyer un petit yak au pâturage. Ce yak sera ensuite remis au clan du yak, *Phur-qi*, au début de la fête du *spre-lo* (en fait, la tête de l'animal.

L'année du singe, *spre-lo*, pendant le onzième mois lunaire, se déroule une grande fête dédiée aux divinités tutélaires. Elle dure 18 jours et débute par le bain rituel des desservants des divinités, les *panre*.

Le *panre* du "yak produit par lui-même", *Yawa ranqchön*, divinité tutélaire des *bhatta-can*, est habillé de noir et porte à la taille une ceinture de grelots. C'est près de Khanti, le premier village Thakali, que le *panre* va rencontrer sa divinité tutélaire sous la forme d'une tête de yak qui sera portée devant lui tout au long de la fête.

Pénétrant dans Gopang, le plus ancien village de la vallée, le *panre bhatta-can* doit manger neuf poignées de sel et distribuer le reste comme bénédiction aux habitants.

Les trois autres animaux mythiques sont représentés par des masques gardés dans de petits temples au-dessus des villages de Gopang et Larjung. Ils sont purifiés pendant trois jours dans une source sacrée au pied du Dhaulagiri (cette source a la particularité de n'être en eau qu'une fois tous les douze ans, au moment du bain rituel des masques).

Le 5ème jour de cette retraite, les *panre* vont chercher les trois masques dans la source pour les apporter à la gompa de Nakung où Lama Kansa entreprend leur restauration.

Lang-ba norbu, "éléphant joyau", divinité des *gau-can*, est de couleur rouge,
Chusing gyalmo, "monstre marin", divinité des *tula-can* de couleur verte,
Senge Karmo, "lionne des glaciers", divinité des *ser-can*, de couleur blanche.

Le 11ème jour, on entreprend la construction des sanctuaires, (sorte de petite cabane à armature de bambou). Dans l'après-midi, lorsque la tête est fixée au "corps", l'animal mythique prend vie et chacun vient demander sa bénédiction. Au soir commence la reconstitution du cheminement au long de l'itinéraire mythique parcouru par les quatre divinités, il s'effectue en huit jours sur une distance d'une dizaine de kilomètres.

Chaque déplacement débute par une triple circumambulation et se poursuit en évitant soigneusement les chemins parcours par les hommes.

Chaque soir, les Thakali sollicitent la bénédiction des divinités. Par la voix d'hommes des clans, elles dialoguent et se livrent à une satire de la société.

Le 13ème jour de la fête, veille de la pleine lune, le sacrifie un bélier blanc aux *ke*, divinités des ancêtres du clan.

Le lendemain, jour de la pleine lune, les divinités arrivent à Kyungkor près d'un arbre sacré. Durant tout l'après-midi, des personnages travestis miment de manière comique des scènes de la vie de chaque jour, les labours, le filage, la chasse ....

A la suite d'une lutte fratricide, les membres du clan *tula-can* avaient été pratiquement exterminés et en signe de repentir, les trois autres clans l'honorent tout particulièrement l'avant-dernier jour de la fête. Le *panre tula-can* raconte une fois encore la légende de l'origine de son clan.

A la fin du 18ème jour, les masques sont déposés dans un coffre avant de regagner leurs temples. La tête de yak est suspendue au-dessus d'une grotte. Quant aux grelots, il faudra attendre douze ans pour qu'ils tintent de nouveau.

Tandis que cette fête se déroule dans le pays Thāk, les femmes offrent des centaines de lampes à beurre dans tous les temples de la vallée, offrandes interprétés comme un apaisement pour les âmes des morts.

Ce n'est pas notre propos d'analyser ici en détail tous les aspects de cette symbolique complexe des rites et du cérémonial mais de donner l'ossature des deux ciné-documents réalisés en pays Thak à l'occasion du *spre-lo*. Montés dans leur longeur de toutes les prises de vues, ils répondent à la nécessité de conserver en archive un certain nombre de détails de cérémonies, mouvements de foule, gestes de vénération qui ne peuvent être qu'imparfaitement traduits par l'écrit et qui ne se répèteront peut être plus.

Le premier document présente en 45 minutes les principales phases de la fête de *spre-lo*, le second, d'une durée de 10 minutes, le sacrifice à la divinité des ancêtres par le *drom*.

Chronologie de la fête

1° jour

Pus 7 B.S. 2025/21.12.1968 - 11ème mois lunaire, 2ème jour de la quinzaine claire (mois de *prum-la* dans le calendrier Thākāli). Bain rituel des *panre* dans le Martsangyü.

2eme jour

Pus 8/22.12.1968 - Après avoir revêtu des ornements, les quatre *panre* et leurs aides se dirigent vers Khanti.
Danse du *panre* du clan du yak, offrandes aux trois autres *panre*. Distribution du sel par le *panre bhatta-can* (yak) à Gopang, les trois *panre gau-can, tula-can, ser-can,* portent les masques des divinités protectrices au torrent où les masques vont rester

pendant 3 jours.

3eme jour

Pus 9/23.12.1968 - Les *panre* sont dans la grotte Pungkyuṅgpu, ils lisent les légendes des quatre clans et de leurs divinités protectrices.

4eme jour

Pus 10/24.12.1968 - Les *panre* sont toujours dans la grotte, lisant les récits des divinités des clans. Offrandes de lampes à beurre par les villageois.

5eme jour

Pus 11°25.12.1968. Dans l'après-midi, trois *panre* vont chercher les masques de la lionne, du monstre marin et de l'éléphant, et les portent à le *gompa* de Nakung où ils sont déposés pour être peints par Lama Kansa.

6eme jour

Pus 12/26.12.1968. Lama Kansa commence à préparer avec de la terre glaise puis peindre les masques des trois divinités. Les *panre* lisent toujours les histoires des divinités des clans dans la grotte.

7eme jour

Pus 13/27.12.1968. Peinture des masques, lecture des récits des clans par les *panre*.

8eme jour

Pus 14/28.12.1968. Peinture des masques, lecture des récits par les *panre*.

9eme jour

Pus 15/29.12.1968. (Calendrier tibétain 11ème mois, 10ème jour). Peinture des masques et fabrication des ornements pour les scénettes. Lecture des récits des clans. Jour de prière dans les *dgon-pa* de Gophang, offrandes de lampes à beurre dans les temples du pays Thāk.

10eme jour

Pus 16/30.12.1968. Les masques sont prêts. Lecture des récits des clans. A la *dgon-pa* de Na-ri Jo-bo, lecture de textes bouddhiques. Réunion des hommes du conseil pour décider de la construction des quatre sanctuaires des clans.

11eme jour

Pus 17/31.12.1968. Confection des quatre sanctuaires (en forme de petites maisons). Chaque clan décore son sanctuaire avec les couleurs du clan.
Distribution d'insignes aux couleurs des clans.
Les *panre gau-can*, *tula-can* et *ser-can* vont chercher les masques de leurs divinités, elles rencontrent le yak près des sanctuaires, le *panre bhatta-can* (du clan du yak) est en transes.
Les masques sont fixés aux sanctuaires, les hommes de chaque clan soulèvent le leur et lui font faire trois fois le tour du champ avant de prendre la direction de *Gaṅgri*.

12eme jour

Pus 18/1.01.1969. Transport des sanctuaires de *Gaṅgri* à *Sonam bianśi*; bénédiction demandée aux masques et présentation d'écharpes de cérémonie.

13eme jour

Pus 19/2.01.1969. Cérémonie propitiatoire par le *ḍrom*, sacrifice d'un bélier blanc au-dessus de *Sonam bianśi*.
Déplacement des sanctuaires de *Sonam bianśi* à Larjung.

14eme jour

Pus 20/3.01.1969. 11ème mois lunaire, 15ème jour (plein lune).
Une foule nombreuse arrive à Larjung.
Déplacement des sanctuaires de Larjung à *Kyungkor*; à midi les sanctuaires sont déposés à *Kyungkor* après avoir fait trois fois la circumambulation de l'arbre. Bénédictions et offrandes se succèdent.
Des scènes jouées par les jeunes de la communauté évoquent la chasse, les travaux agricoles, le mariage Thākāli...

15eme jour

Pus 21/4.01.1969. Déplacement des sanctuaires de *Kyuṅgkor* à un nouvel emplacement à une centaine de mètres vers le Sud.

16eme jour

Pus 22/5.01.1969. Déplacement des sanctuaires à *Kyoṅg*.

17eme jour

Pus 23/6.01.1969. Déplacement des sanctuaires de *Kyoṅg* à *Dhodja Tsobregyung*; ils franchissent à deux reprises la Kali Gandaki

pour arriver à *Dhodja* où les sanctuaires sont déposés.
Le *panre tula-can* lit le récit de la divinité du clan puis les assistants lui offrent des écharpes de cérémonie qui ornent son turban.
Distribution de bénédiction aux assistants.

18eme jour

Pus 24/7.01.1969. Déplacement des sanctuaires à *Gombo'u* (grotte du Gomba).
De nouveau les porteurs sont obligés de suivre le lit de la rivière puis déposent les sanctuaires dans un champ sous la falaise.
Les sanctuaires sont détruits, les masques enlevés et portés jusqu'à la grotte où ils sont enfermés dans un coffre.
Le masque du yak est fixé sous un petit rocher au-dessus de la grotte, le *panre bhatta-can* ayant confectionné auparavant une échelle à neuf échelons.

La signification de ces mythes et de ces légendes échappe à bien des Thākāli aujourd'hui. Les plus jeunes ne parlent déjà plus la langue de l'ethnie et les anciens qui connaissaient la coutume *(lugs-so)* sont de moins en moins nombreux.

Je dois remercier particulièrement les membres des clans Thākāli qui m'ont accepté parmi eux, le drom de Khanti, Govindman Ser-can, Sankarman Ser-can, Omkar Gau-can, Mangalsing Tula-can, Taku Prasad Tula-can, Lama Kansa, Sans eux, cette contribution n'aurait pu être réalisée.

Corneille Jest

NOTES

1. Calendrier traditionnel en pays Thāk

Calendrier Agricole	Calendrier tibétain (divination)		Calendrier tibétain usuel
1 *a-gen-la*	*'brug-zla*	dragon	12ème lune
2 *to-ren-la*	*sbrul-zla*	serpent	1ère lune
3 *ku-bi-la*	*rta-zla*	cheval	2ème lune
4 *lu-la*	*lug-zla*	mouton	3ème lune
5 *pre-la*	*spre-zla*	singe	4ème lune
6 *če-la*	*bya-zla*	oiseau	5ème lune
7 *khyi-la*	*khyi-zla*	chien	6ème lune
8 *phag-la*	*phag-zla*	cochon	7ème lune
9 *pib-la*	*byi-zla*	souris	8ème lune
10 *laṅ-la*	*glan-zla*	éléphant	9ème lune
11 *tab-la*	*stag-zla*	tigre	10ème lune
12 *prum-la*	*yos-zla*	lièvre	11ème lune

to-ren-la est le premier mois *(lo samba)* du calendrier religieux thākāli c'est-à-dire le "nouvel an du roi" tibétain.

phag-la: mois du "milieu de l'été".

Les mois qui sont habituellement numérotés de 1 à 12 sont désignés par le nom d'un des animaux du cycle des douze ans pour la divination (comme au Tibet).

2. D. Messerschmidt a fait une importante recherche sur ce moyen de crédit, voir Bibliographie.

3. Cf. C. Jest, Cérémonie aux ancêtres *Ke*, *Objets et Mondes*, 1969.

4. En tibétain, *lha*.

5. L'origine de ce terme est inconnue de mes informateurs. Il

est utilisé par les Chepang pour désigner leur médium.

6. Une analyse détaillée des mythes et des légendes Thākāli est en cours et doit être publiée ultérieurement.

7. Sinja, ancienne capitale de royaume est située au Nord-Ouest de Jumla, dans l'Ouest du Népal.

8. Venant de l'Ouest.

9. En tibétain classique *mu-le-gaṅs-ri*, nom donné au Dhaulagiri.

10. Dans le Kongpo, province du Tibet, à l'Est de Lhasa, se situe la grande montagne pélerinage de Kongpo Tsari, où l'on doit se rendre l'année du singe.

11. *Yom-gyü* signifie confluent de deux torrents en Thākāli.

12. En tibétain classique: *glaṅ-ba nor-bu*
gyag-pho raṅ-byuṅ
čhu-srin rgyal-mo
gaṅs-la seṅ-ge dkar-mo

13. Ces divinités Thākāli peuvent être rapprochées des divinités du lamaïsme, les *čhos-skyoṅ*(sk. *dharmapāla*).

14. Le torrent du Martsangyü qui naît des glaciers des Nilgiri est sacré, c'est près de sa source que se retirent les *drom* pour leur initiation.

BIBLIOGRAPHIE

Bista (D.B.) - The political innovation of upper Kali Gandaki. *Man*, Vol. 6, n° 1, March 1971.

Haimendorf (C. von Fürer) Caste, concepts and status. Distinctions in buddhist communities of Western Nepal, in *Cast and Kin in Nepal*, India and Ceylon, London 1966, pp. 140-160.

Jest (C.) Les Thākāli, note préliminaire concernant une ethnie du Nord-Ouest du Népal. *L'Ethnographie*, 1964-1965, pp. 26-49.

Jest (C.) Chez les Thakali, cérémonie consacrée aux ancêtres du clan. *Objets et Mondes*, IX, 1, 1969, pp. 59-68

Messerschmidt (D.) Dhikur: rotating credit associations in Nepal. *IX° Congres International des Sciences Anthropologiques et Ethnologiques*, Chicago, 1973.

Parallel Trade and Innovation in Central Nepal: The Cases of the Gurung and Thākāli Subbas Compared

Introduction

A prize for tribal entrepreneurship in the Nepal Himalaya would likely go, by dint of research published so far, to the traders of Thak Khola - the dynamic Thakalis.[2] Their history of economic success in the trans-Himalayan salt and commodities trade and their political ascendancy in the upper Kali Gandaki River region is generally described in the literature as unique and entirely unprecedented (Bista 1971; Fürer-Haimendorf 1966; see also Messerschmidt 1973). But the heretofore unaccounted activities of certain entrepreneurs of the Gurung tribe in Bhot Khola region, directly east of Thak Khola, reveal an altogether new perspective. Not only do questions of significant parallel development between Gurung and Thakali leaders, called *subba* (Nep.), arise, but new data on a successful and far-reaching challenge to Thakali supremacy in west-central Nepalese-Tibetan trade may very well alter the ethnohistorical record of both tribes so far. This paper relates the ascendancy of the first Gurung Subba, Man Lal, and his successors, and compares it with the recorded history of the Thakali Subbas.

The Subba System

The Subba system flourished during the first half of the twentieth century when the Tibetan salt trade was at its height in Nepal. 'Subba' was an hereditary title given to the chief administrator of a region appointed by the central government in Kathmandu. The system initially had a dual purpose: to regulate and control customs on northern trade, and to secure the allegiance of the northern border peoples. By this system, customs contracts (*thekka*, Nep.), which allowed a monopoly over trade in a region, and the title of Subba were jointly awarded to the highest bidder, or to a favoured entrepreneur politician.

> Customs contracts were usually auctioned for periods of three years, and the highest bidder appointed as contractor was awarded the title of *subba*, a designation otherwise reserved for the lowest rank of gazetted government servants. In the case of Thak Khola, an area remote from any of the centres of regular administration, the customs contractor was also invested with the power of a magistrate. As such he wielded political authority in addition to the enormous economic influence derived from his monopoly of the salt trade, and for more than half a century the customs contractors were the

dominating force in Thak Khola.
Fürer-Haimendorf, 1974

The symbol of the Subba's office was a golden crown. Bista (1971) writes that the Subba "acquired the prerequisite for economic and political power: an economic monopoly, a title with influence, and the apparent support of the central government."[3] In both Bhot Khola and Thak Khola the Subbas came to dominate salt trade and regional politics and were agents of significant innovation and change in society and culture. Over time, the Subba system was expanded to accommodate customs contracts on trade at the Indian border in Nepal's southern Terai region as well.

The Setting

'Thak Khola' and 'Bhot Khola' are local names for two high inner valley regions of west Nepal near the Tibetan frontier. (See Maps 1 and 2). They encompass the upper reaches of the Kali Gandaki and the Marsiangdi Rivers, respectively. Both regions have developed as important thoroughfares in north-south trade with Tibet. There are several such high riverine regions in the Nepal Himalaya; they channel social intercourse, communications, and trade, and serve, in effect, as contact zones between the Nepalese and Tibetan culture areas.[4]

Thak Khola, the 'River of Thak', lies north of the Himalayan axis and includes a large portion of the upper Kali Gandaki River in the administrative district of Mustand. It is the home of the Thakali people, agro-pastoralists and traders of Tibetan cultural affinities who speak a Tibeto-Burman dialect. Their immediate neighbours are the closely related people of Panchgaun and several Bhotia groups living in Baragaun (Kag) and Mustang proper (Lo).[5]

As an inner valley of the Himalaya, Thak Khola has certain peculiarities of climate - low rainfall, especially; the effects on local landscape and livelihood are important. The valley is approached from the south along the river route through an abrupt and short gorge above the lower hills. The gorge dramatically bisects the Dhaulagiri and Annapurna Himalayan massifs. The village of Dana, the former trade and customs outpost, is located below the gorge; Ghasa lies immediately above it. The high valley of Thak, stretching north from Ghasa as far as Jomosom, is broad and level, dry, and severely windblown. It lies in the rainshadow of the Himalaya and its semi-aridity makes it amenable to year-round travel by man and pack-animals. Yak trains are the common form of transport between Thak and the border passes (at 6200 meters) above the border outpost of Mustang proper.

The Kali Gandaki River has long been important in the Tibetan trade. Tukche (2600 meters) located on the river is the major town of Thak Khola. It was developed during the last century as a trading mart and caravanasarie by the Thakali Subbas and entrepreneurs. As recently as the late 1950's, Tibetan salt was bartered here for Nepalese grain in large amounts.[6]

The Thakali people have been the subjects of at least nine recent anthropological articles, most of which deal with certain changes in tribal economic, political, and religious life earlier this century (Bista 1967, 1971; Fürer-Haimendorf 1966, 1967, 1974; Iijima 1960, 1963; Jest 1966; Messerschmidt 1973). Many of these authors discuss the apparent unequalled uniqueness of the Thakali phenomenon in place, time and personality. At least three factors emerge which have encouraged Thakali innovation and change: (1) their strategic location on the upper Kali Gandaki trade route, (2) international relations with Tibet which brought the Nepal government into intimate contact with the Thakali and neighbouring Bhotia people whose loyalties it sought to secure, and (3) Thakali leadership vested in their Subbas, possessed of aggressive and far-sighted business and political acumen. In a few short years the Thakali Subbas dominated the economic, political and cultural life of Thak Khola. Their influence eventually reached all the way from Tibet to India. Today, they dominate trade and business at Pokhara and other major western bazaar towns, and their influence on the economy of west Nepal is acknowledged in Kathmandu, the capital.

In comparison, Bhot Khola, the 'River of Bhot (Tibet)', is also an inner valley near the Tibetan border. It is situated along the upper Marsiangdi River some 60 to 80 kilometers east of Thak Khola. As a region, Bhot Khola encompasses Manang District and borders on northeastern Lamjung. That portion of it which interests us most is the subregion of Tinguan to which the village of Thonje is central.[7] Bhot Khola is the home of the Manangba (or Nyeshangba) people who live in the high valley to the west of Tingaun, of other Tibetan-speaking Bhotia peoples, and of Gurungs. The Gurungs are a Tibeto-Burman speaking tribe related to the Thakali; those Gurungs of Tingaun are the northernmost members of their tribe and are considered to be the most Tibetanized (Messerschmidt 1972).

Bhot Khola is geographically dissimilar to Thak Khola in

several important respects. Those dissimilarities must be understood to fully appreciate the significance of the development of Tibetan border trade in the region. Unlike the Upper Kali Gandaki River Valley, the upper Marsiangdi is narrow and precipitous and physically more isolated from the lower hill regions to the south. It is surrounded closely on all sides by high, steep mountainous ranges. The only passes across the border into Tibet are much higher here than those found north of Thak Khola, and they are made more dangerous by the heavy monsoon rains of summer and the deep, long-lasting snows of winter. These combined climatic and geographic conditions seriously impair the flow of trade. The trade route coming north out of Lamjung District follows a long, narrow gorge which is exceptionally dangerous to human porters and totally unfit for pack animals. Formerly, traders climbed over the high Lamjung Himal, west of the gorge, to gain access to the Bhot Khola trade. The various alternative routes sometimes take several days to surmount. This compares unfavourably with the few hours necessary to ascend the Kali Gandaki Gorge into Thak Khola.[8, 9] In Bhot Khola, pack animals are only used to carry loads the short distance between Thonje and the Tibetan border passes in the region of Larkya, at the northeast.

Like their immediate Bhotia neighbours and the Thakalis further west, the Gurungs of Tingaun combine an agro-pastoral economy with trade. By summer they raise wheat, barley, potatoes, beans and a little corn in their high, dry stony fields. They also herd sheep, yak and yak-cattle crossbreeds (*dzo*, Tib.) for their by-products and to serve as beasts of burden. By winter the local Gurungs, Ghale clansmen in particular, traditionally pursue the salt trade, while many of the Bhotia residents leave Bhot Khola altogether to travel and engage in petty trade elsewhere. During summer, the wet season, travel is difficult and trade is nil. In the past, summer has been the season to stockpile Tibetan salt which came down over Larkya Pass in great Yak caravans. By winter, the dry season, Nepali porters trekked north from the lowlands with grain to barter. They still come, but nowadays they sell their grain to Gurung entrepreneurs who hold the contracts to supply the Nepalese civil service stationed in the district.

The socio-economy of these northernmost Gurungs of Tingaun is quite distinct from that of their Gurung cousins to the south. Subsistence in the lower hills, in the districts of Lamjung and Kaski where the bulk of the Gurung population is found, contrasts markedly with that of Bhot Khola. Gurungs of the lower hills are sedentary agriculturalists who raise rice and upland crops. Some tend herds of sheep and cattle in the highland pastures on the southern slopes of the Himalaya, and others pursue mercenary soldiery in the Gurkha regiments.[10] It is only after these secondary pursuits that trade figures at all in their subsistence economy; its utility these days is mainly as a source of salt for the immediate consumption of their small herds of livestock. The differences in the socio-economy of these two Gurung regions is pointed out because it is unique that certain Lamichane Gurungs of Ghanpokhara village in Lamjung District came to dominate the Bhot Khola economy and trade after the nineteenth century.

The Rise of the Thakali Subbas

Before proceeding with the history of the Gurungs of Bhot Khola, the rise of the Thakali Subbas of Thak Khola and their involvement in early Bhot Khola trade of the mid-nineteenth century should be described. In 1854-1856 Nepal was at war with Tibet. Among contributing causes was the desire on the part of the Nepal government in Kathmandu to control the monopoly of trans-Himalayan trade. For a while, after the treaty of 1856, diplomatic and trade relations seemed normal enough, but they soon deteriorated to conditions described by one political historian as "an interminable series of petty disputes" over the salt-rice barter trade along the border and the treatment of Nepali merchants in Tibetan towns (Rose 1971: 123).

Mounting concern over these problems prompted the Nepal government to seek ways to secure the loyalties of the northern border peoples and to tax and control the border trade. Bhotias, because of their strong Tibetan affinities, were considered to have conflicting interests and to be untrustworthy (Bista 1971). But certain members of the Thakali tribe were known and trusted by Kathmandu authorities. One among them, Bal Bir Sherchan (nicknamed 'Kalu') had been an interpreter for the Nepalese during the Tibetan conflict. He was now, in 1869, appointed as a Subba with jurisdiction over trade, customs and local administration (as a magistrate) in Thak Khola (Fürer-Haimendorf 1974). His influence quickly spread to neighbouring regions, including Bhot Khola.

The salt trade through Bhot Khola at this early time was a petty affair, discouraged by the contingencies of the physical environment and by the unscrupulous practices of the parties involved. Tales of weighting the salt and grain with gravel, of wetting it for greater volume, and of outright looting of stockpiles are commonly recounted by the descendants of those early barterers.[11] At first, the trade was pursued locally by the Ghale Gurung clansmen of Tilje village and vicinity and to some extent by lowland Nepalese from Lamjung, with Tibetans from across the frontier. When the Thakalis became interested in this avenue of trade, as small and insignificant as it was, they sent a representative trade agent called a *katkindar* (Nep., 'sub-contractor') with a small but supportive entourage of helpers to settle in Tingaun (in the vicinity of Bagarchap village).

Whereas in Thak Khola their physical proximity to a good trade route and long time involvement in local commerce were important factors antecedant to Thakali dominance, in Bhot Khola neither of these factors was as important. Instead of there being a singular and well-used track to and from Bhot Khola by the south, there were only small tracks leading through the high country of northern Lamjung converging at Namun Pass in Lamjung Himal. Most traders from the lower hills crossed this high pass (6800 meters) in preference to threading their way up the dangerous and difficult Marsiangdi Gorge route below. Many Gurung villages in the lower hills were situated within easy access to one or another of these minor mountain tracks, notably Ghanpokhara in Lamjung District and Siklis in Kaski. But trade was not of significant volume (as compared with Thak Khola) nor did it particularly favour one or another of these villages. Apparently no Gurung villagers of Lamjung were seriously disposed to capitalize on the Bhot Khola trade until late in the nineteenth century when the Gurungs of Ghanpokhara took an interest.

The Rise of the Gurung Subbas

Despite their relative uninvolvement with the trade, compared with the Thakali, and despite the physical contingencies which restricted the development of a major route to Bhot Khola, certain Lamichane Gurung clansmen of Ghanpokhara village in northern Lamjung entered the trading scene in the 1890s. They rose in a few short years to entirely dominate the economy, politics, and social life of the Bhot Khola and northern Lamjung regions. Their leader challenged not only the Thakali agent in Tingaun and drove him out, but seriously threatened the relative autonomy of the Thakali Subbas in their own Thak Khola.

Who are these Lamichane Gurungs of Ghanpokhara and what explains their sudden ascendancy? An overview of Gurung social structure and history helps with the answers.

Gurung society is hierarchically divided into two sub-tribes or strata called the *char jat* (Nep.), or 'four clans', and the *sora jat* (Nep.), or 'sixteen clans'. The Lamichane clan is one of the allegedly superior Char Jat clans. Within the Char Jat there is further differentiated a four-fold hierarchy based on roles of descending status. Ghale, at the top, was apparently the clan of the ancient Gurung Raja, or 'king' (i.e. 'paramount chief'). The second-ranked Ghodane was said to have been a clan of 'ministers' to the king. The third-ranked Lama was a clan of priests. And the fourth-ranked Lamichane was somehow subordinate to the Lama (Allen 1973; Pignede 1962, 1966; Messerschmidt n.d.).

Lamichane status poses a problem, for in northern Lamjung district they, and *not* the Ghodane, are purported to have been the second-ranked chief ministers to the Ghale Raja.[12] This conflicts with Pignede's and subsequently Allen's analyses of the Char Jat hierarchy, but it may be only a relatively recent and successful readjustment of status ranking or a localized phenomenon.

Sometime perhaps as early as the fifteenth century, the last Ghale Raja was deposed by the Nepal Raja of Lamjung.[13] By local accounts, the Ghale's minister at the time was a Lamichane clansman. The Ghale Raja's demise is said to have occurred in the vicinity of Ghanpokhara and in one account there is a hint of Lamichane collusion with the Nepali Raja of Lamjung to deceive the Ghale and lead him into a trap. At any event, since that time, the Gurungs have been subject to the House of Gorkha, the present ruling dynasty of Nepal.[14]

Sometime following these events the Nepalese authorities appointed certain Lamichane clansmen of Ghanpokhara and nearby villages as local administrative functionaries called *jimuwal* (Nep.) delegated to collect the land revenues.[15] Many of the same Lamichanes were also village headmen (*mukhya*, Nep.; *khhro*, Gur.). In these roles the Lamichane gained considerable prestige and power, succeeding, in effect, the fallen Ghales to the first-ranked position of high status among Char Jat, and among the Gurungs overall.

During the nineteenth century, at the time of the Thakali trade agent's presence in Bhot Khola, a Gurung named Man Lal Lamichane (1857-1907) inherited the chieftanship (*chiba*, Gur.) of the maximal local Lamichane lineage, and the combined headmanship and land tax collectorship of Upalo (upper) Ghanpokhara village. Man Lal Lamichane Gurung was, in fact, the single most powerful Gurung of the region. His dominant place was all the more ensured and his influence further expanded geographically by his marriage of alliance with the daughter of a prominent Ghale Gurung clansman of Tilje village in Tingaun. It was Man Lal who came into conflict with the Thakali entrepreneurs and ultimately challenged them for control of Bhot Khola trade and customs.

The story is told that Man Lal's bride was an only child. She came to marriage with a large dowry consisting of two parts. One part gave her husband's lineage hunting rights in a tract of forest near Tilje.[16] The other part was a quantity of salt and other commodities of mostly Tibetan origins. The former part established a Lamichane claim and presence in Tingaun, while the latter set off a confrontation with the Thakalis.

When Man Lal brought his bride and her dowry from Tilje to Ghanpokhara he was stopped at Gaddi Jagat, the winter 'drink-stop custom-house', at the southern end of the Marsiangdi Gorge. There he was compelled by the Thakali agent to pay duty on the Tibetan goods in his possession. This angered Man Lal and he is said to have argued in vain over the inappropriate taxing of personal property. Shortly thereafter, he gathered support from Gurung allies in Lamjung and Tingaun, particularly of the Tilje Ghale clansmen who were already smarting under Thakali control of their trade, and openly challenged the Thakali customs agent, driving him from the region. Somehow the Thakali agent died during the conflict and Man Lal was held accountable. He was taken by government authorities to the Rana royal court at Palpa, but was quickly acquitted and allowed to return to take up his new role as the chief trader and customs collector of Bhot Khola. His power and fame spread quickly through the region, but it would be some years yet before he would be officially appointed to the office of Subba.

Meanwhile, one of Man Lal's first acts was to establish a permanent trading post at the confluence of the Dudh and Marsiangdi Rivers in Tingaun. He called the site Thonje, and built a large house there.[17,18] Thonje (2300 meters) is functionally analogous to Tukche in Thak Khola, although smaller. It was founded in 1892 and it served for a half century as the primary summer customs post of Bhot Khola and as a depot for trading supplies. (The winter custom house remained downriver at Gaddi Jagat.) For years, the salt and animal by-products from Tibetan trade, and the grain and commodities of Nepalese and Indian origins were deposited and stored at Thonje until they could be shipped on by porter or yak in season to their respective destinations.[19]

Much of the actual barter was conducted at Bimthang, on the upper Dudh River a few kilometers southwest of Larkya Pass. Man Lal had acquired rights to the land at Bimthang through his wife's dowry. There he established a summer outpost and storehouse called a *kothi* (Nep.).[20]

At Thonje, Man Lal was in a position to dominate the three main routes of travel to and through Bhot Khola - the tracks going to and from Manang (and Nar), Larkya, and Lamjung. To facilitate trade from Lamjung, he engineered major improvements to the track through the Marsiangdi Gorge, diverting traffic away from the high route over Lamjung Himal.

Turning northward, he sought to further improve relations with the Tibetan traders and to bring more of their business over the Larkya Pass to Bimthang and Thonje. One goal was to draw trade away from the relatively minor trade route along the Buri Gandaki River through Athata-sai Khola southeast of Larkya (in northern Gorkha District). Another goal was to lure business away from his rivals, the Thakalis at the west. He must have realized that the Bhot Khola route down the Marsiangdi could never rival that through Thak Khola in volume of trade because of the physical and climatic limitations, yet he succeeded in setting off a chain of events that brought Bhot Khola trade near to capacity. He accomplished this in two ways.

First, he is credited with personally capturing a notorious Tibetan bandit who had been pillaging the trade along the border for some time. This won him the respect and allegiance of the Tibetan border villagers and of the Tibetan nomads and salt traders who frequented the tradeposts. (It is said that when Man Lal visited Tibet he would be met by 1000 horsemen and offered tribute.) He also negotiated, to mutual advantage, new and more attractive barter arrangements with the traders.

Second, Man Lal became the chief tax functionary, called *talukdar* (= Jimuwal), of Larkya which gave him considerable influence over the economy and peoples of Athara-sai Khola.[21] Soon after, he arranged for two of his sons to become, jointly, the Jimuwals of Nar Khola as well. And, by negotiating as a broker between the people of upper Manang and Kathmandu over local administrative jurisdiction in the west of Manang District, he secured their respect and esteem (although in this case there was no provision for a Jimawal). In a short time the influence of Man Lal and his two sons, Nar Jang and Dilli Jang, had spread throughout these vast border regions.

Man Lal's endeavours to draw trade away from Thak Khola and onto the route through Bhot Khola continued for many years. The

MAP 1 - NEPAL
TIBET
HIMALAYAN
MIDDLE HILLS
Area enlarged in Map 2.
RANGE
Kathmandu
TERAI
REGION
INDIA

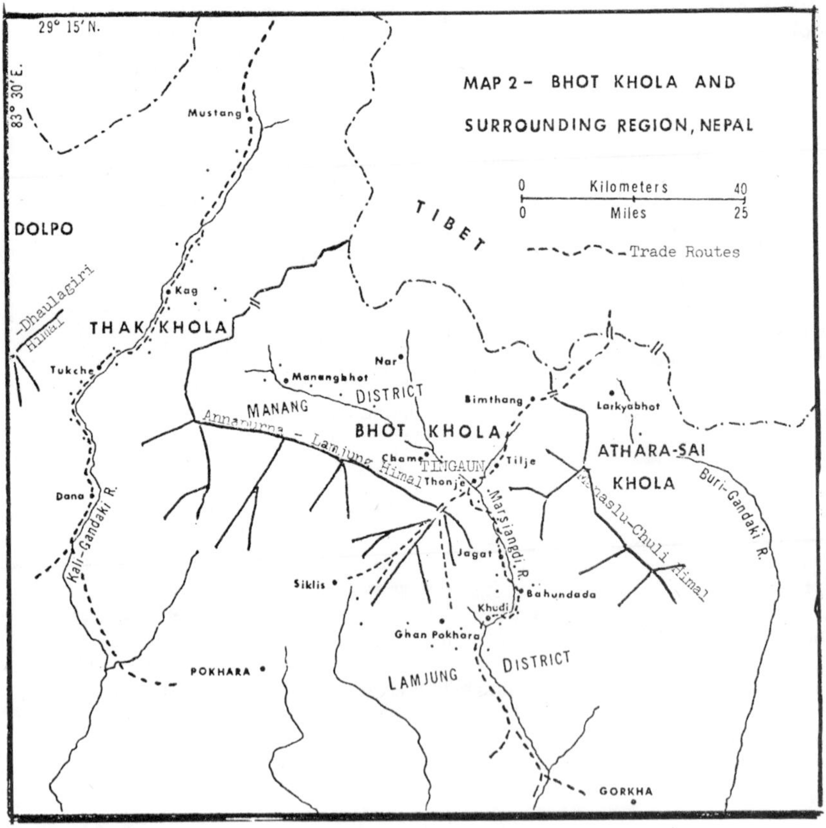
29° 15′ N.
83° 30′ E.
MAP 2 - BHOT KHOLA AND SURROUNDING REGION, NEPAL
0 Kilometers 40
0 Miles 25
Trade Routes
TIBET
Mustang
DOLPO
Dhaulagiri Himal
Kag
THAK KHOLA
Tukche
Nar
Manangbhot
MANANG DISTRICT
Bimthang
Larkyabhot
Annapurna - Lamjung Himal
BHOT KHOLA
Chame
TINGAUN
Tilje
Thonje
ATHARA-SAI KHOLA
Manaslu-Chuli Himal
Buri-Gandaki R.
Marsiangdi R.
Dana
Kali-Gandaki R.
Jagat
Siklis
Bahundada
Khudi
Ghan Pokhara
POKHARA
LAMJUNG DISTRICT
GORKHA

FIGURE 1.

LAMICHANE GURUNG 'SUBBA' PATRILINEAGE

GHANPOKHARA, LAMJUNG DISTRICT, NEPAL

▲ - Official 'Subba' (total: 5)

Δ - Other members of the patrilineage

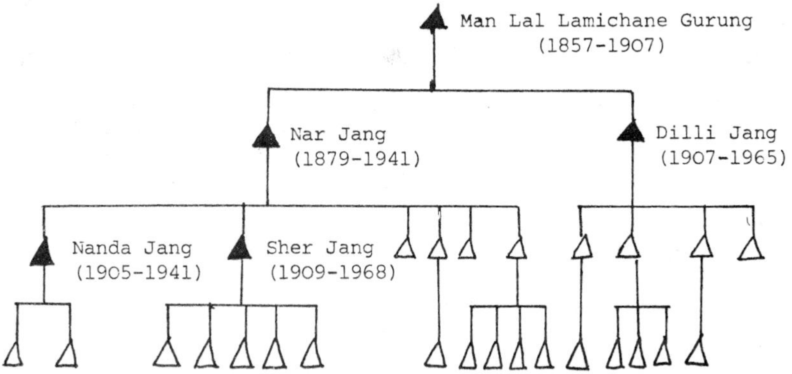

FIGURE 2.

SHERCHAN THAKALI 'SUBBA' PATRILINEAGE

THAK KHOLA, NEPAL

▲ - Official 'Subba' (total: 14)

Δ - Other members of the patrilineage

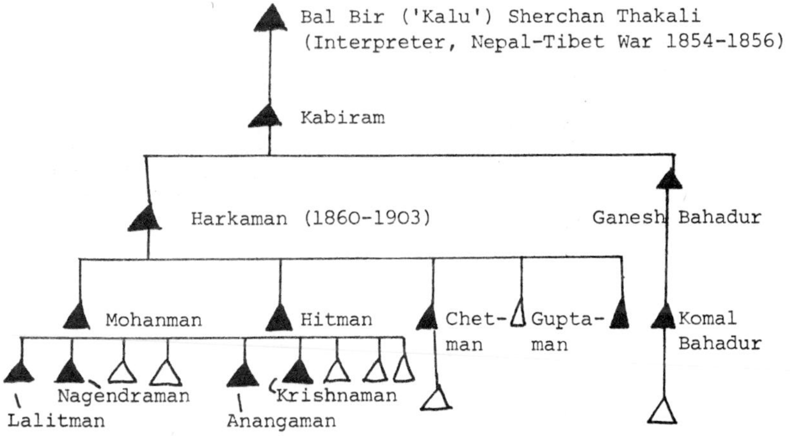

precise measure of his success will probably never be determined, but the fact of it may be reflected in this comment about the decline in Thak Khola trade in the early twentieth century:

> The reason for a decline of the salt trade was not a fall in the demand for Tibetan salt - the competition of Indian salt being not yet effective - but a sharp, drop in the amount of salt exported by Tibet from the area north of Thak Khola. Fürer-Haimendorf, 1974

Readers familiar with the history of the Thakali Subbas will by now have recognized several parallels in the ascendancy of Man Lal Gurung. For one, the rise of the Gurung Lamichane clan from a fourth rank position (if we assume that to be their original place) within the Char Jat hierarchy is analogous to the Thakali Sherchan clan rising to first place through their own four-fold clan system. This status mobility was both part and parcel to the rise of the Subbas from these respective clans. And at the same time that Man Lal's power was spreading throughout the Bhotia areas along the border in and near Bhot Khola, his Thakali contemporary, Subba Harkaman Sherchan (1860-1903) was consolidating his own leadership within and adjacent to Thak Khola. Between 1869, when Harkaman's grandfather was awarded the customs contract for Thak Khola and became the first Thakali Subba, and the turn of the twentieth century, the Thakali Subbas established themselves as head (Mukhya) of all the Thakalis and as paramount chief (*chikep*, Thk.) over a loose confederation encompassing the whole of Thak Khola, Baragaun, and part of Dolpo.[22]

But there was one far-reaching difference in the personal circumstances of Man Lal Gurung as compared with the Thakali Subbas. This was the important matter of patrilineal succession. Where the Thakali Subba Harkaman Sherchan had a brother and many sons and nephews to help administer and ultimately inherit a widespread network of trade and political control, Man Lal Gurung had only two sons to succeed him, and to only one of them, the elder Nar Jang, did he apparently give any real responsibility and trust. (See Figures 1 and 2.) This situation was detrimental to the Gurungs and severely limited their ability to continue on a par with the Thakali entrepreneurs later on.

In the meantime, in 1902, under circumstances not yet fully documented, the government in Kathmandu awarded the Thak Khola customs contract to Man Lal Gurung. Some Gurung informants relate that it was at this time that the Thakalis fell temporarily out of favour with Kathmandu by their inability or unwillingness to live up to the financial obligations of the customs contract. Writing from the Thakali perspective, Furer-Haimendorf (1974) notes that "on the strength of his reputation as a reliable and successful customs contractor in the area of the Marsyandi Valley, he Man Lal obtained the customs contract of Thak Khola for an annual royalty of Rs. 75,000 and established himself in Tukche." That royalty was a much higher figure than what was paid by the immediately preceding Thakali Subba.

The direct descendants of Man Lal Gurung tell a more detailed and interesting story of the event. They relate that at the turn of the century there was a high ranking Gurung officer in the Royal Nepal Army who was an aide to the Rana Prime Minister. This aide suggested that the Gurung Man Lal be called upon to replace the Thakali Subba as the next contractor of Thak Khola. The Prime Minister beckoned Man Lal to an audience at the court in Kathmandu, awarded him the contract and title of 'Subba', and dispatched him to take up his extended duties in Thak Khola.

The account of the audience is interesting in that it sheds light on the legendary character of Man Lal and indirectly on government distrust of the Bhotias, a point made earlier:

> Intending to look his best, Man Lal appeared at the Prime Minister's Palace dressed as a Tibetan, riding a horse. When the Prime Minister saw him he took his aide aside and reprimanded him. "I told you to call in a Gurung and you have brought me this Bhotia instead!" he said, to which the Gurung aide replied, "It is only because he has taken the customs contract of Bhot Khola that he dresses this way."
>
> The Prime Minister offered Man Lal the Thak Khola contract for a prescribed amount. When Man Lal showed hesitation in taking on so large a responsibility, the aide reminded him of his unquestioning duty to the King:
>
> *"raja le dieko tel, kasto ma thapnu."* Literally: 'for the oil which the King has offered, you must hold open your wrap to receive.'

The story continues that although Man Lal was unable at short notice to purchase the customs contract lease at once, he was, nevertheless, allowed to register the contract in his name (and subsequently in the name of his eldest son, Nar Jang)[23] and to pay in full at a later time. He raised part of the required money from Gurung supporters in the districts of Lamjung and Kaski.

According to records from the time kept by the Lamichange Subba lineage of Ghanpokhara (and recently uncovered), Man Lal's initial tenure as Subba of Thak Khola was quite short, from 1902 to 1903. It was returned after that to the Thakalis for a year. Twice again, however, it was granted to Man Lal and his sons, once from 1905 to 1910 and again from 1918 to 1920. In 1910 an agreement was reportedly made whereby the two contending parties would hold the contract in alternate turns. Nevertheless, the Thakalis held the contract continuously from 1910 to 1918. Meanwhile, in 1907, Man Lal had died (at Ghanpokhara). He left his son, Subba Nar Jang, as principal hier. Subsequently, Nar Jang's own eldest son, Nanda Jang, was also registered as Subba of Thak Khola.

The office of the Subba of Thak Khola was alternately called the 'Dana *bhansar*' (Nep., 'customs collector'). When Man Lal arrived at Dana to take that post for the first time in 1902, he replaced the former Thakali Subba's subordinates by his own with one exception - he retained the Thakali's chief agent, a man who was a close affine of the contemporary Subba, Harkaman Sherchan. Man Lal and Harkaman also became bond brothers (*mit*, Nep.) as did Man Lal's son, Nar Jang, with the son of the Thakali customs agent. The mit bond is ideally an amicable brotherly relationship between two men and by extension between their lineages and clans (Messerschmidt n.d.; Okada 1957). Just how amicable it remained in this case is the subject of conflicting reports. Nar Jang Gurung also took a Thakali wife (not closely related to the Thakali Subbas, however) and owned land near Cherok, north of Tukche. At a site on the west bank of the Kali Gandaki River near Cherok he built the summer off-season customs house.

During their short hegemony over customs contracts in Thak Khola, the Gurung Subbas were mainly accountable to the government for the price of the contract lease. And although they had some magistratical powers as Subbas, the Thakalis maintained their strong interest in the trade and virtual full control of local political affairs.

It is apparent that the Thakali Subbas took no chances with the Gurung interlopers in their midst. An affine of the Thakali remained chief agent of the customs post, and both the mit bonds and the marriage alliance were sanctioned for their potential as leverage with the Gurungs. Gurung informants maintain that the Thakalis also worked quietly in Kathmandu to defame the Gurung

Subba, a move which ostensibly led to the eventual abolishment of the customs contract system in Thak Khola in the 1920's in favour of a direct tax on the populace called *loka bhar* (Nep., 'social debt'). The timing of this change of taxation system corresponds to the consolidation of political authority in Thak Khola by the Thakali Subbas and a grand plan to establish an independent Thakali state - a plan looked upon with disfavour by Kathmandu (Bista 1971).

Following closure of the Thak Khola customs post, the Gurung and Thakali Subbas also contended for the customs contract on the growing Indian border trade in the Terai at Butwal and Bhairawa. The Subba there was alternately called *chautaro bhansar* (Nep.), or 'stopping-place customs collector'. The Terai contract was successfully bid for alternately by both parties over the next two decades. During that time, the Gurung Subbas controlled it for fourteen years, and both they and the Thakalis alike developed wide ranging networks of private business. Shortly after taking the last Terai contract, Subba Nar Jang died (1941). Within thirteen days his son and direct successor, Subba Nanda Jang, also died. This left the Gurungs without a successor knowledgeable of their far flung business enterprises. Subba Dilli Jang, Nar Jang's only brother, was primarily involved in the Bhot Khola trade, and the brothers and sons of Subba Nanda Jang were too young yet to have gained requisite experience to carry on (although one brother, Sher Jang, had been made Subba under the Terai contract).

Within a few years the entire customs contract system and the office of the Subba were abolished in the Terai as well, and customs collection was placed under the direct control of the central government civil service. This marked the end to a half century of Gurung-Thakali confrontation.

Recent Developments

In the quarter century since the end of the customs contract system, the Thakali and Gurung Subbas and their descendants have continued to dominate the economy and politics of Thak Khola and Bhot Khola, respectively. All men directly descended from the original Subbas are honorarily called 'Subba' themselves, although the title is now devoid of its former authority. All Subba's wives and daughters are called 'Subbini'. Among the Thakali, but not the Gurung, the title of Subba is now widely and arbitrarily applied to all adult men. The titles and roles of the Thak Khola regional headman (Mukhya), Thakali paramount chief (Chikep),

Gurung village headman (Mukhya, Khhro), and of land revenue collector (Jimuwal) have been retained by the Subbas in Thak and Bhot Kholas, respectively.[24]

In some respects parallel developments between the two parties have continued, although the Thakalis have surpassed the Gurungs in depth and breadth of their involvement, particularly in business. For the Gurungs, the lack of an experienced successor after 1941 coupled with a family feud impaired their ability to hold large-scale business interests together. As a result, during the 1940's and 1950's they concentrated mostly on localized business and politics in and near Bhot Khola. The Thakalis, on the other hand, capitalized on the vacuum in business leadership created by the death of the Gurung Subbas and expanded their interests far beyond Thak Khola, into the Terai, to Kathmandu, and to India. Only recently have the descendants of the Gurung Subbas and their affines moved into the developing economies of Kathmandu and the Rapti Valley region of southern Nepal.

Despite waning interest in business affairs, the Gurung Subbas' descendants have applied themselves quite successfully to local, regional and national politics and government. To date, one of Subba Nar Jang's sons has been appointed twice as an assistant minister in His Majesty's Government of Nepal. The two sons of Subba Nanda Jang have been successfully elected to represent Lamjung and Manang Districts in the national assembly, the Rastriya Panchayat. Several other members of the patrilineage are actively engaged in more local level politics in both districts, and one is a high ranking officer in the British Army. The Thakalis have had a comparable history of involvement in politics and government as well.

A dominant factor in the great attention given to Thakalis by anthropologists is the existence of a cohesive sense of Thakali ethnic identity. This ethnicity is encouraged by a relatively small population led by strong headmen, and by a definite geographic homogeneity.[25] The Gurungs, on the other hand, are a large and diffuse group spread over a vastly larger territory in the hills. No single Gurung leader has ever been in a position to dominate the entire tribe, and the mere fact of Man Lal's ascendancy is a remarkable achievement.

These various situational and personal conditions serve to highlight the fact that parallel developments did occur between the Gurungs and the Thakalis in trade and politics, developments which can be primarily attributed to the aggressive and innovative personalities of a few dominant men.

Before concluding, religious and material acculuration and change related to the Subba phenomenon should be briefly mentioned. Upon his ascendance to power in Bhot Khola and the establishment of Thonje, Man Lal Gurung adopted Tibetan Buddhism, to the neglect of the Gurung tribe's own style of Lamaism and older Shamanistic tradition. He also wore Tibetan costume in exchange for Gurung dress. Then, in an attempt to maximize religious and cultural options, the Gurung Subbas embraced Hindu orthodoxy, gradually abandoning Buddhism. Concomitantly, they adopted the Nepali national costume. To this point, their religious and material acculturation roughly parallels that of the Thakalis described by Iijima (1963) and Fürer-Haimendorf (1966). More recently, however, members of the Gurung Subba lineage and other prominent Lamichane and Ghale clansmen of Ghanpokhara and Tilje have been attracted to a new Hindu sect called Adwaita led by the charismatic reformist, Kshitis Chandra Chakravarti. But contrary to the situation in Thak Khola, few if any of the Gurung Subbas' innovations in these areas have had far-reaching effects among Gurungs at large. As a reference group to inspire or dictate significant change, the Gurung Subbas have been emulated only locally, restricted, by and large, to the region of Bhot Khola and their own northern Lamjung District.

Recapitulation

These data on the Gurung Subbas demonstrate that the Thakali phenomena of innovation and change in Thak Khola and abroad are not entirely unique in Nepal. The data reveal three hitherto unrecorded aspects of the Thakali-Gurung Subba confrontations: (1) the early role of Thakalis in the trade of Bhot Khola, (2) the successful encroachment of the Gurungs in the Thak Khola trade, and (3) the more recent roles of both groups in the Terai and Indian border trade.

In addition, future research may turn up other parallel developments in similar Himalayan regions. An obvious first choice for such investigations would be in those regions where other Subba or Subba-like administrative appointments were made during the nineteenth and early twentieth centuries, and where local authority of one degree or another was vested in a select few resulting in the establishment of a rural elite of the nature discussed in this paper.[26]

Don Messerschmidt
Nareshwar Jang Gurung

NOTES

1. This paper was prepared for presentation to the Symposium on Nepal and Adjoining Himalayan Regions at the School of Oriental and African Studies, University of London, June 28 to July 2, 1973. We are indebted to Professor Christoph von Fürer-Haimendorf, Chairman of the Symposium.

   The paper is based on original research among the Gurungs of northern Lamjung District and adjacent Bhot Khola in Manang District in 1971-72. It was generously supported by a grant from the U.S. Public Health Service National Institutes of Health NIH Grant No.5 TO1 GMO 1382 (BHS) , through the Department of Anthropology at the University of Oregon. We are indebted to the living descendants of the first Gurung Subba and to various members of their agnatic and affinal kin groups, particularly Narendra Jang Lamichane and Komal Ghaley. Important points in the data were cross checked with Thakali informants. We are also appreciative of the constructive critique of an earlier draft of the paper by our friend and colleague, Dr. James W. Fields of Kathmandu.

2. Of course, the merchants of Newari ethnicity who originated in Kathmandu Valley and who have spread far and wide throughout the Nepal hills have long been the most far-reaching force in Nepali trade and commerce. In this paper, however, we consider only the more remote hill tribes west of Kathmandu who engaged initially in Tibetan salt for Nepalese grain trade across the northern border.

3. The practice of appointing local or regional revenue administrators and functionaries was widespread in Nepal. They have been called by a number of titles: Subba, Subedar, Ijaradar, Mukhya, Jimuwal, and others (Regmi 1963, 1971). Caplan (1971) describes Subbas among the Limbu people of east Nepal as traditional headmen who were apparently absorbed into the local administrative structure and given responsibility for Kipat land revenue collection. Regmi (1963) distinguishes three types of Subbas: (1) Limbu headmen, (2) district administrative heads in the early nineteenth century, and (3) top ranking civil officials. The Gurung and Thakali Subbas of the early *twentieth* century seem to fit the second category.

4. For a botanical-geographical description of these inner valley regions of the Himalaya see Stainton 1973.

5. All place names are given in Nepali, with their Tibetan equivalents - where applicable - in parentheses.

6. Detailed descriptions of Thak Khola and the entire upper Kali Gandaki River region may be found in Bista 1967, 1971; Furer-Haimendorf 1966; and Snellgrove 1961.

7. Local Nepal-speakers in Bhot Khola (mostly lowlanders engaged in the trade) differentiate between three sub-regions within Bhot Khola: (1) Tingaun, the 'three villages' (see Note 17), reaching from the Marsiangdi Gorge below Thonje to Chame at the west and up the Dudh River Valley at the northeast, (2) Nar Khola, the 'river of Nar', a small Bhotia valley at the north, and (3) Manang (sometimes Manangbhot), the high westernmost valley of the Marsiangdi River headwaters. Tibetologists will recognize these places as Gyasumdo, Nar, and Nyeshang, respectively. Larkya (sometimes Larkyabhot) is the border region east of Larkya Pass (northeast of Tingaun) on the upper Buri Gandaki River in a region known in Nepali as Athata-sai Khola, the 'eighteen-hundred rivers' (Nup-ri in Tibetan) (see Dobremez and Jest 1970, and Snellgrove 1961).

8. During the winter of 1971-72, the Nepal government completed major improvements to the Marsiangdi River Gorge track, levelling and widening large portions of it and making it passable for pack animals and safer for porters in all seasons. Similarly, improvements have been made on the shorter Kali Gandaki Gorge track between Dana and Ghasa. There is recurrent talk of making these routes to the border jeepable.

9. Besides the Marsiangdi River route there are three alternative routes to and from Bhot Khola via high passes (all over 6800 meters) linking it with neighbouring regions of Nepal and Tibet. These passes are open only from late spring until first snow in the fall. (1) Namun Pass crosses the Lamjung Himal southwest of Thonje. It is little used these days except by Gurung shepherds fetching salt for their herds during the monsoon season. In earlier times this route was favoured over the dangerous Marsiangdi Gorge track. A customs post was established for summer use near the southern approach to Namun Pass on a mountainside at 6200 meters to accommodate the traffic. (2) Nyeshand Pass crosses Muktinath Himal at the extreme west of Bhot Khola. It is primarily a pilgrim route to the shrines at Muktinath and the main thoroughfare for Bhotias going to Thak Khola, Baragaun (or Kag), and Mustang (Lo). (3) Larkya Pass is adjacent to the Tibetan frontier northeast of Tingaun, crossing between Manaslu and Larkya Himals. It has become the major salt trade route to and from Tibet via Bhot Khola.

10. A detailed description of Gurung economy in the lower hills is given in Macfarlane's dissertation, 1972.

11. There is an interesting note in Buchanan (1819: 243) indicating an earlier curtailment of the trade from Tibet through Lamjung by the Nepal government (i.e. the House of Gorkha) in Kathmandu:

> The Kingdom of Lamjun ... was a cold country bordering on the snowy peaks of Emodus i.e. the Himalaya, 'Emodus of the Ancients' , and inhabited by Bhotiyas, with some Brahmans and Khasiyas in the warmer vallies. It contained no mine of any importance, nor any town of note, except the capital; and the chief advantage, after the loss of Gorkha, that the Raja enjoyed, was the commerce with Bhotan or Thibet, which was carried on through a passage in Emodus called Siklik. Many goods were conveyed bynthis route south to Lamjun, and from thence, by the way of Tarku, Tanahung, Dewghat, and Bakra, into the low country i.e. via the Marsiangdi and Narayani River Valleys ; but this trade has been interdicted by the present government of Nepal, which is very jealous of the Raja of Tanahung Tanhu , to whom Bakra is secured by the East India Company's protection. Siklik, however, is still the residence of a Subbah or civil governor ... The name merely implies a frontier place, but among the hills is used to imply a place inhabited by barbarians; that is, such as reject the doctrines of the Brahmans. In both meanings the term is applicable to Siklik, as its inhabitants, Bhotiyas and Gurungs, adhere to the Lamas, and it is the frontier town towards the empire of China.

Siklik, now Siklis, is the name of a Gurung village on the former trade route over Namun Pass (alternately called Siklis Pass) on the high route between Lamjung and Bhot Khola. We have encountered no other reference to the 'Subah of Siklik', and he apparently bears no relationship to the Subba of Bhot Khola of a century later.

12. The problem is discussed more fully in Messerschmidt, n.d. Briefly, Pignede's date indicating the Lamichane fourth rank position in the hierarchy are based on his findings among the Char Jat Gurungs of Kaski and Parbat Districts, west of Lamjung. In those districts, Ghodane clansmen are numerous and Lamichane are relatively few. There the Ghodane clan is accorded the second rank status position, and today Ghodane clansmen are frequently found to be village headmen (Pignede 1962). In northern Lamjung, however, the Ghodanes are scarce and the Lamichanes are quite numerous. Not unexpectedly, local legends accord the Lamichanes the role of ministers to the Ghale Raja. Many Lamjung village headmen are Lamichane clansmen.

13. The Nepali Raja of Lamjung was a progenitor to the House of Gorkha. His kingdom was one of the three most powerful princely states among the *chaubisi raja* (Nep.), or 'twenty-four kingdoms', founded in the Sapta Gandaki region of west-central Nepal by descendants of Rajput immigrants from the plains. Lamjung Principality dates from the mid-15th century A.D. (Hasrat 1970: 111). It was formally annexed by the government in Kathmandu in 1778 A.D. (Regmi 1971: 72-73).

14. A published version of a legend describing the fall of the Ghale Raja is recorded by Pignede (1962: 106-107, Legend III). See also the discussion of this and other versions of the event in Messerschmidt, n.d.

15. This probably occurred between 1830 and 1837 when the central government instigated basic changes in the system of revenue collection in the hill districts (Regmi 1963: 173 ff.).

16. This entitled them principally to all profits from the sale of musk from the Musk Deer (*kasturi*, Nep.) shot in that tract. It was interpreted or amended later to allow for the establishment of a trading mart at Bimthang.

17. The original 'three villages' from which Tingaun takes its name are the Gurung settlements of Taje, Naje, and Tamrong. Tamrong is uninhabited today; its site is between Thonje and Tilje on the Dudh River. Wodargaun, Gelangchok and Thanchok are more recently settled Gurung villages. Chame, Bagarchap, Thonje, Darapani and Tilje are mixed Bhotia and Gurung trading towns. These towns and villages are situated in a narrow, often sunless valley between Chame (at 2400 meters), the Manag District Headquarters town at the west, and Tilje (at 2300 meters), 15 kilometers east on the Dudh River. About three quarters of Tinguan's population (of a total of about 200 households) is Gurung. The Bhotia minority (some 60 households) of Tibetan origins settled here four or five generations ago. There are also several households of Kami (Blacksmith) and Damai (tailor) castes, and of the Thakali and Tamang tribes. All the rest of Bhot Khola is populated by Manangbas and other Tibetan-speaking Bhotia peoples. (At the time of my visit to Bhot Khola in 1971, I was restrcited from visiting any towns or villages except Thonje and Darapani. All figures are rough estimates given me by local informants see Messerschmidt 1973 .)

18. Thonje derives its name from the pine trees (*tho*, Gur.) growing on the relatively flat place (*tshe*, Gur.) where Man Lal chose to establish his trading post. 'Thonje' is the spelling found on Survey of India maps.

19. Since the 1950's, when the Chinese curtailed the Tibetan trade, Thonje's importance has diminished. For a few years in the 1960's it served as the administrative headquarters for Manang District, but in 1971 the main offices were moved up the Marsiangdi River to Chame. Prior to their establishment at Thonje, Manang's administrative offices were temporarily housed at Bahundada in northern Lamjung District.

20. The place is designated Bimthakothi on Survey of India maps. Here is how a Western traveller saw the market there at the height of trade:

> At Bimthakothi there was a frequent coming and going of herds of zos and flocks of sheep, to or from either Larkhya Pass or Thonje ... The man in charge of the store, the 'Subah', a relative of our rich friend at Kudi a small bazaar near Ghanpokhara , told us that during the short season he weighed more than 3000 animal loads. The rate of exchange was 16 measures of rice for 25 of salt; but over the pass at Larkhya, where the Tibetans arrive with their salt, 12 measures of rice are enough to buy 25 of salt ... Tilman 1952: 197-199

The Tibetologist, David Snellgrove, passed through Bimthang in 1956 during one of its last seasons. He writes:

> This is Bim-t'hang, 'Plain of Sand'. It is simply a small trading mart, occupied only during the summer months like Babuk (Larkya) across the pass eastward. From Tibet via Babuk come yak-loads of salt and wool, and from the Nepalese side rice and other food grains, cotton cloth, cigarettes, matches and other useful oddments. One meets here Tibetans from across the political frontier, Tibetans from Gyasumdo Tingaun and Tibetans from Nup-ri Athara-sai Khola , all seeking to make profit out of the loads they have brought. Yaks and sheep graze on the mountain-sides round about ... It was a forlorn place, much as one might imagine the limits of the inhabited world to be. 1961: 239-240

21. At first Man Lal's jurisdiction encompassed all of Athara-sai Khola, i.e. the whole northern sector of Gorkha District east of Manaslu Himal along the upper Buri Gandaki River. This proved to be too much of a financial and administrative burden and he very soon had the jurisdiction reduced to the immediate locale of Larkya on the Tibetan frontier proper.

22. Bista (1971) also describes how a fictive kin bond called *mit* (Nep.) was arranged by the Thakali Subba with the Raja of Mustang, a semi-autonomous Bhotia kingdom north of Thak Khola

(on the trade route). This relationship gave the Thakalis access to the Mustang Raja's wealth and the administration of his domain. This ultimately led to the Raja's decline as a power figure and to the rise of the Thakali Subba to local preeminence in his stead.

23. Ostensibly the customs contracts were awarded to the highest bidder, but in actuality appointments were manipulated by favouritism at the highest levels and nepotism at the level of the Subba. It was the custom among Gurungs, as among the Thakalis (Bista 1971) to reregister the contract periodically in the name of sons and brothers of the Subba. In this way the title was perpetuated and its privileged status was enjoyed throughout the immediate patrilineage.

24. The functionary role of Talukdar (Jimuwal) of Larkya was dropped by the Gurungs after Tibetan border trade diminished in the 1950's. Also, hereditary succession to Mukhya (headman) has been undermined by the 1962 enactment of the Village Panchayat Acts which now make village headmanship (i.e. Village Panchayat Chairmanship) elective in the rural districts (Messerschmidt n.d.).

25. A good example of the extent to which Thakali ethnic unity has been carried is found detailed in a paper on the *dhikur* (Thk.), a type of rotating credit association (Messerschmidt 1973). In that paper Thakali credit associations, the role of the Thakali Social Reform Committee, and the use of auxiliary funds to finance worthy communal projects are described.

26. See Note 3.

BIBLIOGRAPHY

ALLEN, N.J. 1973 "Four-fold Classifications of Society in the Himalaya", *IXth International Congress of Anthropological and Ethnological Sciences*, Chicago. (In Press)

BISTA, Dor Bahadur 1967 "Thakalis" in *People of Nepal*. Kathmandu: H.M.G. Department of Publicity. Pp. 80-88.

BISTA, Dor Bahadur 1971 "The Political Innovators of Upper Kali-Gandaki", *Man* 6: 1: 52-60.

BUCHANAN (HAMILTON), Francis 1819 *An Account of the Kingdom of Nepal and of the Territories Annexed to the Dominion by the House of Gorkha*. Edinburgh: Constable.

CAPLAN, Lionel 1970 *Land and Social Change in East Nepal* Berkeley and Los Angeles: University of California Press.

DOBREMEZ, J.F. and C. JEST 1970 *Carte Ecologique de la Region Annapurna-Dhaulagiri (Nepal)* (Ecological Map of Annapurna-Dhaulagiri Region, designating linguistic, ethnic, and caste groupings). Grenoble: Laboratoire de Biologie Vegetale, Faculty des Sciences de Grenoble.

FÜRER-HAIMENDORF, Christoph von, 1966 "Caste Concepts and Status Distinctions in Buddhist Communities of Western Nepal", in C. von Furer-Haimendorf (Editor), *Caste and Kin in Nepal, India and Ceylon: Anthropological Studies in Hindu-Buddhist Contact Zones*. Bombay and New York: Asia Publishing House. Pp. 140-160.

FÜRER-HAIMENDORF, Christoph von, 1967 "A Challenge to Buddhist Values", in Chapter 7, "Morality and the Quest for Merit", of *Morals and Merit: A Study of Values and Social Controls in South Asian Societies*. Chicago: University of Chicago Press. Pp. 197-202

FÜRER-HAIMENDORF, Christoph von, 1974 *Trans-Himalayan Traders*. (forthcoming) London, John Murray.

HASRAT, Bikrama Jit (Editor) 1970 *History of Nepal: As Told by Its Own and Contemporary Chroniclers*. Hoshiarpur, Punjab, India: B.J. Hasrat.

IIJIMA, Shigeru 1960 "The Thakali, a Central Himalayan Tribe", *Japanese Journal of Ethnology* 24:3: 1-22. (Japanese text, English Summary)

IIJIMA, Shigeru 1963 "Hinduization of a Himalayan Tribe in Nepal", *Kroeber Anthropological Society Papers*. 29: 43-52.

JEST, Corneille 1966 "Les Thakali. Note préliminaire concernant une·ethnic du Nord-Ouest du Nepal", *Ethnographie* 58-59. (1964/5): 26-49.

MACFARLANE, Alan 1972 *Population and Economy in Central Nepal: A Study of the Gurungs*. Unpublished Ph.D. Thesis, University of London.

MESSERSCHMIDT, Don 1972 "Rotating Credit in Gurung Society: the *Dhikur* Associations of Tin Gaun", *The Himalayan Review* (Nepal Geographical Society, Kathmandu) 5: 23-35.

MESSERSCHMIDT, Don 1973 "*Dhikur:* Rotating Credit Associations in Nepal", *IXth International Congress of Anthropological and Ethnographical Sciences*, Chicago. (In Press)

MESSERSCHMIDT, Don n.d. *Social Status, Conflict and Change in a Gurung Community of Nepal*. Unpublished Ph.D. Dissertation, University of Oregon. (Forthcoming)

OKADA, Ferdinand E. 1957 "Ritual Brotherhood: A Cohesive Factor in Nepalese Society". *Southwestern Journal of Anthropology* 13: 212-222.

PIGNEDE, Bernard 1962 "Clan Organization and Hierarchy among the Gurungs", *Contributions to Indian Sociology* 6: 102-119.

PIGNEDE, Bernard 1966 *Les Gurungs: une population himalayenne du Nepal* (The Gurungs: a Population of the Nepal Himalaya). Paris: Mouton.

REGMI, Mahesh Chandra 1963 *Land Tenure and Taxation in Nepal*. 4 volumes. *The State as Landlord: Raikar Tenure*. Volume 1. Berkeley: University of California Institute of International Studies.

REGMI, Mahesh Chandra 1971 *A Study in Nepali Economic History: 1768-1846*. New Delhi: Manjusri Publishing House.

ROSE, Leo E. 1971 *Nepal: Strategy for Survival*. Berkeley and Los Angeles: University of California Press.

SNELLGROVE, David 1961 *Himalayan Pilgrimage: A Study of Tibetan Religion by a Traveller through Western Nepal*. Oxford: Bruno Cassirer.

STAINTON, J.D.A. 1972 *Forests of Nepal*. New York: Hafner.

TILMAN, H.W. 1952 *Nepal Himalaya*. Cambridge: Cambridge University Press.

Shamanism among the Chantel of the Dhaulagiri Zone

One of the smallest groups among the Tibeto-Burman speaking populations of Nepal are the Chantel (approx. 5000). Their outstanding characteristic lies in their former occupation: they were exclusively engaged in copper mining. Although they started some agriculture around 1900, the definitive change took place abruptly in 1930-31, when the government closed the copper mines. Probably this is one of the most important socio-economic changes in Nepal in recent times. Except for a short survey by C. Jest no research has been done among the Chantel.[2] They are often referred to by their neighbours as Magars and appear as such in the Census and other reports. This may be due to the fact that those Chantel who enlist in the Indian or British Army adopt the name *Poon* (Magar sub-tribe) because Magars have an excellent reputation as soldiers.

My aim was to investigate the inter-ethnic relations between Chantel, Thakali and other Magar sub-tribes of this region, including the impact of Hinduism on these ethnic groups, but soon I came to realize that the Chantel are a group apart, that many of the Thakalis had left this region because the copper mining stopped in 1930-31 and trade with the Chantel was no longer profitable; there are almost no inter-ethnic relations between the Chantel (of Āṭh Hajār Parbat) and the surrounding castes and ethnic groups. Therefore I tried to find out the characteristic features of the Chantel to provide a general introduction to them, and to examine the implications caused by the change of their economic basis from mining to agriculture. It should be mentioned that during my stay the Chantel of Āṭh Hajār Parbat experienced the worst famine for three generations and that this situation might have had some influence on various information collected.

The Chantel can be divided into two groups: western Chantel and eastern Chantel. The main difference between them lies in the language; the Chantel of the West, being a minority among Nepali speaking castes and tribes such as Brahman, Chetri, Kāmi and Magar have given up most of their specific traditions and also forgotten their own language. They live in the region around Bhuji Khola, Nissi Khola and Taman Khola, in the north-western part of Baglung District (28°20' - 28°30' latitude north; 83°22' longitude east), at an altitude ranging from 5000-65000 ft.

The eastern Chantel region is limited in the North by the steep slopes of Dhaulagiri Himal, in the South and West by Myagdi Khola and in the East by Rahughat Khola (28°26' - 28°35' latitude north; 83°23' - 83°40' longitude east). This region belongs to Myagdi District and is known as Ath Hajar Parbat (Eight Thousand Hills). These Chantel speak their own language exclusively (Chantel Kura) but most of them have sufficient knowledge of Nepali to communicate with Kamis, who live in nearly all Chantel villages, and with the Nepali speakers of the valleys. The total number of Chentel speakers lies between 1800 - 2000 only.

One of the largest Chantel villages lies outside the two areas mentioned: Gurjakhāni at the foot of Churen Himal and Gurja Himal. It is the remotest village in Myagdi District, access to it is rather difficult and the next Chantel village is two days' walk away. Gurjakhāni plays an intermediary role between western and eastern Chantel having marriage relations with both parts (whereas today western and eastern Chantel hardly know of each other's existence). The oral tradition of the Chantel there is still alive and most of the old people at least understand Chantel Kura. There are about 90 Chantel houses and 17 Kāmi houses at Gurjakhāni; its altitude is 8500 ft. The Chantel population is increasing steadily and has almost tripled in the past ninety years. At present they number about 5000 persons.

In the West, villages are composed of several small groups of houses and isolated farmsteads around one to three nuclei; these villages extend over several hundred yards. In the East, houses are clustered compactly together, ranged in parallel lines horizontally to the mountain slopes. Often the gap between two houses is less than one yard. In every line of houses there are one or two stone-paved platforms of 10-30 sq. yards; these are the centers for social and working activities. Wherever space is available it is used to store fodder or firewood and for sheep and goat sheds. The Kāmi houses are grouped together and located at the village border; Kāmi workshops are situated outside the main village. Nearly all Chantel villages lie at the end of a small valley surrounded by steep, rocky hills on three sides thus making communication rather difficult. In comparison to other ethnic groups of the region the Chantel occupy the highest settlements.

As to agriculture and house building there is almost no difference between the Chantel and the neighbouring Magars. In the past, when the main occupation of the Chantel was copper mining, their houses were only one-storeyed, with stone walls and roofs of thatch or bamboo mats. Agriculture was unknown to them at that time and all necessities were provided by Thakali merchants in exchange for copper. When the copper production declined (the mines were nearly exhausted) they gradually started agriculture and adopted the solid, mostly two-storeyed stone houses of the northern Magars. Grass-thatched roofs have nearly disappeared and been replaced by solid slate roofing. The upper part of the house is used for storage, the lower room, completely dark, serves as kitchen, living and sleeping room. In the cold season, young sheep, goats and chickens are kept there too. Verandahs on one or two sides form an integral part of every house. There is no restriction for anybody to enter any part of the house (except for untouchables) and no shrine or special place for gods and worship inside the house.

Today, all Chantel can be considered settled agriculturists but because of the environmental conditions we can speak of a transhumant pattern to some extent as well. Chantel depend on subsistence economy and their only cash crop (on a modest scale) is potatoes. Potatoes, maize, barley, wheat and buckwheat (the bitter variety) are the main food crops. Millet is grown only in a few villages and is of a poor quality. Another food crop - *Amaranthus leucocarpus (latay)* - is common among all Chantel but only eaten on certain occasions. Paddy is purchased in a bazaar or obtained in exchange for potatoes, bamboo mats or baskets, and is only used during festivals and on ceremonial occasions. The forest offers a great variety of edible roots and plants which are used as vegetables; radish, garlic and pumpkins are planted. Hemp *(Cannabis sativa)* grows wild in the forests and fields but only during the last few years, when traders began to collect hashish in the Chantel region, has this plant become a small source of income.

An average farmstead keeps 5-10 cows and a pair of oxen for ploughing; well to do families have a few buffaloes as well. Milk production rarely exceeds half a litre for either cow or buffalo per day and is almost exclusively made into clarified butter *(ghyu)*. Buffaloes need more fodder and care than cows; they are kept largely for the sake of prestige. After harvesting, cows and buffaloes are herded near the village to graze on the fields. During the rest of the year they are moved to different grazing areas every 6-8 weeks. The highest grazing land (10-1200 ft.) is used during the monsoon. Each family establishes its own temporary cattle shed made out of bamboo mats, and one or two persons take care of the herd. Sometimes a cattle shed can be as far away as two days' walk and small families will leave the village to stay there. That means that between 25-50% of the inhabitants live outside the village most of the year.

Every family keeps a small flock of sheep and goats in sheds inside the village. Goats are never milked and sheep very rarely; their main purpose is to provide wool as well as meat for festivities. Herding sheep and goats in the surroundings of the village and at the same time collecting firewood is the first regular activity for Chantel boys and girls starting at the age of 8-10. Thakali merchants and a few rich Chantel families own sheep herds of a hundred animals and more, and during the warm season these are herded on the remotest grazing lands up to the snow line (ca. 15000 ft.). Chickens are the most important animals for sacrifices and mainly kept for that purpose.

Many village names in the Chantel region contain the word *khānī* (= mine), which indicates the relation between the Chantel and mining. According to oral tradition, the Chantel came from the West over the Chantu Pass (near Dhorpatan) long ago and since then they have been engaged in copper mining.

The Chantel claim to be Hindus but it is obvious that they are much less influenced by Hinduism than their nearest neighbours, the Northern Magar (mostly Poon). In interrelations with the Kāmi they observe strictly the regulations of the Nepalese Caste System regarding commensuality, less strictly those concerning touchability; in one case I could even observe the participation of a Kāmi (soldier in the Indian Army on leave) at the cremation of a Chantel. The Kāmi participate in most of the feasts and religious ceremonies and it is not unusual to see the Chantel Jhā̃kri praying together with a Kāmi on the occasion of a *pujā* for the welfare of the village. Among the deities worshipped by the Chantel only a few belong to the 'classic' Hindu Pantheon, the most important being local deities like Bhume, Bāra and Siddha. Witches (*boksi*, *ḍayani*), goblin- or demon-like beings (*bir*, *māsān*) and spirits of the dead (*moc*[2], *pret*, *siyo*) play a dominant role in the religious life of the Chantel. There are no temples for any of those gods in the Chantel region of Āṭh Hajār Parbat; only some bushes with a small shrine made of some stone plates and decorated with cotton straps or occasionally with a small bell indicate the places of the gods.

The Chantel pretend to employ Brahmans for every important life cycle ceremony such as birth, marriage and death, but during my six months' stay, Brahmans performed sanskritic rites in a Chantel village only once (on the occasion of the death of a Chantel woman, mother of a District Assembly member). Only a few Chantel own a *janma patra* (astrological birth certificate) written by a Jaishi Brahman. In my records about Chantel-marriages over the past 60 years not a single case appears where a Brahman was employed for a wedding-ceremony.

The Jhā̃kri is the most important religious expert among the Chantel. In Āṭh Hajār Parbat there are four of them including one *jharini* (woman shaman); the Kāmi-Jhā̃kris are more numerous but it is difficult to give the exact number because - as I was told by the Chantel - every Kāmi is a potential Jhā̃kri and communicates with ghosts and spirits anyhow. Among these Jhā̃kris one, Kumma Siha Chantel of Kuinekhāni village, has achieved an outstanding position, and he is the only one who can live entirely on his income as a shaman. The way he became a Jhā̃kri does not differ much from that of other Jhā̃kris (both Chantel and Kāmi) and will be best presented in his own words:

"I started this profession when I was 15 years old. I was in a *goth* (cattleshed) up there in the mountains. The *guru* also lives there, - in the eastern side of Kuine. During the night when I was sleeping the *guru* entered my body and caused my body to tremble. For some days, because of the sudden change, I felt some pain and was a little bit sick. While I was sleeping I was trembling, and after getting up I was still trembling. After that, still trembling, I went to other places where a *jhā̃kri basnu* (séance) was going on. Sometimes I also looked after someone's headache, for the pain of the heart and for other troubles. Once somebody recovered from that [treatment] and from then on everybody called me '*jhā̃kri*'.

"For two years I worked in the same way [that means without playing the *dhyāngro* (drum)]. In the third year I started playing the *thāl* (metal disc) [which belonged to his grandfather who also was a Jhā̃kri]. After that I made a *pujā* to the *guru* . After making *puja* to the *guru* I waited for the *dhyāngro* and the *gajā* (drumstick) and continued playing the *thāl*. Once it happened that the *thāl* clashed with a tree covered with creeping plants [and got stuck in it]. After that I took some *akshatā* (holy, unbroken rice for offerings), chanted some *mantra* and threw the *akshatā* on that tree. While throwing *akshatā* in that way, it was told that the tree trembled. Because of the God in me, I did not see the tree trembling, but the *mūrkha* (expression for all 'ordinary' people at the moment when a Jhakri communicates with gods or spirits, also in the meaning of 'foolish, ignorant people') told that it [the tree] trembled.

"Then I told them to cut the tree and then those *mūrkha* cut the tree and [I] made the frame for the *dhyāngro*. Then, after hunting the *ghoral* (wild goat) and having fixed [the skin] on the frame I started playing [the drum]. The *gajā* was also brought on the same day."

An initiation under the guidance of a teacher *(guru)* as mentioned by Hitchcock (1967: 154 ff) and Höfer/Shrestha (1973: I ff) is unknown among the Jhā̃kris of Āṭh Hajār Parbat. For them the *guru* is identical with the tutelary deity and they deny any initiation by a human being. Kumma Sĩha admits that he has acquired some knowledge about religion in general through Brahmans and Magar but insists on the fact that all the ritual techniques and *mantra* were taught in dreams by his spiritual *guru*. Any God or spirit can be a *guru* and that God who caused a Jhā̃kri at the beginning of his career to tremble for the first time will become his *guru* for lifetime.

The *guru* can be called at any time, no special offering or preparation is necessary. At the very moment when the *guru* enters the Jhā̃kri's body (through the head, sometimes through the heart) his head begins to shake. When he intends to perform a seance he will put on his *chā̃cā̃mā̃cā̃* (Jhā̃kri's costume and equipment), offer some *dhupā* (incense; any kind of leaves or flowers may be used) to the *guru*, put some ash from the fireplace on his forehead to purify himself, and plants the metal *trisula* (trident), decorated with red and white cotton straps, beside him. Then he begins to chant the 'main *mantra*'. These 'main *mantra*' vary according to the different *gurus*; its main purpose is to improve the communication between *guru* who speaks through him. Kumma Siha's *guru* is *siram* ('the dumb god of the forests') and so he makes no sound but only moves his lips when *siram* is speaking through him. With the help of his *guru* the Jhakri can call other gods, too, and they will speak through him. The Jhā̃kri's speech during a seance is called *bakhā̃unu bhā̃shi* (*bakhā̃unu* = to speak through somebody). When communicating with the Jhā̃kri, the gods and the *guru* will address him by the term *dā̃ge* (Turner: "dā̃ngā-daṅgi, adj. overjoyed, ecstatic. daṅge, adj. quarrelsome;" p. 301).

The *guru* protects the Jhā̃kri against witches (*boksi, dāyāni*) and other evil spirits such as *bhut, rākas, pisāch*, etc. In return the *guru* expects strict obedience, and if the Jhakri does not obey he will be punished severely. The Jhakri will offer *dhūpa* to his *guru* from time to time but at the beginning of a seance this offering is compulsory.

As to the costume and equipment there is no strict rule for the Jhākris of Āṭh Hajār Parbat. According to Kumma Sĩha the complete *chā̃cā̃mā̃cā̃* is given by the *guru* and he decides what a Jhā̃kri needs. The *chācāmācā* is considered as 'the robe of the God' and will protect the Jhā̃kri against the attacks of evil spirits. Two kinds of necklaces are used: *riṭṭhā* (black, shining seeds of a tree) and *rudrācchī ko mālā* (Turner: "rudrācche, l. rudrākṣa s. a variety of Elaeocarpus, the seeds of which are used for rosaries"). Each necklace should contain 108 pieces or 54, but of all the necklaces I have seen, not a single one had the 'right' number of pieces (no Jhãkri could tell me something about the meaning of these numbers). On certain occasions Kumma Sĩha also wears a necklace made out of the skeleton of a snake (which he killed on the order of his *guru*). In both necklaces other items are also fixed: horns of *ghoral* (wild goat), teeth of *sarā* (kind of deer) and of wild boar, 8 small bells and one round big bell and a *kawadā* (shell conch).

On his left arm Kumma Sĩha wears a *bholṭo* (a kind of wooden bracelet that protects the hunter's arm against the string of the bow, made out of *nyāmal* wood; Turner: "bholṭo, s. gauntlet, mail-glove." p. 484). This too protects against evil spirits. *Dhyāngro* and *gajā* (drum and drumstick) are the weapons of the Jhãkri. The one-sided drum is held with two loosely fixed crossed handles. When drumming, the drum is moved as well as the drum-sticks. The skin of the drum must be from a *ghoral*, preferably from a male animal, it must be replaced every 2 or 3 years. Besides the *dhyāngro* a metal disc *thāl* (mostly a brass plate) is also used by some Jhãkris. (I was told that *thāl* is mostly used in the region around Pokhara). The use of the *trisula* has already been mentioned. For a seance the Jhãkri will put on clean clothes that do not differ from his ordinary clothes: (cloth forming a sack on the back and crossed at the chest) and a short *lungi*. Both pieces can be made out of cotton or of *phuwa* (nettlecloth).

In comparison to the shamanism in the Bhuji Khola - Nishi Khola region presented by Hitchcock (1967: 1972), shamanism in Āṭh Hajār Parbat is less influenced by the "classic inner Asian tradition";[3] there is no headgear at all and no feathers or other signs of flight on the costume. Skin and horns of the wild goat, the bells and to some extent the 'climbing plants' mentioned in Kumma Sĩha's account point to an inner Asiatic tradition, but the Jhakris of this region are not aware of its origin. *Trisula, rudrācchī ko mālā* and shell conch indicate the influence of Northern India.

Ecological conditions in Āṭh Hajār Parbat are rather hostile to human existence; the micro-climate of Dhaulagiri is well known because of its rapid and violent change. Hailstorms with hail-stones up to the size of a chicken egg destroy the harvest, whole flocks of sheep and goats are killed by lightning, heavy rain transforms the steep mountain trails into small streams, takes away the thin layer of fertile soil and causes landslidings. Leopards living in the large forests surrounding the villages kill sheep, goats, and even small cows and buffaloes. In the night jackals *(shyāl)* come into the village and take away chickens. The Chantel believe that all these troubles are caused by angry gods or evil spirits. One of the tasks of the Jhakri is to find out the cause of these troubles and how to appease the gods and spirits. In most cases he will fix a date for a *pujā* and at least one member of each household should attend. The costs for such a *pujā* will be shared by the whole village. For such kind of service the Jhākri does not receive any compensation it is for the welfare of the village.

His main task, however, is to diagnose difficulties of individuals or families who call upon him for information and kill or drive away harmful ghosts and spirits by the use of various magical techniques. The Jhākri does not hold regular sessions; if a client needs his service he will go to the Jhākri, inform him of his difficulties and also tell him what in his opinion is the source of it. Then they will agree on a date for a seance (always performed at night). Payment is arranged after the seance; it depends on how long a seance lasts, and that cannot be known in advance. The charge also depends upon the financial condition of the client, varying from 3 to 20 Rs; the Jhākri also receives one meal and one *mānā* of rice (poor people may also give maize or buckwheat).

At the end of the séance when the Jhākri has found out the cause of the trouble through his contact with the supernatural world he tells the client which measures are necessary to appease the angry gods or to kill or drive away the evil spirits. In most cases a small offering is necessary which is performed immediately after the seance or even during it under the guidance of the Jhākri. Sometimes two or more gods or spirits may cause trouble and then one offering for each of them has to be given. There is no inquiry of the client or a relative by the Jhākri during the seance; neither are they ever possessed by spirits. If the client is not satisfied he can seek another Jhākri but first he will carry out the (first) Jhākri's recommendations. For the killing of a *syo* (spirit of an adult man who died an unnatural death) several sessions sometimes over the period of several years are necessary; for *syo mārne* (*syo* killing) always the same Jhākri is employed.

One of the most frequent sources of troubles are *boksi* (witches). In the village of Kuinekhāni (about 450 inh.) nine women between the age of 22 to 73 are supposed to be *boksi* but people talk about *boksi* only secretly. They have supernatural powers, their 'spirit' leaves their body in the night and troubles other people especially in their own village, mostly small children and pregnant women. If the Jhākri's diagnosis shows the cause of the trouble to be a *boksi* he always speaks of *boksi* in general without giving any details. During a seance the Jhãkri never mentions names of living persons thus avoiding social conflicts that might result from his diagnosis and have consequences for himself as well.

In his paper "A Shaman's Song and some Implications for Himalayan Research" (Hitchcock, 1974) Hitchcock compares the dual relationship between wife-givers and wife-receivers with shamanism and says: "In the domain of shamanism we find a status which similarly is ambiguous, because like the status of wife-giver, it also is associated with power that can be either beneficient or punishing." (Hitchcock 1974: p153). From the structuralist's point of view this is a very interesting thesis. Although the focus of my research was not shamanism I must say that I did not find any indication that could support this thesis. In no case could I register that the shaman's powers were directed at individuals within the community or that "the shaman's status .... with respect to good and evil is ambiguously colored." (Hitchcock 1972: pp 4-5).

According to their tradition the Chantel have never had any leader and my investigation revealed that Chantel society is rather egalitarian. Even after the introduction of the Panchayat System decisions are made by the village assembly (one male member of each household); the influence of the elected Village Panchayat Members is still insignificant. (The problem of dependance on Thakali merchants cannot be treated here). As every aspect of daily life, economical, social or other, is based on the religious background, the opinion of the religious specialist is the most important. The Jhākri in Āth Hajār Parbat does not act as a leader, he is an important adviser. I must admit, however, that this is mostly true for Kumma Sĩha, but the other Chantel or Kāmi Jhãkris of Āṭh Hajār Parbat play only secondary roles. In quarrels between distinct groups or individuals he tries to 'depersonalize' the conflict and blame it on 'unpersonal' spirits as far as possible. This task as well as the services he renders to the whole community is fulfilled while remaining in the background. He might be characterized as a kind of leader, but I think he is best characterized as an integrating factor in Chantel society and to some extent also in regard to interethnic relations: he decides whether a Kāmi may participate in a ritual or not, and among his clients are also Magar and Thakali.

The Jhãkri of Āṭh Hajār Parbat (again mainly Kumma Sĩha) is also a religious policy maker. As a result of his pronouncements, "particular deities appear, gain prominence, lose prominence, and disappear in the village pantheon." (Berreman, 1964: p.59)

Wolf D. Michl

NOTES

1. Research was carried out in 1971-72 with the support of the South Asia Institute. Heidelberg.

2. Turner: "moc,s. A partic. disease or visitation or evil spirits which causes the death of children before the age of nine in the family afflicted by it." p.519

3. Hitchcock 1967: p.149

BIBLIOGRAPHY

Berreman, G.D. Brahmins and Shamans in Pahari Religion; in: *Religion in South Asia*, Harper, E.B. (ed) Seattle 1964.

Hitchcock, J.T. A Nepalese Shamanism and the Classic Inner Asian Tradition; in: *History of Religions*, Vol. 7, No. 2, Chicago 1967.
A Shaman's Song and some Implications for Himalayan Research; *Contributions to the Anthropology of Nepal*. Warminster, 1974.

Höfer, A. and Shrestha, B.P. Ghost Exorcism among the Brahmans of Central Nepal. (Manuscript) 1973.

Turner, R.L. A Comparative and Etymological Dictionary of the Nepali Language, London, 1931.

Myths and Facts: Reconsidering some Data concerning the Clan History of the Sherpa

"Das wahre Bild der Vergangenheit huscht vorbei. Nur als Bild, das auf Nimmerwiederschen im Augenblick seiner Erkennbarkeit eben aufblitzt, ist die Vergangenheit festzuhalten."

Walter Benjamin *Illuminationen*

If you have left a place, you cannot definitely say, I'll never return. For even if you don't return physically, the place might still be on your mind. Sudden flashes of thoughts bring it back: a scene, a smell, a bell, someone saying a word. Writing a book and finishing with it is like leaving a place. Many books are written with this motivation - to clarify a particular problem and in that way to bury it forever.

It is now several years since I left Nepal behind and the ethnological questions aroused by my stay. The book stands in its shelf and the subject matter has faded into the distance.[1] And yet, there are a few themes which I dealt with then and which since then have come back to my mind time and again. I think that these are the ones that must have troubled me most, i.e. the ones that have turned out to be the most problematic.

Some of the questions that were underlying my work on the Sherpa and partly motivated it might be formulated in the following way:

1. Is it possible to get some knowledge on the historic composition of a tribe, its time and place of origin, by merely relying on its own oral or written traditions, provided there are any?

2. If so, is it possible, to find the demarcation line between mythographical and historiographical accounts?

3. What is the nature of an historical fact, comparing native and western history?

4. Can the historical study of a social institution help to understand that institution theoretically or sociologically?

The simplest approach to these questions is to resume briefly the results of my work.

Until the discovery of a number of local documents found in several villages of Solu back in 1965, which were partly mythological and partly historical in nature, the knowledge about the past of Solu-Khumbu's inhabitants was scarcely more than a blank page. This fate has been shared till now by other regions and populations of Nepal. The Sherpa documents, most of which are written in Tibetan, helped to change this situation a little. We have now some data at hand.

To begin with: the area in Eastern Nepal called Solu-Khumbu, now the main dwelling place of the Sherpa, has not always been inhabited by them. Nor by others. It was not until the middle of the 16th century that the first ancestors of the Sherpa immigrated into this region. These ancestors had come a long way. According to written accounts and oral information their original homeland was a region in the Eastern Tibetan province of Kham named Salmo Gang, that is a region approximately 1300 miles away from their present home. One of the reasons for this migration can be guessed from a statement in one of the documents, according to which the emigration took place at a time of politico-religious tension between the Kham people and their powerful neighbours in the North, the Mongols.

The migration itself can be divided into two successive phases first, the march from Kham in Eastern Tibet to the Tinkye region in Central Tibet; then, from Central Tibet to the present dwelling places in Nepal. The intermediary stay in Central Tibet appears to have been intended by them as a final one. Another politico-religious pressure seems to have caused the Sherpa ancestors to have left their newly acquired homes for the second time. In the years 1531-33 Mirza Muhammed Haidar Dughlat, the General of the religious Muslim zealot, Sultan Sa'id Khan from Kashgar, invaded Tibet with his army from the west and although he did not quite achieve his aim - the destruction of the City temple of Lhasa - the army generated a lot of fear and turmoil in those parts through which the martial campaign led. Supposing that this foreign invasion was directly related to the Sherpa's escape across the Himalayan mountain range into Nepal, as the indications suggest, we can date their arrival in Solu-Khumbu very precisely. It must have been round 1533.

With the migration of the Sherpa ancestors across the Nangpa La pass into the valleys south of Mt. Everest begins the history of the colonization of Solu-Khumbu. The first chapter of this colonization is identical with the separate movements of the first clans to arrive. They number four, each of them composed of not more than a few families. A general pattern of settling can be observed:

- Each of the different clans selects a clearly defined locality for settlement and demarcates the boundaries of its clan-property;
- the number of a clan's members increases and the small settlements develop into the first discernable clan-villages, the centers of clan activities;
- from the first clan-villages new satellite settlements are founded within the confines of a clan's area;
- the new settlements also grow and become independent clan-villages;
- the dislocation from the old villages produces naturally an increasing disintegration of the original homogeneous proto-clans;
- the final result of disintegration is the split of the proto-clans into several sub-clans which, by adopting new clan names, become independent social units.

Two of the four original or proto-clans - the Minyagpa and Thimmi - first occupied the eastern and western parts of Khumbu, the remaining two - the Serwa and Chappa - proceeded immediately to Solu, later followed by the majority of the others. In the course of their geographical dispersion only the first two proto-clans mentioned split up into a number of independent sub-clans, which however preserve to the present day their common ancestry. This can be seen from the fact that members of sub-clans belonging to a common proto-clan do not intermarry, just as if they still were one single clan, which by definition strictly follows the rules of clan exogamy. The descendants of the four proto-clans, including their different split branches - lineages or sub-clans - now form the core of Sherpa society, in rank, in age and in number.

The next historical and hierarchical stratum of Sherpa society was created by the immigration - almost exclusively to Khumbu - of people who had formerly lived in the surroundings of Dingri, the adjacent area north of the main Himalayan range. They started to move into Nepal from about the middle of the 18th century. Because of their general cultural similarity they were easily integrated into the tribal community.

Dating back to about the same time another set of people made its way into Sherpa society. It consisted in members from other

Nepalese groups such as Tamang, Gurung, Chetri and Newar, who had entered into marital or casual unions with Sherpa girls. The offspring of these alliances, now mainly living in Pharak, were also assimilated into Sherpa culture despite the fact that they had come from distinctly different cultural background. They started to wear Sherpa dress and ornament, took Sherpa names, were converted to Buddhist religion and adopted the Sherpa language. The ultimate feature of their assimilation, however, was the transformation of their original tribal names into substitutive clan names. Formerly being an indicator for tribal endogamy the name now changed into a sign of an exogamic practice. This shift of the name's function was a necessary tribute to the social practices of the group into which these newcomers entered. To distinguish them from the newer clan or family groups immigrating from the Tibetan side, I have called these newly formed units pseudo-clans.

The last group of immigrants - predominantly to Khumbu - that was integrated into Sherpa society were the so-called Khamba. Although the word originally means 'those from Kham', Khamba is a relatively empty category in local terminology. For all people who had within the last four generations moved into Khumbu from the north were labelled in this way. Some of them were just northern neighbours, whereas a number of them had their place of origin as far away as the west Nepalese areas of Mustangbhot and Manangbhot. Lacking the most important status symbol in the eyes of the Sherpa, i.e. an acknowledged clan name, these Khamba were looked upon as socially inferior.

Finally there were settlers from other ethnic groups of Nepal who shifted into the regions of Solu-Khumbu, maintaining their own cultural traditions and not mingling with the Sherpa. Most of them came from the west. This movement started in the 19th century and continues into the present. Nearly all of them now live in Solu.

To give a numerical idea of the people I have been speaking of here some general figures from the demographic charts I collected in 1965 are given. The present population of Solu-Khumbu amounts to about 30,000 persons, half of whom are constituted by the non-Sherpa ethnic or caste groups such as Chetri (4,700), Tamang (2,200), Magar (2,000), Kami (1,600), Newar (1,000), Rai (700), etc. The other half is Sherpa of which 13,300 persons belong to the offspring of the proto-clans, 450 to the newer clans, 350 to the pseudo-clans and about 1,000 to the Khamba.

I

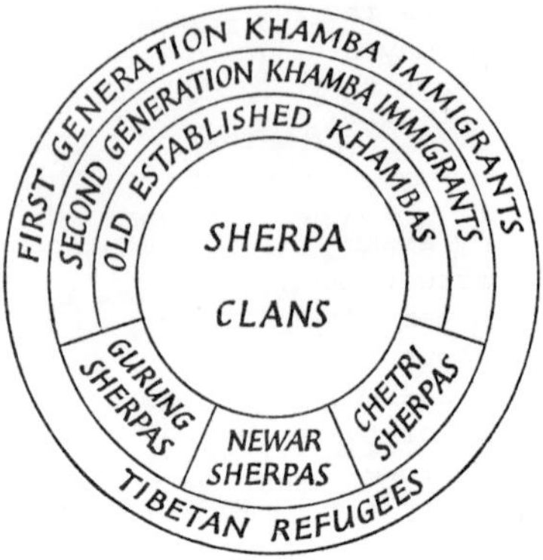

II

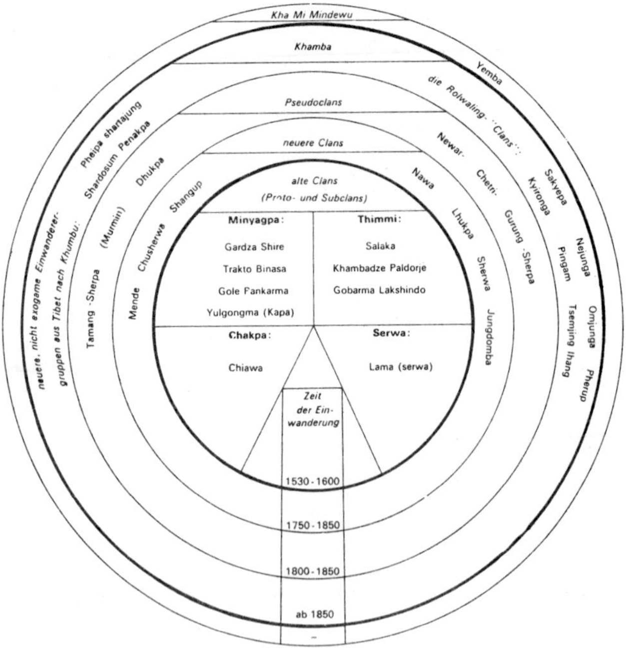

Reproduced from: (I) C. von Fürer-Haimendorf *The Sherpas of Nepal*, London 1964, p.27 and (II) M. Oppitz *Geschichte und Sozialordnung der Sherpa*, Innsbruck/Munchen 1968, p.100.

The subjoining chart summarizes the foregoing discussion. It has been juxtaposed by the older one in Furer-Haimendorf's book on the Sherpa,[2] together illustrating two phases of fieldwork, one before and one after the discovery of the native historical documents. Besides the utility of historical investigation this juxtaposition may also indicate that it is never too late: even if a tribe seems to have been thoroughly studied it is in no way superfluous to revisit it again.

As already assumed the first ancestors of the present Sherpa did not migrate from Eastern Tibet to Nepal as a whole tribe. They came in very small number. Therefore, and this was my final hypothesis about the history of their colonization, what now is known as the Sherpa, a considerable hilltribe of Eastern Nepal, is the result of the numerical expansion of a very small population that followed mechanically its own rate of growth (doubling rate for population: 49 years) within the confines of a single area (Solu-Khumbu) and a demarcated period of time (ca 450 years).

So much for the resume.

Let us now go back to the four questions posed at the beginning of the present paper and see if the ethnographical material provides a glimpse of an answer to them or if in turn the material itself can be slightly illuminated or x-rayed by them.

If one asks the first question and the answer is yes, the second comes immediately up; so let us postpone this possibility till we talk about the second. But if the answer is no, one would like to find our what other auxiliary means can be offered to rescue native history from the level of mere conjectural guessing. In the Sherpa case there were two such auxiliary means to support the local oral and written reports on the past: alien historical sources and statistics. The first of these two means is common practice among historians: dealing with a particular period of time, one of their primary efforts will be to enlarge the quantity of independent sources that reflect the time in question. In a few instances the Sherpa material allowed a cross-checking from other - mainly Tibetan - historical accounts. Some of the events and persons mentioned in the Sherpa documents also figured in chronicles, unrelated to them. This situation was not only an affirmative point for their existence, it also helped to provide markings for the time scheme. The other auxiliary tool - statistics - might seem a little uncommon in this connection. In fact, when I did my demographic enquiries amongst the Sherpas, I could not foresee that later they would aid the historical ones. Given were some historical data, for the correctness of which there was evidence from other sources. Also given were several genealogies of some of the clans and lineages, which either I extracted from the historical accounts themselves or which existed in pure form, in the guise of written ancestral enumerations. These genealogies comprised 10 to 35 generations. Now, if I could give a fairly precise mean for an average generation amongst the patrilineal Sherpa, that is the time span between a man and the son who carries on the lineage, then the historical markings and the genealogies, the generations of which would further on serve as rungs of a chronological ladder, could be connected and mutually tested. The answer was provided by my demographic questionnaires. In other words: three different and in isolated form dead sets of information - historical dates, genealogical charts and demographic details - could be assembled towards making a joint message: together they formed the time scheme for Sherpa history.

If on the other hand we look upon the local (native) historical documents as they stand on their own, it is necessary to investigate their nature, i.e. to examine where they belong to, to the realm of history or that of mythology. Otherwise one would risk the charge of naivete. In the case of the Sherpa material this investigation is simplified by the native's own distinction between the two spheres. In most cases the learned people among them are quite definite about which parts of an account are to be taken as serious historical report and which ones are mythological. And for some, this in fact, is quite easy. I will give two short examples. One of the texts deals with the ancestors of the Chakpa clan before and at the time of the emigration from Kham. Speaking about the founder of one of the lineages, who himself is apparently an historical figure, the text suddenly deviates into telling an adventure this man had with an eagle. Both the form which instantaneously changes into verse and the fantastic content clearly unmask the interpolation as a mythical story, the aim of which is to establish the eagle as the protective clan deity and the man as the one who first met that supernatural animal. Other documents have their mythological parts in the beginning. For they start with well known and standardised genealogies, borrowed from Tibetan mythological genesis, such as the derivation from the monkeys. That is to say, in the case of the Sherpa documents the demarcation line between historical and mythological account is usually sharp enough to be recognised.

But it would be oversimplifying the matter if one stuck too rigorously to a strict dualization of the two mentioned spheres. In fact, one may ask if not history itself has mythological qualities. Or to put it into more direct terms: isn't it inevitable that historical data in the moment they are presented take on the quality of mythical, that is to say ideological statements? That leads us right into the third question, the one about the nature of an historical fact. No one has gone into it with more radical vigour than Levi-Strauss in his famous controversy against Sartre at the end of *La Pensée Sauvage*. The last chapter entitled Histoire et Dialectique reveals the various descriptions of the French Revolution as inevitably mythological. Since a total history is impossible or would confront us with undistinguishable chaos, history by definition has to be partial. A historical fact therefore is not just what really has happened, it is what it is only through the declaration of the historian. In a way it is made by him, because it is he who selects what is to be considered as historically relevant; it is he who cuts out other events and puts the ones selected together. In short, history is always *a* history, depending on who is talking. It is a conscious or unconscious ideaological collage of what has happened, an interpretation of it. It is a demonstration. And exactly at this point the mythological features of history become apparent.

The difference therefore that normally is made between historical and mythological fact is much less sound than at first sight would appear. Both types of facts serve at times exactly identical purposes: they want to tell and thereby prove something. The lofty attitudes which western interpreters of indigenous societies often take towards the native's incapacity to distinguish between the two spheres - an assumption that probably is more often wrong than right, as the Sherpa case suggests - return to them like a boomerang: not seeing the inevitable ideological dimension of historiography they themselves become automatic victims.

Moreover, it can be observed that the distinction between historical and mythological fact, instead of simply separating what actually happened from what happened in people's imagination, indirectly serves to establish and confirm another opposition that apparently is one of the dearest to run-of-the-mill anthropology: I mean the opposition between civilised and primitive. In fact, the most general criterion for this distinction is historical consciousness, which according to a widespread agreement, the civilized people possess and the primitive people don't. This extends to the point of making the assumption that there are societies which have no history at all.

All societies have their history, be it written or unwritten, stored or not. What differs is the importance they invest it with. This again depends on the different concepts people have of history. Some of the concepts may be described as linear, according to which all events of the past form a necessary line of development that runs parallel to their chronological order. Others may be described as circular, according to which there is a certain amount of events that happen and after exhaustion happen again. The first of the two concepts attributes a teleological quality to the film of history, the other conceives it as repetitive. It can be easily deduced from conditions like these - and they are only two out of many - that the attention paid to the sum of historical events changes from one concept to the next. One could even say that the concept a society has of history in general determines its own history in the same way as the historian makes or manipulates it. As a matter of fact he is rarely more than the official spokesman of that particular concept.

To sum up: I don't think it is acceptable to introduce the qualifying opposition between primitive and civilized by the sole criterion of historical consciousness, because this would equal a voluntary critique on alien forms of consciousness in general. For the neutral denomination of different levels of techno-economic status however the opposition might be practical.

Apart from historical consciousness the question remains whether there is a difference between say western and native historical facts. And here, I think, one must make a distinction, which mainly results from the size and specification of a population. In a relatively small, unspecified and homogeneous society like that of the Sherpa events could be called historical that in our society would rank as anecdotal or biographical. Our societies have, as Levi-Strauss would put it, a kind of strong history, whereas the native's history more often than not is weak, that is to say, situated on a less explicative scale. "L'histoire biographique et anecdotique est la moins explicative; mais elle est las plus riche du point de vue de l'information, puisqu'elle considère les individus dans leur particularité, et qu'elle détaille, pour chaqun d'eux, les nuances du caractère, les détours de leurs motifs, les phases de leurs délibérations. Cette information se schématise, puis s'efface, puis s'abolit, quand on passe à des histoires de plus en plus "fortes"".[3] In other words: history reaches a higher degree of potency the more extended and diversified the society is, with which it deals.

Before we conclude let us now turn to the last of the four

questions that headed this paper. It brings us directly into contact with the principal sceptic, concerning the study of history in the anthropological field. This man was Radcliffe-Brown. On the very first page of his most influential work[4] Radcliffe-Brown makes a distinction between historical and theoretical studies of social institutions. The first type of enquiry he calls idiographic. The second one he labels nomothetic. The difference between the two is defined by the conclusions they aim at, which are particular or factual statements in the one case and general propositions in the other. Among the idiographic enquiries besides historical studies he names ethnography, which in turn differs from the former in that it derives its knowledge from direct observation rather than from written accounts. A field for nomothetic enquiries is comparative sociology; we may add theoretical or just social anthropology.

Now, having made these more or less academic distinctions Radcliffe-Brown warns us, never to confuse historical explanation with theoretical understanding. And in the primitive societies, he goes on to say, "that are studied by social anthropology there are no historical records"[5], which means that from an historical point of view in anthropology not even an idiographic study is possible.

There are some objections to be raised against these assertions. First of all, there are historical records, at least in some of the primitive societies. They only wait to be discovered. The Sherpa are one example. The first ethnographer who did a thorough study on them, Fürer-Haimendorf, concluded slightly disappointed on this matter: ... "Traditions and myths relating to the Sherpa's migration to the regions of Khumbu and Solu and to the establishment of the present villages are almost completely lacking."[6] This was written one year before we went to Nepal and collected just about twenty such documents, aided by the fortunate choice of having stayed mainly in Solu, where nearly all of the scriptures stem from, rather than in Khumbu.

The second objection against Radcliffe-Brown is of a more epistemological nature. Contrary to his statement I maintain that an historical study of social institutions can very well support theoretical understanding of them. This does not at all mean that historical explanation is or necessarily leads to a generalised comprehension; or that it could replace theoretical reflection that is sociological understanding. Let us confront my assertion with concrete ethnographic experience.

If one compares the present clan system of the Sherpa as it appears to direct observation with the one of the past that can be deduced from the written traditions, the first impression one gets is that there are no major contradictions between the two. Although not identical they share the same features. For both the most outstanding one is the clan name, which every person belonging to Sherpa society must have. If a person has not got such a name, he or she can either choose a substitute or else will not be admitted to the social life of the people. The clan name designates whom one can marry and whom one cannot. The Sherpa stick strictly to the rules of clan exogamy. This feature is at present as marked as it was in the past. As a social unit the clan manifests itself in various domains: it has an own and clearly defined clan territory, its exclusive clan villages, its own pastures. As a result of the topographical unit the clan undergoes common economic enterprises. Finally each clan has its own religious habits. Besides the universal deities each clan worships its own. However, it must be borne in mind that these last mentioned features don't have the same density today as they did in the past. Nowadays clan territories exist only in Solu. In the whole of Khumbu and Pharak there are no such things as clan territories, clan villages and clan pastures. And of all the villages in Solu only one half have remained pure patrician villages. On the other hand, the long list of mountain deities that are worshipped clanwise in Khumbu, is very short in Solu. In other words; the tightness of the clan as a social unit now is partially reduced or even left in ruins.

It is here that historical studies of social institutions become valuable. For if one wants to get a full account of the functions a clan may have as a social unit that is a general understanding of 'clan', it is a prerequisite, first to enumerate them. And if one does not find them in the present it is legitimate to search for them in the past. Thus the idiom: Spuren der Vergangenheit can be inverted: Die Spuren der Gegenwart that is,the residues of the present can be compounded to complete images by the past. Discoveries made in this way serve to explain the historical development of a single case just as much as they increase the possibilities for general sociological understanding; they are of equal use for both restricted ethnography and comparative anthropology.

Michael Oppitz

NOTES

1. I was in Nepal in 1965 and the result of my stay was the book: *Geschichte und Sozialordnung der Sherpa*, Innsbruck/München 1968.

2. Ch. von FÜRER-HAIMENDORF: The Sherpas of Nepal, London 1964, p.27

3. C. LEVI-STRAUSS: La Pensée Sauvage, Paris 1962, pp.338-348

4. C. LEVI-STRAUSS: La Pensée Sauvage, Paris 1962, p.346

5. A. R. RADCLIFFE-BROWN: Structure and Function in Primitive Society, London 1953

6. op.cit.p.3 (second edition)

7. Ch. von FÜRER-HAIMENDORF: The Sherpas of Nepal, London 1964, p.18.

The Divinities of the Karnālī Basin in Western Nepal

A. Introduction

I

In its religious practice western Nepal offers some striking features, which no other region in Nepal presents. Most of its leading divinities manifest themselves through a human medium, the oracle, who in the local parlance is called the *Dhāmī*. The institution of *Dhāmī* is based on the principle of reincarnation. When an old *Dhāmī* dies, the vacated position is filled, after a certain time, by another person of the same family or clan group in whom the divinity chooses to reappear *(autinu)*. However, the claims of a new *Dhāmī* are not accepted without verification: this means the *Dhāmī* has to pass certain tests by performing miracles. During the time he is possessed, which is called *paturnu*, the *Dhāmī* acts as the god-incarnate for the divinity he is supposed to represent; he fulfills the god's various socio-religious roles in the village towards his clients as a priest, an astrologer, a dispenser of medicine, an arbiter of village disputes, etc. Spells of possession take place at the time of the big worship *(Paiṭh)* or on any other occasion when the deity is invoked for special consultations by the villagers.

II

The author of this article was able to collect preliminary information on these religious practices during two trips to Jumla in the years 1967 and 1970. The facts included in this study derive mainly from the two districts of Dailekh and Jumla, with a few additions from the adjacent districts of Mugu and Tibrikot. Information about more distant places is derived from hearsay accounts collected in those regions. All this region is more conveniently described by the more comprehensive term "the Karnālī basin".

For the study of the religion based on the cult of Maṣṭa,[1] the core territory would be formed by the three districts of Jumla, Mugu and Tibrikot. The inventory of divinities given in a tabular form below is by no means an exhaustive list; nor is it even complete concerning those places through which the author actually passed. In each of the villages there is such a variety of names of divinities that it was not possible to do justice to all of them in a short time. Nevertheless, it is hoped that the present inventory, however incomplete, might be useful for doing more extensive studies on the subject in future.

III

The divinities worshipped in this region resolve themselves into five classes. In the first category come the Maṣṭās (Nos. 1 - 16). In the second category are included those divinities whose names do not bear any Maṣṭa suffix but who nevertheless wield the same prestige as the former (Nos. 17 - 36). In the third category fall the deified spirits (Nos. 47 - 51). These are Brahman men and women, who have died in certain unhappy circumstances. Such deceased men and women are said to revisit the village as spirits and cause sufferings to the families till they are honoured by the assignment of a fixed place of worship within the village. One or two of these spirits, like the Jagannāth of Pādma (No. 47), in Bārabis darā of Jumla have a cult built up around them with their life story widely told in the area. But the majority of these spirits are usually centred on a single village. The practice of oracle consultation is known to exist only in respect to the deities of the first three categories. The divinities in the fourth category consist of females who were most likely established in the region because of the expansion of the Sakti Cult there, the central concept of the goddess having been provided by Durgā, Devī or Mahiṣamardinī (Nos. 52 - 58). In the last category are included Chandan Nāth and Bhairav Nāth, the presiding deities of Jumla, Khalaṅgā, the headquarters of the district. (Nos. 59 and 60). The functions and mode of worship in temples of the last two categories of divinities are like those in any other Brahmanical or Buddhist temples of Central and Eastern Nepal.

IV

None of the divinities acclaimed in the Karnālī basin has a fame or influence which is uniformly distributed in the whole area. Exceptions to this rule are the several pilgrimage centres of this region such as Chāyānāth, Riṇamokṣa, Thākūrjī and Muktināth, which everybody seeks to visit at least once in a life time. The influence of Chandan Nāth (addressed as Guru Mahārāj or Gosāiñ) is also widespread. He is considered the protective deity who bestows rain and plenty to the people. But there is no place for this divinity in the every-day religious life of the common people living in outlying villages. He is venerated but not worshipped except by wealthy Brahmans, Ṭhakuris and Chetris living close to the temple. Holding a special type of *pūjā* (i.e. worship) in this shrine; a *pūjā* known as *Rudrī* or *Saptāha* is considered a prestigious act enhancing the person's social status. Chandan Nāth has been actually much more patronized by outsiders and by the ruling family based in the Kathmandu valley than by the local people in terms of the organisation of *pūjās* in this temple.

Regarding the influence exercised by other divinities, their popularity differs from region to region. Some are more renowned in one area than in another. If plotted on the map, this might yield an interesting picture.

V

In Jumla and its surrounding districts the Maṣṭas and the divinities of their rank are worshipped and patronized by members of a specific clan or clans or in some cases by castes living within a village. It is a common thing to come across villages containing shrines of more than one divinity which shows that the villagers, in terms of sectarian loyalty, are split up into several groups. However, this is not the only phenomenon which one observes. For there are other villages which may or may not be composed of a single clan but which worship only one divinity. We may cite the village of Bābiro and Thārpā as examples of this. Here the entire village is a votary of one god. In the author's opinion, the religion of the Karnālī basin may have provided the nucleus for the evolution of the religious system of the *Kula-devatā* among the *Pahāḍī* caste-groups of Nepal. Worship of one's *Kula-devatā* (divinity worshipped by a lineage) is an important and intimate event for a person of this social group in Nepal (Bista, Khem Bahadur, 1). Families up to seven generations in a lineage assemble at a site having some connection with the family ancestry for this worship. The *pūjā* is done after great activity and important preparations. Many beliefs and superstitions are linked to this worship and each divinity seems to have its own preferences and eccentricities. This worship is done at one, two or twelve yearly intervals, differing from family to family. Many of the *Kula-devatas* in central Nepal can be traced to the divinities still being worshipped in the Karnālī basin. Elsewhere in Nepal, the days or years between the performance of the worship of the *Kula-devatās* of these people are given to performing a multiplicity of other religious activities. But in the Karnālī basin the sole religious preoccupation known to the villagers up till now is to organise the *paiṭh* for their village gods.

VI

The circumstances in which each clan came to invent and adopt its individual divinities cannot be properly explained here. These beginnings lie buried in the layers of time. What may still be said in respect of them is guess-work concerning the various social groups which may have been responsible for introducing and popularising them in the area.

A divinity travels from his original abode to other villages through the migrating villagers who are his votaries. Thus it is these migrants, who set up the divinity's shrine in the new village of their settlement. If the migrants form only one or two households, they may not set up their shrine at once; in this case they would return to worship their divinity in their original village at the time of the *paiṭh*. If the migrants have a large number of households in the new village which would enable them to pool their resources for maintaining and manning the management of the shrine, they may very well have a separate shrine erected there. This will not necessarily mean the end of relationships with the parental shrine so that sending from one place to another of *pūjā* (which means sending of *dhaj* i.e. pieces of red and white cloths and *Sik* meaning husked rice grains) will continue. Another instance of linkage binding the two shrines is provided by the fact that the *Dhāmī* of the off-shoot shrine must seek formal recognition of his position from the *Dhāmī* of the main shrine in a ceremony called *Chāpbido* which consists in placing a bell of bronze on the forehead of the supplicant, once in his life-time.[2]

In the process of migration some divinities were no doubt taken out of their home to new areas, but many others were completely forgotten by the migrating families as they were drawn into the influence of new local divinities. It is the author's belief that the hills of Nepal were widely settled by the *Pahāḍī* caste groups starting from their early base in the Karnālī basin (Sharma, Prayag Raj, 6, pp. 12 - 13). Many small incidents which happened to these families on the move may have had a profound bearing on their religious outlook and instincts. What is surprising is however the fact that many families could still preserve the memories of their early deities, so far away from their home in the Karnālī basin. In many cases the migration to distant places could have happened in fewer stages and over a shorter period of time.

VII

It is not possible to be definitive about the history of the religion centred on Maṣṭa or the divinities of his rank. First of all it is not clear from what root the name Maṣṭa is derived.[3] However, one or two aspects of the cult lead us to make some suppositions. One such supposition would be that the Matawālī Chetris of the Karnālī basin are primarily responsible for popularising the Maṣṭa cult. The villages which have the shrines of some of the leading Maṣṭas such as Bābiro, Thārpā, Buḍu and Kawa are all Chetri villages and the entire management in these shrines is looked after by them. The other region where Maṣṭas are popular and a religion based on oracle widely prevalent is the Chaudhabis *Kholā* to the north-east of Jumla, which is an exclusive Chetri settlement. (Sharma, Prayag Raj, 5). Although it is true that followers of the Maṣṭa are found in all castes including the low service-castes, the number is fewer among them. The number of *Dhāmī* among the Brahmans and the Ṭhakuris is comparatively fewer. Therefore, the cult always points to a connection with the Chetris. The Chetris of Dailekh district worship two forms of the Maṣṭa; the Dāḍyā and the Dudhyā. (Once outside of Jumla in Dailekh, one ceases to hear about all these varieties of Maṣṭa). It has already been said above that most Chetris in central and eastern Nepal still have one or the other name of the Maṣṭa as their *Kula-devatā*. One very popular name is Bārā-Maṣṭā, although there are other names too (Bista, 1, p. 63). Bara Masta in all probability is a collective reference to the group of Mastas whose number is said to be twelve in the Karnālī basin. (e.g. *Bārabhai maṣṭa nau durgā bhavānī*).

What is the origin of this religion? Is it of Brahmanical derivation or is it a local religion? It is not easy to give a clear-cut answer to this question. One guess is to suggest that it is a relic of the religion of the Khasas, who were settled in the region since a long time back, in the medieval period and earlier. There is some reason to think that the Chetris of the Karnali basin descend from the historical Khasas. The Karnālī basin in the records of the 13th century A.D. was called a *Khasadeśa* or Khasa country. (Sharma, Prayag Raj, 6 pp. 14 - 15). The fundamental aspects of this religion are unfamiliar to either Brahmanism or Buddhism. What are these points? First, the names of the Maṣṭas are not of Sanskrit derivation and they do not correspond to any gods of the Brahmanical pantheon. Attempts at Sanskritizing the names of one or two of them must be regarded as later acts. Secondly, there is no iconographic representation of the Maṣṭas or other divinities of the same order in the Karnālī basin. There is not a single stone or a piece of wood which represents the divinity in the shrine; only an empty niche. These divinities are not accorded any physical forms even in stories or songs sung in praise of them. In the stories Maṣṭas are known to wander in human forms sometimes impersonating an ascetic or a diseased person. The stories give a strong flavour of pastoral background. But they have no other special features or identification marks. The only symbol known to be associated with Maṣṭas is a bronze bell called the *jiughānt* (first heard in Tharpa and mentioned in story F, Gaborieau, 2, p. 22). Bells are used in this religion by the *Dhāmī* at other times also. Thirdly, the oracle idea, which is the central feature of the religion of the Karnālī basin is totally non-Brahmanic in character. The *bhāns* (vehicle) of the main divinity do not correspond to the idea of the *vāhana* of the classical gods of Brahmanism. All the *bhāns* are considered lesser divinities and malignant forces controlled by the main *Dhāmī*. The greater the variety of these evil spirits, which a *Dhāmī* can control, the greater becomes his prestige and fame. As these *bhāns* cause all illness and suffering to the villagers, the *Dhāmī* can easily cure them as soon as they are brought to his notice. Masta or the main divinity is regarded as a kind and benevolent deity completely different from his *bhāns*.

The Khasa country of the Karnālī basin came under strong Brahmanical influence between the 12th - 14th century A.D. New groups of people arrived there and set up a kingdom. These were the Mallas and people of other houses of the Ṭhakuris. They built temples of stone dedicated to Brahman and Buddhist gods (Sharma, Prayag Raj, 6), paid obeisance to these divinities in their numerous records and gave land-grants to the Brahmans. It must be during this time that an interaction between the two sets of religious traditions took place. Brahmanism has persisted in the region ever since its first introduction. But its distinctive features have been blunted in this remote and isolated land. All the temples of stone built in this region stand deserted and desecrated today, with no sign of any idol in them. Their place is taken by tumbled-down structures of rubble and timber with a low sloped roof and a facade placed at the gable end. These are the shrines of the Maṣṭas and other divinities in this area today. It may not be reasonable to regard this cult as having arisen only after the decline of the Malla Kingdom for no factor was present to generate a less evolved form of religion there after a phase of higher religion had already been experienced. It might be safer therefore to consider the cult of Maṣṭa as an older religious instinct in the area nurtured mainly by the Khasas and which had perhaps remained unemphasized or ignored in the records of the Mallas, but which reasserted itself again and this time assimilated a lot of influence from Brahmanism. The complete silence about this religion in the records may not be as significant as it appears at first sight. There is a possibility that the word *Dharmabhāṇaka* used in the two inscriptions of Prithvī Malla (Tucci, 7, p. 49 and *Itihāsa Prakāśa*, 3, p. 61: 69) refers to the *Dhāmis*.[4]

In the records from the Karnālī basin, the oldest reference to the Maṣṭa by name is to Bhuvānī Maṣṭa in a document of Saka 1547 (A.D. 1468) and to Kṣetrapāla Mastho in a writing interpolated in a document of Śaka 1768 (A.D. 1689) (*Itihāsa Prakāśa*, 3, p. 137; 367). Both these dates are posterior to the end of the Malla regime in western Nepal. The first name is clearly a conjunction of Bhavānī and Maṣṭa. The association of Bhavānī with Maṣṭa is a result of interaction between the two religious traditions. The second reference shows a Sanskritized form of Maṣṭa. The Brahmans of Sijā and Ukhāḍī worship the Maṣṭa under this very name.

Attempts to Sanskritize the names of the Maṣṭa can be seen in two other cases (Nos. 5 and 8). Other Brahmanical influences can also be detected as inserted in this religion. One part of the *paiṭh* requires the performance of a *homa* (a rite in which a Brahman priest puts oblations into a sacred fire while pronouncing vedic incantations). The author even saw the Bābiro Maṣṭa being given a *gotra* at the time of this *homa*. In the story of the Maṣṭa as narrated by the Ṭhakuris of Dāhān, Khāpar Maṣṭa is portrayed as the son of Indra (the Brahmanical king of gods). Maṣṭas are also identified with the Pāṇḍava heroes (story listed in Gaborieau, 2, story G, p. 22). There is another belief which says that the Masta recites forty chapters of the *Veda* (meaning the *Śukla Yajurveda*) through the person of his oracle who, in fact, is completely illiterate. Brahmanical values like these were assimilated in order to obtain the faith of the Brahmans in the divinity.

VIII

The deification of deceased Brahmans furnishes another interesting instance by which Brahmanical values were spread among a racial group mainly represented by the Khasas. One sees shrines of these Brahmans in the *Matawālī* settlement of the Chaudhabis *Kholā* (No. 51). The author was told that the offering in this shrine must include among other things, a sacred thread (*janai*). Jagannāth who is a popular deity of Bārabis dara, Kālikot darā and Dailekh district is the spirit of a Brahman boy who had been driven to commit suicide after an injustice suffered at the hands of the local ruler. In an interesting story narrated to the author by the Brahmans of Chilkhāyā in Jumla, their ancestor upon coming to the village for the first time refused to accept Jagannāth for a divinity - a fact which offended the population of the Tharis (i.e. Chetri) in the area who had accepted Jagannāth with all their faith. The Brahmans of Chilkhāyā have resisted this cult even to this day and the resentment of the Tharis against their behaviour is preserved in a formalised custom under which they do not give milk, curd or any of their dairy produce to the Brahmans of Chilkhāyā (these Brahmans belong to the Upamaṇyu *gotra*).

IX

The introduction of female divinities under various names and the introduction of Chandan Nāth and Bhairav Nāth again seem to be a legacy of Brahmanical influence. In this area the priests in all the shrines of these goddesses whatsoever their names are the Brahmans. The spur of Kanaka Sundarī māi in Hāṭsijā, which represents the palatial site of the Mallas, has a shrine consecrated to the goddess of that name in which the priests are the Brahmans. There is a shrine of Tripurā Sundarī māi in Talphi in

Chaudhabis *Kholā*. A Brahman comes from Ukhāḍī to worship here two times a year in Asoj and Chaitra. The shrine of Jālpā Devī in Ukhāḍī is similarly priested by a Brahman. Apart from Bhāvāni, who is associated with the Maṣṭa; another very popular name under which Durga is worshipped is Mālikā. The most famous shrine of Mālikā lies on the borders of Jumla and Bājurā districts. Her shrines can be found in other places also and these are always located on the summits of high mountains. These goddesses are not represented by an oracle so that even the Bhavānī in the shrine of the Maṣṭa is unattended by this custom.

The twin temples of Chandan Nāth and Bhairav Nāth are considered in local beliefs, to be very old. However, inscriptions found in these shrines are not earlier than the early 19th century A.D. (*Itihāsa Prakāśa*, 3 pp. 86 - 100). Offerings to these temples have been made by kings, queens, prime-ministers, officials of Kathmandu serving in Jumla and other well-to-do local people. Both the shrines have land endowments donated by the rulers at different times, the income from which is spent in the maintenance and worship in the temples. The state has also granted the right to raise levy from each house on behalf of these temples in Jumla, Mugu, Karān and Tibrikot districts. By similar arrangements, free labour can be extracted for temple works from specified villages. Thus the state has been directly involved in promoting the status of these two divinities in Jumla.

The identity of Chandan Nath is not quite clear. In a popularly known story, he is held to be a saint who came from Kashmir and who did for Jumla the same thing that Mañjuśrī did for the Nepal Valley in a different tradition. Thus he drained the water which had accumulated like a lake stretching from Khalāchaur to Dānsānghu and rehabilitated the place. He introduced the cultivation of rice in Jumla. The real object of worship inside this shrine is a pair of footprints. But there are also a number of small statues of different divinities including those of Buddha and the Buddhist divinities. But there is one image which is regarded as the chief one. It is a three-headed image of Dattātreya who is said to be a synthesis of the Brahmanical trinity - Brahmā, Viṣṇu and Maheśvara (Śiva). Festivals held in the shrine fall on days commemorating Viṣṇu as well as Śiva. The priest in it is a Giri from the *Dasanām Sanyāsī* group and should be an unmarried person. The characteristics of the temple present a confusion of the Śaiva and Vaiṣṇava traditions (or a harmony?).

Chandan Nāth's companion Bhairav Nāth presents no problem of identification. Bhairav is a well known form of Siva. Bhairav is also a very popular deity in the Dailekh district where there are many shrines of this deity. The priests in these shrines are everywhere people belonging to the *Kānphaṭṭa* order i.e. ascetics with pierced ears. Western Nepal has a large population of the *Kānphaṭṭas*, who are married and live a household life. The *Kānphaṭṭas* may have been the people instrumental in popularising Bhairav Nāth in this area.

The details of the cult have not been described in this article. For this the reader is referred to the brief literature mentioned in the bibliography at the end of this article.

B. <u>Inventory</u>

The Gods of the Karnālī Region

	Name of Divinity	*Vāhana or carrier*	*Location Premier*	*Time of worship*
1.	Bābiro Masṭo	Dhamādī, Hānikhole Amilāsagāḍi Sātsaya Lāṭī Chaudhasaya Goruneṭyā Bhāt Kundyā Tali chauḍyā Dui Masān Bāman and Maiyān	Bābiro village (Pānch Saya darā)	Baisākh and Kārtik F.M.
2.	Buḍu Masṭo	Phuṭāsillī	Buḍu village (Sijā darā)	Kārtik F.M.
3.	Kawa Masṭo	Phuṭāsillī	Kawa village (Khaṭyāḍ darā)	
4.	Thārpā Masṭo	Gumdeo Gañgaḍo	Thārpā village (Gum darā)	Baisākh, Śrāv-an and Māgh F.M.: Minor worship in Kā-rtik F.M. and on many other special occasions.
5.	Ukhāḍi Masṭo (Gaḍulasiddhi Masṭo)	Sātsallo Lāto/Dudyā Bāṭho, Bhiñgār	Ukhāḍī village (Asi darā)	Main worship in Māgh F.M. worship also in Baisākh, Asoj and Kārtik F.M.

6.	Ḍhañḍar Maṣṭo (Kṣetrapāla Maṣṭo)[5]		Ḍhañḍār (?)	
7.	Bānṭapāl Maṣṭo		Pauni village (Sijā darā)	
8.	Kālāsillo Maṣṭa (Vināyaka Maṣṭo)		Vināyak village and (Kunnā darā)	
9.	Lvāchari Maṣṭo	Bāligāḍyā Samaiju Gum Deo	Talphi and Pere village (Chaudabis kholā)	Kārtik F.M.
10.	Bijulī Maṣṭo[6]		Bijulī dānḍā (?)	Śrāvan and Asoj F.M.
11.	Kurmi Maṣṭo		Dāhān (?) (Kālikoṭ darā)	
12.	Bānjhkoṭ Maṣṭo		Bānjhkoṭ (Palāntā darā)	
13.	Baḍḍākotī Maṣṭo	Pānī Kholyā bhūt Amarālyā bhūt	Chautho	
14.	Khāpar Maṣṭo	Khābgāḍī	Śrīnagar (Gumdarā)	Asoj F.M.
15.	Dāḍya Maṣṭo		Dailekh district	Śrāvan, Kārtik F.M.
16.	Dudhe Masto (Dudhe Sillo)		Dailekh district	Baisākh, Śrāvan, Māgh, F.M.
17.	Kailās		Binhi (Palāntā Darā)	
18.	Talikoṭī Kailās[7]		Kolti Pandeyar (Kunnā Darā)	
19.	Guro	Sātsaya Kālī Sātsaya Gorī Chaudhasaya Gorunetyā Aṭhārasaya Gopālgirī	Binhi (?) (Palāntā darā)	Śrāvan and Bhādra, F.M.

20.	Gaurākoṭi	Mhelyā Pāmbhanyā	Talphi (Chaudhabis Kholā)	Bhādra F.M.
21.	Mābu/Mahābahī	Bhāmākhānī Bhāmākhaḍyā Pāḍgyā Jhyāngaḍyā	Mābu Pass (between Dailekh and Jumlą)	Śrāvan F.M.
22.	Mahādeo[8]	Muraule Suraliṅgo	Bārabis, Pānchsaya and Chaudhabis darās	Bhādra F.M.
23.	Mahārudra		Paḍmārā (Chaudhabis)	Bhādra and Māgh F.M.
24.	Lāmā + Viṣṇu	Poribinyā Hiunkhole	Lekhpara (Sijā darā)	Śrāvan, Asoj, Māgh F.M.
25.	Ḍhalpuro		Dāhān (Kālikoṭ darā)	Bright forthnight of Bhādra ekādaśī.
26.	Hyānçadyā		Chaudhabis Kholā	Bhādra F.M.
27.	Hyānkarvarmā/ Hyānkar deutā[9]		Chaukī (Sijā darā)	Bhādra and Māgh F.M.
28.	Sujjaman		Chaudhabis Kholā	Māgh F.M.
29.	Baḍuwa		Tibrikot District	Baisākh, Śrāvan, Kārttik and Māgh F.M.
30.	Dāhāl		Hāuḍī (Kalikoṭ darā)	?
31.	Nainyāl	Haṭanya	Poripālī (Kalikot dara)	Jeṭh, Bhādra, Kārtik F.M.
32.	Panchālo		Khaddu/Rāmnākoṭ (Palāntā darā)	
33.	Parālyā		?	?
34.	Ligāsaini	Nāk Kholyā Samaijyā Rānkā Bāchulo	Dasalāgaon, Pānkhā, Ruchukoṭ (Bārabis darā)	

35.	Bhāmā Sainī[10]		Nāgmā (Rakāl darā)	
36.	Gum Deo		Talphi (Chaudabis Kholā)	
37.	Sunnare[11]			
38.	Nirālgo		Dāhān (Kālikoṭ darā)	
39.	Khodāi		Dullu (Dailekh district)	
40.	Agni Betāl)		Śrīnagar (Gum darā)	
41.	Lāṭo Betāl)		"	
42.	Sāṇḍh Betāl)		"	
43.	Bhuñyer[12]		Dailekh, Jumla and Chaudhabis Kholā	Jyeṣṭha, Āshād, Bhādra and Marga
44.	Bagaulyā bubā		Chaudhabis Kholā	
45.	Rumāl		Baḍa Lamjee (Dailekh district)	Āshāḍ F.M.
46.	Maiñyāñ[13]		Jumla district	
47.	Jagannāth	Pāmnyā Bhāmā Sainī Jhyāngaḍya Majiṭhā Lāṭā and Lāṭī	Pādma (Bārabis darā)	Jeṣṭha, Śrāvan and Pauṣh
48.	Deutī (also named as Satī and Satyavatī or Vāmanī in certain villages)		Jumla (Asi darā) Chaudhabis Kholā	Śrāvan
49.	Vīrajaiśī		Okharbhiṭā, Pānkhā (Bārabis darā)	
50.	Kālyā Jaiśī		Jumla (Asi darā)	

51.	Lāṭā Varman or vāman		Chaudhabis Kholā	
52.	Naudurgā Bhavāni[14]		Attached to all the Maṣṭa Shrines	Same as the time of Maṣṭa worship.
53.	Baḍī Mālikā[15]		Mālikā lekh (borders of Jumla and Bājurā districts)	One day preceding the Śrāvan F.M.
54.	Kanakasundarī		Hāt Sijā (Sijā darā)	Daśain and Chaitra
55.	Tripurā Sundarī		Chaudhabis Kholā	"
56.	Jālpā devī		Ukhāḍī (Asi darā)	Daśain, Āshāḍ F.M.
57.	Devī/Bhagavatī		Jumla, Chaudhabis Kholā Dailekh districts	
58.	Kālikā	Bairukhe	Litākoṭ (Pānchsaya darā)	
59.	Chandan Nāth		Jumla Khalaṅgā (Asidarā)	Akṣaya Tritīya, Krisnāṣṭamī Śivarātrī, also in Daśain
60.	Bhairav Nāth		"	"
61.	Ratna Cūḍeśvar[16]		Jumla Dansānghu (Asi darā)	

Dr. Prayag Raj Sharma

MAP SHOWING SOME OF THE DARAS OF OLD JUMLA

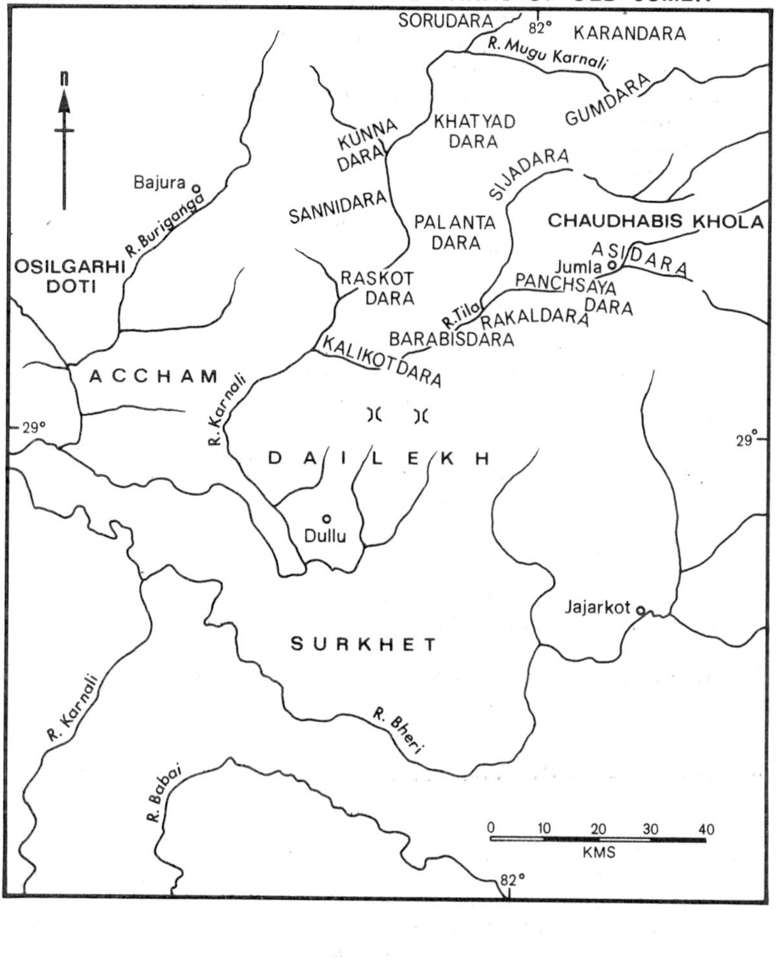

NOTES

1. The deity is called Maṣṭo (or Maṣṭa) in a singular form of address or Maṣṭa in a plural form of address which in Nepali is also used honorifically.

2. The persons directly concerned with the works and upkeep of the shrine are the *Dhāmī*; the *Dāngrī*, the custodian and the person charged with the management; the *pūjārī* or the person who does the *pūjā* in the shrine. In Tharpa, there is a *Khāwā* instead of a *pūjārī*. The *Khāwā* is the interpreter between the divinity and his votaries.

3. The twelve Maṣṭas are said to have first descended onto the earth at Ḍhā̃ḍār and to have dispersed at Khaptaḍ *(Ḍhā̃ḍār phuṭyā Khaptaḍ phāṭyā)*.

4. Mr. Dhana Vajra explained to me the possibility of this interpretation. The word *Dhāmī* in the Nepali dictionary edited by Bal Chandra Sarma has been derived from Prākrit *Dhammi* (*Nepālī Śabda Kośa*, Royal Nepal Academy, Kathmandu, 2019 V.S.).

5. Kṣetrapāla Maṣṭo is the *Kuladevatā* of the Acārya, Pyākuḍe and Neupāne Brahmans of Sijā. There is no *Dhāmī* of this god at Sijā, but there is a Brahman *Ḍāngrī*, who is the chief custodian of the shrine.

6. Bijulī Maṣṭo is worshipped by the shoemakers' caste at Pere, a village in Chaudhabis Kholā.

7. It is possible that the name Talikoṭi refers to the Tibetan town of Taklakot (Parang).

8. The three names (Nos. 22, 23 and 24) are names of the main Brahmanical gods. But the rites and festivals which attend them are not different from those of the Maṣṭās. So their identity is only founded in their names. The Lāmā-Viṣṇu (No. 24) is a curious combination of two deities of Lamaism and Brahmanism. There is only one *Dhāmī* for both of them and they are said to possess him turn by turn. The story of their origin mentions the Lama having come from the north. In the course of time he meets Viṣṇu and is able to win him over and make him his brother. Viṣṇu's sacred thread is snapped and he is forced to take alcohol as a result of his tie with the Lama. The story establishes the superiority of the social practices of the Matawālī Chetris.

The Chetris of Lekpara, where the shrine of Lāmā-Viṣṇu stands, are Matawālis.

9. This divinity (No. 27) is said to be the nephew of all the gods in the area as believed in Hāṭsijā.

10. Nos. 35 and 36 are the *bhāns* of Jagannāth and Thārpā Maṣṭo respectively also worshipped in some places as independent deities.

11. No. 37 is worshipped by the *Kamsālyās* i.e. the untouchable service-castes. No. 38 is worshipped by the tailor-musicians *(damāi)* and No. 39 by the shoe-makers *(sārkī)*.

12. This divinity is connected with agricultural fields. He is not a major divinity and has no big shrine; nor has he any *Dhāmī* or *pūjārī*. In his shrine worship is done by individual families. But he is known widely in Western Nepal. In the author's village of origin in Tanhu in Central Nepal, there is a small place consecrated to *Bhañyer* called the *Bhañyer thān*, where occasional worship is made by individual families of the village. Macdonald mentions a Bhãyar thān in a Thāru village in Dang (See A.W. Macdonald: 'Note sur deux fêtes chez les Thārus de Dāng'; *Objets et Mondes* Tome IX, Fasc. 1, 1969, pp. 69 - 88).

13. Maiñyān̄ is an evil spirit which can cause illness.

14. It is difficult to ascertain the names of Nava Durgās. Most of the following names were given to the author at Dāhān: Bhavānī, Mālikā, Ambikā, Caṇḍikā, Kālikā, Tripurāsundarī, Kanakasundarī, Jālandharī, Setī.

15. Mālikā is known by other names such as Cuḍālnī Mālikā and Pugyālnī Mālikā.

16. It is a modern temple of Śiva and those who go for a ceremonial bath in the confluence at Dansānghu visit it.

BIBLIOGRAPHY

1. Bista, Khem Bahadur: *Le Culte du Kuldevata au Nepal en particulier chez certains Ksatri de la vallée de Kathmandu;* R.C.P. 253 C.N.R.S., Paris, 1972.

2. Gaborieau, Marc: 'Note préliminaire sur le dieu Maṣṭa! *Objets et Mondes,* Tome IX, Fasc. 1, Paris, 1969; pp. 19 - 50.

3. *Itihāsa Prakāśa:* edited by Yogi Naraharī Nāth, vol. 2., No. 1, Kathmandu, 2013 V.S.

4. Sharma, Prayag Raj: 'Paschimī nepālko himālayamā pūjine kehī devatāharu tathā tyas bhek ko dhārmik rūpko euṭā sāmānya carcā, (Certain divinities worshipped in the Himalayas of Western Nepal and a general description of the religious features of that area)'; *Karnālī Pradeśa, ek biṭo adhyayana,* published by Sāmājik adhyayan samudaya, edt. by Bhim Prasad Shrestha, Kathmandu 2028 V.S. pp. 91 - 104.

5. Sharma, Prayag Raj: 'The Matawali Chhetris of Western Nepal', *The Himalayan Review,* a journal of Nepal Geographical Society, Kathmandu; vol. IV, 1971, pp. 43 - 60.

6. Sharma, Prayag Raj: *Preliminary Study of the Art and Architecture of the Karnālī Basin, West Nepal,* R.C.P. 253 C.N.R.S., Paris, 1972.

7. Tucci, G.: Preliminary Report on two Scientific Expeditions in Nepal, Is.M.E.O., Roma, 1956.

Name of Nepali Months	*Corresponding dates in English Months*
Baisakh	April 15 - May 15
Jesth	May 15 - June 15
Ashad	June 15 - July 15
Sravan	July 15 - August 15
Bhadra	August 15 - September 15
Asoj	September 15 - October 15
Kartik	October 15 - November 15
Marga	November 15 - December 15
Paush	December 15 - January 15
Magh	January 15 - February 15
Phalgun	February 15 - March 15
Caitra	March 15 - April 15

Abbreviation F.M. = Full Moon